PPG-2266: A SURGEON'S WAR

PPG 2266

A SURGEON'S WAR

NIKOLAI AMOSOFF

Translated & Adapted by George St. George

Henry Regnery Company · Chicago

Library of Congress Cataloging in Publication Data

Amosov, Nikolai Mikhailovich.
  PPG-2266: a surgeon's war.

1. World War, 1939-1945—Medical and sanitary affairs.
2. World War, 1939-1945—Personal narratives, Russian.
3. Amosov, Nikolai Mikhailovich. I. Title. [DNLM:
1. Surgery—Personal narratives. 2. Personal narratives. WZ100 A525p]
D807.R9A4813   940.54′7547′0924 [B]   74-30472
ISBN 0-8092-9055-3

Published by Henry Regnery Company
180 North Michigan Avenue, Chicago, Illinois 60601
Manufactured in the United States of America
Library of Congress Catalog Card Number: 74-30472
International Standard Book Number: 0-8092-9055-3

Published simultaneously in Canada by
Fitzhenry & Whiteside Limited
150 Lesmill Road
Don Mills, Ontario M3B 2T5
Canada

To the wounded soldiers, wherever they fought

Translator's Note

Professor Amosoff, who recently was awarded the title Hero of Socialist Labor, the highest Soviet civilian award, is an internationally known heart surgeon and medical cyberneticist. But he is probably even better known as a writer, particularly as the author of *The Open Heart*. Now Amosoff has written another book.

PPG-2266 is not "new" and it was "found" rather than written. Moving to a new home three years ago, Amosoff came upon several thick folders: his wartime diaries about which he had completely forgotten. From the first day of the war, in 1941, Amosoff, then a young surgeon, kept a diary. True, many days and even weeks are missing, but these lapses do not affect the continuity of the narrative.

Two years ago, in Moscow, Amosoff read me some of the entries. And since I had adapted two of his books into English, he asked my opinion about the material. I was deeply impressed with its raw, artless sincerity. To me the diary was a unique human document.

Of course, millions of words have been written about World War II. Politicians, marshals, generals, officers, historians, and novelists all have written about it. But this young army surgeon saw the war not as generals, historians, and politicians saw it, but as millions of nameless soldiers confronted it: with all its filth, blood, and death.

Twenty million Soviet men, women, and children died during World War II. The terrible holocaust that threatened the whole civilized world was doused partly by their blood. Yet few people remember this today. To younger generations, especially, the horror of war has been reduced to statistics. This book is a timely reminder of how statistics look at close range, and few people were closer to them than Amosoff, a novice surgeon in an obscure army hospital where he had to perform desperate surgery, often under appalling conditions.

As you read Amosoff's account, the quiet courage of simple soldiers, without tinsel heroics, stands out as a monument to human spirit that neither fire nor steel nor death can break.

PPG-2266 is a shocking document. From many pages comes the stench of sweat, stale blood, urine, chloroform. And yet it is permeated with the profound faith in life that so many Russian writers describing human beings *in extremis* have been able to convey to their readers.

This is a very personal document, intensely subjective, and yet it mirrors the vast tragedy that involved millions of human beings. There are no heroes in Amosoff's book, but in a small way everyone is a hero, in a purely human sense. In this lies the strength of this unusual narrative, not a "well-written" book in the traditional sense but, I believe, a great book.

George St. George

PPG-2266: A SURGEON'S WAR

JUNE 22, 1941

Through a dark corridor I enter a large, bare room. A few benches, a battered desk, a square radio horn in the corner.

The last words of an announcer: ". . . Comrade Molotov."

A brief pause. Then: "The Soviet Government and its head, Comrade Stalin, have authorized me to make the following statement. This morning at four o'clock . . . "

War. *War!*

Instantly everything is changed. A memory: in a mobile motion picture tent a film comes to a stop. The actors freeze on the screen. Then, a dark, dirty-pink spot starts to spread from one corner of the screen. A hysterical cry: *"Fire!"*

No more film, no more actors, no more hot little hand in mine, no more feeling of warm shoulder next to mine. Panic. And a quick thought: "Don't lose your head."

For a moment I stand spellbound. I have come to this place to inquire about my half-brothers. Years ago my father left us—my mother, my sister, and myself—remarried, and not so long ago died of alcoholism. The original hurt has worn out and has been replaced by curiosity: who are they, these little half-brothers of mine, 13 and 15?

I have been putting off my quest, and finally I have chosen this unfortunate Sunday. No one appears in the room. Just as well! I have forgotten why I came. My inquiry has no meaning now. This is noon. For eight hours now men and women have been dy-

1

ing. "This morning at four o'clock . . . " Why have they waited so long to tell me?

I go out. A beautiful day. Both May and June have been cold, but today golden summer has come in.

The town is quiet. Small wooden houses sleep under linden trees. The staccato clicking of a girl's heels on the pine sidewalk. The barking of a dog. From a distance, accordion music.

The streets are deserted. Those who heard the news are now sitting at home, stunned. But there are those who do not yet know. Sunday—some have gone fishing or hiking in the woods.

I don't yet fully understand what has happened. My thoughts run along usual channels, except that, now and then, snippets of new thoughts break in.

I must go to my hospital. Yesterday I operated on an old man who had a pinched hernia. I should go and look at him. *Now I will have plenty of surgery.*

Yesterday I spent a wonderful evening. It is good to be young, single, strong. Ida is so tender.

I will volunteer for front-line duty. When Lina comes back, she won't find me here. When she left for Moscow two months ago to attend a course, neither one of us shed tears. And now there is Ida. Betrayal? No. There were no promises; neither of us swore fidelity.

We feel no bourgeois sentiments, and yet there is a feeling of relief. Now I won't have to explain anything.

Women are strange creatures. To me there are more important things than women—science, for instance. I have had a fine year after the tedium of post-graduate drudgery. I've found I can think; I've begun to develop theories—about the body's physiological functions, about the self-regulating mechanism of the human system, about the human psyche, programs of human behavior. I needed advanced mathematics and physics to understand it all, but I am an engineer. It should be within my reach.

Big ideas! Actually, my scientific baggage is light, no learned papers to my name, just an old notebook with my "theories." In a few years I will be ashamed to read them, I expect. Still, Professor

Petroff hadn't laughed at my work, even when he had demolished my theories. A noted physicist, Petroff had even done some work in Leningrad with Joffe. In medical school he had almost flunked me. "You can do better than this, Amosoff. You have that spark in you," he'd said. But he was interested in my mechanical heart project. "It will never work, but one can see you have had engineering training. Concentrate on surgery. That is where engineering is important," was his advice. I'd taken it. And he'd wound up in Arkhangelsk. Denounced?

Men have been dying for ten hours. People die differently. I know. I've seen them go. Sometimes quietly, like falling asleep. The breath rate slows down, the pulse grows weaker, then stops. Their eyes are closed, but they remain alive. Then suddenly the jaw sags, the eyes sink in. A corpse. Others fight death with frantic thrashing, terror in the eyes, cries, entreaties, prayers—"God, God." Then convulsions and death. A surrender.

Actually, it is very simple. Tolstoy knew. His last words were: "This is death, and it's nothing." Chekhov simply said: "I am dying."

Some people, of course, can't get used to it—Alla, for instance. She cried every time. *Has she heard the news yet?*

We were married for four years and have been divorced for one. Perhaps we married too early. But we had such love; we couldn't wait a single minute. It lasted for two, well, almost three years. We parted peacefully, respecting each other. She was a good person, and our love was real. It could have worked, had we been older and had life been easier. Crowded dormitories, student's allowance, no place of our own, all that didn't help. Perhaps if we had had children? But it is better that we did not.

In half an hour the town has changed. Quiet uneasiness is in the air. Women hurry along, shopping bags in hands. Small lines form in front of stores. Salt, soap, candles, matches, there is not much to buy in a tiny provincial town, though life has improved dramatically over the last few years.

There are few men. They're probably sitting at home glued to their radios, waiting for the word that this has been a mistake, a border provocation. But it's unlikely. Molotov would not have quoted Stalin.

The hospital is some distance from the town center, and there is no public transport in Cherepovets.* I walk along beside the fence of the town park.

Last night I was there with Ida. A military band was playing. She danced with some tall fellow. I watched them, suffering. An awkward misfit, I don't know how to dance.

But then the tall man went home, and Ida came to my place. And everything turned out well.

Or badly? I don't know. Ida is a last-term medical student here for the summer, a sensible, mature girl. I didn't break any promise. Still, a worm of guilt stirs inside me. *Why should it?*

We made a date to see each other again tonight.

Our district hospital is a fine building built by Dr. Rozhdestvensky, a good physician, they say, a humanitarian. His daughter Tomka, a fat, cheerful girl, was in grade school with me. We all thought she was very rich: she brought cheese and sausage from home and had several dresses. I had one shirt and a torn sweater.

I saw her father only once, when I took my mother to the hospital with an abdominal bleeding. He refused to operate. "An abdominal ulcer," he said. "It can be treated." It was cancer, and it was too late when they diagnosed her problem.

All this is no longer important. My mother died seven years ago. Rozhdestvensky also is dead.

The reception hall is crowded. Sundays usually are rather pleasant. Relatives visit recuperating patients; there are smiles, gossip. In the reception hall or on the benches in the garden among the trees patients eat things brought from home.

But today all faces are strained.

Nina, the supply nurse, hands me a white gown, saying, "Boris Dmitrievich is upstairs."

A small town in northern Russia where Amosoff was working. Now an important metallurgical center.—Trans.

He's sure to say, "Amosoff, you're late." He's right. I should have been here at eleven. But this is an unusual day. Anyway, he shouldn't have been here on Sunday.

There he sits in the hall, tall, bony, old, closely cropped gray hair, bristling whiskers: Boris Dmitrievich Stasov. He's a fine person, a good physician, and an indifferent surgeon, in my opinion. He has forty-five years of experience, and I not yet two, but that's my opinion. He looks at me through his gold-rimmed glasses. His old, colorless eyes are sad. "Have you heard?" he asks. No reprimand.

"Yes, that's why I'm late." Playing it for what it's worth.

He lets that pass. "Now it will all begin again. This is my fifth war. I know it all by heart: no beds, no medications, no bandages, no blankets—all for the front. And people here get sick just the same, war or no war."

Nina runs in: "Dr. Amosoff! You're wanted at the *voenmat*.* They just telephoned."

The old man winces. "Here we go. You'd better look at your patient before you leave," he says. Pedantic, never misses anything—that's part of the problem.

My patient is fine. We have no difficult cases in our wards: fractures, hernias, appendectomies. Mostly men. A young peasant lad catches my sleeve. "I must get out, doctor! War!"

I look at him. Blue eyes, snub nose. Full of life.

"They'll remove your stitches tomorrow. Don't worry. You won't miss your war." I sound old, reassuring. Why *not* worry about it when you're young?

I make a list of those young men who can be discharged soon. Perhaps this will be my last day here.

Nurses are talking in the corridor. "I'm going to volunteer for the front." "Me, too. I missed the Finnish war. Had pneumonia." "I'll stick here, with the old man. They will probably move us over to the tuberculosis dispensary. This place will go to the wounded."

District army office.—Trans.

I am ready to leave. Boris Dmitrievich takes my list, nods his head.

"Good. I'll go over it. If you get free, come to the house tonight. Vera Mikhailovna's cooking a meat pie ... perhaps for the last time for a while. Flour will be short."

I promise. Young doctors often drop in at the Stasovs' little apartment. Mostly to listen to the old man. He's had a very interesting life. As a young doctor he was in Manchuria during the Japanese war. He still cannot understand how we lost that one. "At Mukden we had two corps in strategic reserve. . . . We retreated without using them. . . . " Yes, in our history we've done a lot of stupid things.

Again I walk along beside the park fence, past the vodka distillery. A militia man stands on duty. Cherepovets has always been a drunken and disorderly town; they looted one wine store during the Finnish war. Some foodstalls are already closed. Small knots of women stand around those still open. Conversation snatches: "They will stop selling vodka, like during the German war ... " "No use, those Herods will find it anyway ... " At least they still have their husbands to drink the stuff.

Music comes from open windows. Patriotic songs. I must map out my strategy before I get to the army center; they can only want me for mobilization.

Of course I know what I want: the front. Surgery under fire! I am 27, and "nothing done for immortality"—Caesar's words, I think—just some obscure theories and a lot of self-assurance. I've had just one fist fight in my whole life, and I was beaten. Will I panic under fire?

No, I won't. I know. I have had crises in my life, and I kept cool even when others lost their heads.

First of all I must formalize my status, which is a little ambiguous.

I have a white card—"unfit for active military duty"—which I got by a ruse, avoiding military service, which seemed such a waste of time in peacetime. First, the institute and deferment. Then, post-graduate work, another deferment. During the Finnish campaign, they almost caught up with me. I could smell it all: soldier's greatcoat, barracks, obscenity, stupid bantering. I started to look for medical loopholes. Blood analysis, perfect. Heart, perfect. Blood pressure, normal. Urine, stop!—*excess sugar*. Diabetes. I was sure it was a lab mistake, but I latched onto it. Our chief physician didn't want to lose me—he needed interns—and he backed me up.

The result? A white card (re-examination within a year). The chief signed it, even though I suspect that he knew there was nothing wrong with me.

Was I ashamed? A little. But that wasn't a real war. I was 26, and I was just starting to enjoy my work. I had had a difficult youth. Poor, I had had to work at an electric station and to study at night. In five years I had two diplomas—both with top scores. Poverty helped, in fact. Study was the only thing I could afford. I felt that no one had a right to make me throw away two years in the army.

That was my argument *then*.

Now it is different. This is *real* war. No Russian can stay out of it. So I must take a side excursion on my way to "immortality." Anyway, do I really want fame? No. Of course, I would not refuse it. But the main thing is to work, think, search, learn new things. Now all this will have to wait.

I'll just say: "I have been cured. I am ready to go. Please send me to the front."

What will it be? Trenches? Would I be afraid to work there? No. But that would be a waste—anyone can dress wounds. I am a surgeon.

A crowd in front of the army office in Engels Street: men, both civilian and military, a few women, children, one new automobile parked in the street. There's an armed sentry, and on the back door there's a fresh notice: "General Mobilization."

Inside, a squat major wastes no words: "To Public School #7. The emergency induction point. The medical commission! Right away!"

It is three o'clock and hot, and I am hungry. The one public dining room on the way, in Sovietskaya Street, is jammed. I will have to miss a meal. There will be many missed meals now.

School #7 is quite new. With four floors, it is the pride of our town. All the other doctors called are already there. I know them all: general practitioner, eye specialist, osteopath, neuropathologist, and me, the surgeon.

The induction post commandant, a fat lieutenant-colonel, gathers us around him. "Comrades," he announces portentously, "this is war. Our people are conscientious, of course, but be on the lookout for malingerers. No consultations or analyses. We must mobilize this town in twenty-four hours."

We are divided into two groups. With me are the eye specialist, Dina Semenovna, young and good-looking, and a rather dull man, the neuropathologist, a medical school classmate.

The most important person around is the military clerk, Ivan Trofimovich. He keeps all the lists. We know each other well, since we last worked together on other medical commissions.

"You see, Comrade Amosoff," he says, "our work hasn't been wasted." He pats his thick file of folders. "Our government has been getting ready for this."

Getting ready. Yes, we've been working a seven-day week. We are going to need all that preparation. We've had just fifteen years of industrial development—from nothing—and Germany has had two hundred years. *And* Hitler has all European industries in his pocket now. The prospect is more than a little frightening.

We'll win, but it will not be that easy.

After four o'clock men start coming. Ivan Trofimovich checks off their names against his lists.

"Are you in good health?"

"I think so."

A stamp, and a man is a soldier. Some are eager; others less so. Only those who complain or are uncertain are sent to us. According to law, everyone should be examined, but this is an emergency.

They pass before me, future defenders of our Motherland—peasants from nearby collective farms, workers at the local industrial plants, small clerks and functionaries, cobblers and tailors from artisan cooperatives. Many of them I know, from the hospital, from previous examinations, or from encounters in the streets.

Men from 25 to 45, our people. They're all simply dressed, but not unkempt. Almost all wear clean shirts, following the old Russian tradition of dressing neatly "to face God." The ones I see speak little. There's no enthusiasm, but also no attempt to escape their fate. Imbued with a touch of traditional Russian fatalism, they're ready to do some difficult work.

The fatalism is the same as that Russians have affected for generations, but there is a difference between these men and "the holy gray cattle" of the Czar's armies. All of them are literate, and many have worked on industrial projects. Some have graduated from seven-year school. They all have had their share of political education.

Cherepovets has never seen a foreign enemy. Not even the Tartars reached it. The people are of pure Russian blood; northwood peasants, they're taciturn, tough, used to hardship.

They undress in a classroom, putting their things on the floor—battered boots, homespun pants and shirts, underwear. Then they go to the doctors, covering their "shameful parts" with their hands.

A naked man is utterly defenseless. He can't even lie convincingly.

"What are you complaining of?"

"Well, not much. . . . When the weather is bad my shoulder aches . . . a pressure in the chest . . . "

He is 36, has three children, a pregnant wife, and hands so calloused they look as if they're covered with oak bark. He speaks timidly, hoping against hope that the doctors will find something wrong and send him back to his woman, to his village to gather his crop.

I listen to his heart. Tough body, not a bit of fat. He does not try to simulate anything. Generally he's as fit as a man of his age could be.

"You can serve, Comrade."

"If I must, I must . . . just like all the others."

He goes away to dress. Probably he's relieved. He did not want to complain, but he had to for his wife's sake. She was crying and wailing when he left home. Now it is all over. Now Mother Russia will make all decisions for him and his pregnant wife. *Will he ever see his fourth child?*

It makes me sad to look at these men. Some are short and thin, with signs of rickets—the generation of "the hard years." World War I and the Civil War left the country in shambles; hunger was our way of life. These men were raised on potatoes, thin cabbage soup, coarse black bread.

Now all this must be defended. Potatoes, cabbage soup, black bread.

A young man with a shock of unruly blond hair, grinning, eyes sparkling.

"No, no military training. They let me off because of a bad heart. But I'm all right, Doctor. . . . I feel fine. I want to fight the goddamned Fascists!"*

I listen to his heart. Diastolic murmur. An obvious defect.

"They'll need people to work in the rear," I say, trying to soften the blow.

"Oh, no! Please, Doctor!"

"You have a bad heart."

"So what? I can still smash the fuck . . . damned Fascists! I'm as strong as a bull."

I stamp his card: "Fit for active duty." Who am I to stand in his way? They can re-classify him later on—if he's still alive.

There are many men like him, usually young; the rumor is that the army center is jammed with volunteers, very different people from those who try to get out. In a rather naive way, without much hope, the latter say, "Colic . . . . Pain in the stomach . . . . Spasms." But they do not insist.

"You can serve, Comrade."

In the Soviet parlance the Nazis were called Fascists.—Trans.

"Maybe I should be treated for a few weeks first, Doctor?"

"No, it's too late. There's a war on. Next!"

By seven o'clock the crowd has grown considerably. There's a constant babble of voices in the hall. Already there are drunks; those who are really soused are put in an empty classroom to sleep it off. There are no recriminations; raw recruits are protected by an unwritten law. "This last day I'm making merry with you, friends."* Those who have passed the commission are formed into platoons in the yard and marched off by sergeants. Most of them have had some military training.

By late evening the area around the building looks like a gypsy camp—peasant carts from faraway collective farms, men, women, children sitting around, talking, eating, and, of course, drinking. Now and then, someone bursts into song, usually from a recent film: "If war comes tomorrow," "Moscow, my Moscow," "With little blood—by one mighty blow!" Of course, there's obscenity from the men. Women clasp their hands over their men's mouths. And complaints: "Why didn't they tell me about this before? Were they blind?" And again the women shush them.

Everyone has learned to be careful. Even though Stalin's purges have not affected simple people very much, mostly the party cadres and various "specialists," the people are well aware of the old Russian saying: "God takes care of those who take care of themselves."

As a platoon is marched off, men hold children by their hands, wailing women break through the ranks and hang around their men's necks, sergeants yell and swear. Street boys trying to march in step walk beside the soldiers. There's a mingling of tears, shouts, curses, and now and then a cry: "Death to the Fascists!" And another squad is off to the war.

We hear that women and children are sitting all around the reserve regiment barracks. They will sit there all night, maybe longer, numb with grief, until their men are loaded into freight cars and taken away. Then they will drift home, lost, bewildered,

---

*The words of an old Russian soldier's song.—Trans.

to start again the difficult task of survival without their men.

Soldiers' wives. Women without men. During some previous wars, the word *soldatki* had a slightly derogatory connotation: sex-starved women, easily seduced. War and sex have a peculiar correlation. In ancient times women were included in the spoils of war.

My father was mobilized in 1914, when I was still too young to remember. Mama told me how she saw him off, followed him to Cherepovets from our village, sat around the army center waiting for the medical commission's decision. Then she went back to live with her mother-in-law, a cruel and miserly old hag.

There is no point in thinking about that. They are dead, shadows of the past.

At nine o'clock they bring in some tea and sandwiches for us. We eat without stopping our work. It seems that there will never be an end to this stream of naked men. "Cannon fodder." Terrible words, when you see it so literally.

And they are *not* impersonal. Each has his own story, his own bewilderment, pain, fear, and, sometimes, anger. "You want to examine me? What for? I know you people. Fit, and that's all. All right, look—two toes missing. The Mannerheim Line. And look at my leg—blue. And this scar in the chest—the cuckoo's bullet!* But what the hell does it mean to you?"

Judging by the scar, it was a bullet through the chest wall, barely missing a lung.

"Did you lose much blood?"

"How do I know: I keeled right over. That's where my feet got frozen off. Why the hell do you ask?"

"Why are you so angry at us?"

"Not at you. At the whole world. Just think—three months at the front, six in a hospital. Then my wife runs off with some bastard. And now back again. There's no end to it."

"Then what d'you do? Surrender to Hitler?"

That stops him.

"All right, Doctor. Do your work."

Soldiers' slang for Finnish snipers perched on trees.—Trans.

I stamp his card: "Fit for inactive duty." They'll find some place for him. He had four years of school, is a trained mechanic. He takes his card, looks at it, walks off, still angry. But he will serve well, work hard, conscientiously, without complaining. There is some great inner strength about these people. They are used to suffering. For generations it has been bred into them. It takes a great deal to break them.

The newspapers have been assuring us: "Any aggressor will be smashed at the border." I hope so, but I can't forget France. It had the best army in Europe, the Maginot Line, the Verdun tradition. And in six weeks it was all over.

Of course, this cannot happen to us! Our people are different. And then they say much has been done since the Finnish war in the way of new armaments. And our frontiers have been pushed farther west.

"An unexpected perfidious aggression . . . . " That sounds odd. Everyone knew that this would come. The government must have known it better than anyone. Perhaps they have made some plans about which we know nothing? Some real surprise for the Germans?

There are no real "white nights" in Cherepovets, but when the sky is clear in summer, there is enough light at night to see, though not enough to work inside by. When we switch the lights on, soldiers nail blankets over the windows—a blackout. Why? Surely no German planes can fly this far into Russia?

A state of emergency is proclaimed in the town. Soldiers try to disperse people outside, but without much success. The women will not budge, and who will make them go?

At ten o'clock ("Twenty-two-zero-zero" in military parlance) I have to go to the toilet. The scene outside is upsetting, bacchanalian. The classroom "dehydration ward" is filled with sleeping drunken men. Knots of men near open windows throw out loops of string and hoist up bottles from women in the yard. The sentries on duty outside are helpless to do anything. The colonel is walking about, red-faced, sweating, angry, utterly frustrated. No one pays the least attention to his shouting, returning his outbursts with mumbled epithets: "Bastard . . . Fat pig . . . Lardass."

Ivan Trofimovich grins. "There's no law against it—as long as they are not in uniform," he says.

Another platoon is formed and staggers away, the last for the night. Though it is now too late to collect another one, we continue to work until two o'clock in the morning. All the men now are more or less drunk. But they don't argue, don't resist. Some seem to be actually eager to pass. It's all routine: check eyes, listen to the heart, feel for hernias and look for hemorrhoids, ask a few questions. Our eye specialist, Dina Semenovna, is dead tired, and I am trying to help her.

I am quite proud of myself. I know how to talk to these men, to assert authority, without swearing or shouting, having learned this skill at the electric station where I worked for three years, one of them as a shift supervisor. Men instinctively respect me. And if necessary, I can swear with the best of them. The colonel seems to be impressed with my "efficiency."

By two o'clock it is quite light outside, and we remove the blackout blankets: it is hot and smoky inside, and it stinks. More work is senseless—all the remaining "patients" are asleep in the "drunk tank." All of them are probably fit anyway: those who had any hope of getting out were careful not to drink, and there were surprisingly few of those. The colonel orders the building cleared and the doors locked.

Then he comes into our room and slumps on a bench, exhausted. "Thank you, Doctors," he says. "At least you didn't create any extra difficulties for me."

I don't know whether this is a compliment or not. They say that when military superiors praise you, you'd better be careful. Perhaps we were too offhand with all those men, too careless, too negligent. Some of those we passed didn't look very fit.

"Try to sleep now, Comrades. Tomorrow, at six-zero zero—reveille. We must get through with this as quickly as we can. There's a war on."

Of course. Everyone knows there's a war on. And yet it is hard to believe. We knew this would come, but now that it has come, it is too much of a shock.

We stretch out on divans and benches, anywhere. I lie down on a table, but for a long time I can't go to sleep. I'm too tired, too keyed-up. The endless procession of peasants' faces passes before my eyes, hairy chests, flat stomachs, knotty legs. Especially faces—like old icons.

Can this *really* be war?

Birds are beginning to chirp outside. Another beautiful day is dawning. For many this will be the last in their lives.

And my first day of the war has come to an end.

JULY 3, 1941

Tonight, at long last, we're going to the front!

Thank God. One can't just sit back and do nothing. It has been a nightmare. Those communiqués! "Heavy defensive fighting... The enemy has penetrated local areas." How local? What does the "Minsk direction" really mean? Have we lost Minsk? Why don't we counterattack? Why, why why?

Millions of questions and no answers. We are behind a solid brick wall, and there is not a crack in it. All radios have been requisitioned, and no one is allowed to listen to foreign broadcasts. Anyway, I don't *know* any foreign languages.

So many things have happened in my life during the last ten days. Suddenly I have become "The chief surgical officer of PPG-2266"—Mobile Field Hospital #2266. "Mobile," that's funny. We haven't been moving anywhere.

I still can't understand how it all happened, though I am not afraid of the responsibility. I should be, I suppose; I've not had much experience. But I do have common sense and, I think, some talent for surgery. Anyway, I like the challenge.

The head of our PPG is Boris Prokopievich Khaminoff, military physician, third class (we all have military titles now). He is imposing, this Khaminoff: a double chin, but firm, and a fat stomach that doesn't look too flabby because of his height and military bearing. We will see soon enough how well he stands up.

I'll try to remember the events in sequence.

On the morning of June 23, at the induction center, we heard the first communiqué. "Heavy fighting . . . The enemy has penetrated local areas . . . " Why? How? We'd always been told that the Red Army would smash the aggressor at the border. We were depressed. We avoided looking at one another and spent the morning processing our men. Gradually we calmed down. It must be a small, temporary setback, we reasoned; in a few days our troops will be across the border.

In the evening I went to the district army office, looking for information. A captain with red-rimmed eyes brushed me off with: "A doctor? Go to your hospital and wait. Next!" There was nothing to do. I was no longer a boy; I could not just "run off to war."

I was back at the hospital by six o'clock and found everything in turmoil. The talk was incessant. Young doctors and nurses had their orders assigning them to various military establishments. Old nurses and aides were packing up. They had orders to move over to the old dispensary across the town. There was nothing for me.

Boris Dmitrievich was grim, tired. "I wish they'd leave you here. Just my luck. . . . I was going to retire this year. Now it will be impossible. Too much work. And we couldn't live on my pension in wartime anyway."

He has worked for almost fifty years and accumulated nothing—a shabby apartment, books. Yet I could not help thinking of Boris Dmitrievich as a living piece of history. During the Japanese war he entertained Count Ignatiev, whoever he was.

I stopped at our ward. Ida walked toward me with red, hard eyes. I smiled, but she froze me with one look. "I can't see you tonight," she said.

"I understand. I'm sorry."

A delayed guilt complex. Was I a cad? It just happened. There'd been no real feelings: loneliness on her part, masculine vanity on mine. It was a little ugly, I suppose, but it didn't matter now.

Instead of going out, I went back to my room. An iron bed, a table, two chairs, a bench, an open suitcase with books—my "library"—another suitcase under the bed—my wardrobe—and a record player on the table where Lina had left it: not much. But I was happy in this room. I could think. No one disturbed me in my solitude, and that struck me as being more valuable than comfortable furnishings.

The next morning I sat on the examination committee at the Medical Technicum. It was a mere formality; we passed everybody. The country needed them: boys in front-line medical stations, girls in base hospitals.

The evening communiqué was terrible: fighting near Grodno, Vilnius, Kaunas; the Finns and Rumanians have joined Hitler. I could not eat, could not sleep.

I spent the next day at the hospital operating on old women and children—small stuff. The communiqué mentioned Baranovichi, Chernovtsy. We retook Peremyshl (we had not been told that we had lost it). Then there was that "Minsk direction," and Minsk is over one hundred miles from the border!

When I got home, there was a surprise. Lina, home on an emergency pass. She had spent two days traveling from Leningrad on a trip that usually took a few hours. The traffic, she said, was incredible, everyone going everywhere.

Our reunion was all right, but there was no word of love. To make matters worse, she found one of Ida's red buttons in my bed. She pretended to be amused, and it was unpleasant.

We ate in my room—bread and sausage. Then we listened to records. Lina's favorite was "Don't speak of love—all has been said." Appropriate. I put on "La Cucaracha," but Lina switched it off. "Vulgar," she said, putting on another one of her sentimental favorites.

Women are strange. She missed the curfew. We slept on my bed without undressing and without the slightest suggestion of intimacy.

The next day everything changed after they called me at the

hospital: "Report immediately to Kommunisticheskaya #5. See Dr. Khaminoff, the head of Mobile Field Hospital #2266. Your orders are waiting for you there."

So they hadn't forgotten me, after all.

I knew #5, a large squat building. Before the revolution, it had been the home of a merchant; now it was some sort of military staging depot.

The "hospital" was an old desk with Khaminoff behind it. There were other men around, but you couldn't mistake the chief. I noticed his size at once and his slightly protruding gray eyes and a large wart on his left cheek.

I also noticed his disappointment at seeing me—so young, thin, short. He started to question me, and my answers clearly did not impress him. Graduated in 1939. From December, 1940, a junior surgeon at Cherepovets Hospital. Herniatomies, appendectomies, one major intestinal and two abdominal operations. I did not mention that I got to do those only because Stasov had been ill. Yes, I was familiar with traumatology, I said. I mentioned my two diplomas. Divorced. No children. Not a Party member. Headed a shift at the electric station in Arkhangelsk, successfully. (This was true; my superiors and workers respected me.)

Khaminoff rubbed his nose. "I am taking you as a head of a surgical department," he said. "I'll be frank: I hoped to get someone . . . er . . . more experienced. A man was coming from Leningrad, but he was intercepted on the way." He smiled, and suddenly his fleshy face became appealing. "There's open season on you surgeons. We'll be loading tomorrow at 1400 hours on the third siding. Minimum baggage."

I ran out, happy as a child at the end of school year.

At the hospital I said goodbye to Boris Dmitrievich and to the nurses, including Katusha, a marvelous nurse who used to blush so prettily when I looked at her. I'd walked her home several times, but I'd never tried to kiss her. You couldn't do that with a girl like Katusha.

Boris Dmitrievich tried to give me some pointers about field surgery, but I didn't listen. Finally he just kissed me on the cheek and made the sign of the cross over me. Pleasant.

Then I went to the Policlinic to see Lina. I thought it woud be easier with people around, but she wasn't there. She had been called to the army office.

I felt a flood of relief. "Tell her I'll try to stop by and see her tonight," I said blandly to a mutual acquaintance.

I collected my back pay from the hospital and the Technicum and went shopping. First I bought a field pack—a blue canvas bag with a leather top—then a penknife with several blades. In a commission store I paid 500 rubles for box-calf boots. They cost more than my month's pay, but they were beauties, real officer's boots. And I was lucky. Stores were emptying of goods fast.

Then I went home to pack.

Minimum baggage. Well, some underwear, old shoes, and, most important, books. But which ones? Finally, I selected two books on surgery to go with me. All the rest I decided to leave with Vera Mikhailovna's parents, along with my suitcase there. My "theories" went to the bottom of the suitcase. After the war it would be different. Then it would be medical research, theories, brain work only. Meantime, into the suitcase went everything: photographs—mama, Alla—some letters. Lina had already taken home her record player and records.

The suitcase weighed a ton. The new boots were tight. It was very hot. And I had to cross the town to reach Vera's parents' home, a little wooden house half-buried in the ground.

Vera and I are pals. A man-woman friendship has a certain quality. As long as sex is excluded, it can be tender and enduring.

Vera's mother, frail little woman, wanted me to have something to eat, but I declined. There was no time. She kissed me and promised to come to see me tomorrow at the station.

I wanted to get away so that I could get about fulfilling a rather awkward duty: saying goodbye to Lina.

I found her packing.

"Where to?" I asked.

She laughed. "I've been assigned to PPG-2266, as an assistant surgeon! Did you think you could get rid of me so easily?"

A bit of a shock. So Khaminoff had caught her in his net!

I didn't know how to react. Our relationship had been complicated. Officially: "Full equality, independence, no moral obligations." Actually, it hadn't worked out that way.

"Don't worry. I won't divorce my husband for you," she said.

I never knew why she had got married. I never asked her and she never told me. Her husband had stayed in Leningrad. And she had married him when something already had begun brewing between us.

Actually I should have been glad to have Lina with me. An old friend and a good surgeon, she would be a great help except for that false relationship.

Apparently she felt it, too, because she said: "Don't worry, my dear. Consider me as your fellow soldier. Remember that song of ours: 'Let's banish worry; who can live without love and little lies?' "

That was another thing that irritated me about Lina, her song quotes: terribly schoolgirlish.

I had to say something. "I'm glad you'll be with me, Lina. I really am. We've been good comrades. Let's keep it that way. Till we win this war."

Win the War. That sounded stilted, trite. Every day the communiqués became more alarming, and there were terrible rumors. No one believed in quick victory any longer. The town had changed, become calm, grim, determined. There was no patriotic braggadocio, but no despair, either. This is the test we have to endure. After all, we are a great people.

On my way home I thought about that stupid song. "Little lies." I detest lying, but I have lied. I could never understand those treason trials. Old Bolsheviks, Lenin's comrades—foreign spies? That was unbelievable. Stalin's sycophants turned my stomach. But I lied by silence. And when it was necessary, I got up and applauded—not very hard, but still I applauded.

I knew what was going on. My own uncle, a dedicated Communist, was arrested and sent away; we never learned where. But what could a little man like me do?

We learned to live silently, sharing our thoughts only with our closest friends—Boris, Vera, my classmates, my sister, my aunt Natasha, Alla. I was even careful speaking to Lina. And all because one man had put himself above the revolution. He could not stop progress, but he made it painful when it could have been joyful.

The next day I was at the station at noon, carrying my stuff. And there it was—our famous PPG-2266. About twenty freight cars, boxes, barrels, bales of hay, horses. *Hay and horses?* Yes, under the care of some soldiers, an assortment of oldish men. A lot of people were standing around, some in uniforms, some not.

Khaminoff was standing near a pile of boxes. Tall, straight, in a military uniform complete with belt, revolver holster, and all, he struck me as a Napoleonic figure.

He called me over, and we shook hands.

"What are those horses doing here?" I asked.

He grinned. "We're a horse-drawn unit. Didn't you know?"

I didn't. The word "mobile" suggested to me Red Cross vans, green ambulances.

Khaminoff was undismayed. "Just wait till we hit those country roads when the autumn rains start. No automobile can move in good Russian mud. That's when the Fascists will get stuck."

Perhaps. But I still felt let down.

Khaminoff introduced me to his second in command, Dr. Zvereff, and to our political commissar, Shishkin. Then he called a sergeant and ordered some "proper equipment" to be issued to me.

In the supply freight car I was given my gear. Some things were obviously out of season: short naval peacoat and woolen foot wraps. I liked my summer uniform except for the canvas belt. The supply sergeant smiled. Probably I didn't cut a very dashing figure. But he liked my boots, even clicked his tongue.

Then I went looking for my colleagues. I found a group sitting on a pile of railroad ties behind the train. Three women and two men, in uniform. They watched me approach in silence.

I introduced myself: "Dr. Amosoff, the head of the surgical department," I said.

One of the men saluted. He introduced himself: Dr. Chernoff, a former surgeon of some Leningrad hospital. "A veteran of the Finnish war," he added pointedly. He was tall, dark, much older than I, probably more experienced. He presented the others: Dr. Isaac Solomonovich Mech; Dr. Ann Kokina; the pharmacist, Sarah Abramovna (I didn't catch her last name), a very full-breasted bleached blonde; and her assistant, Galia, an intense little thing. "We all came from Leningrad," Chernoff told me.

Probably as a "head" I should have made a speech. Instead, I just saluted awkwardly (my first military salute), turned, and walked away. I thought I felt ironic glances on my back.

I kept walking along the train. Suddenly, I heard my name called: "Nikolai Mikhailovich!"

There were some old friends: Tamara, from our gynecological clinic, and Nina, the operating room nurse, and a very young, very pretty student nurse, Zoya. They greeted me warmly. Probably they were happy as I was to see a familiar face.

We sat down on a bale of hay to gossip. "Those Leningraders don't approve of your appointment... A snooty bunch, a clique... They look down on us provincials... But we're for you. And Lina will be with us."

Small town, Cherepovets. No secrets.

According to the girls, our hospital was an empty shell—no medical equipment, not even first aid kits. Kostia, the veterinarian, they said, had one kit. The *veterinarian*? Of course, the horses—state property.

"We are going to get everything later on," was a constant refrain. We already had our soldiers, who, with the horses, came from Bielozersk, near Cherepovets. Khaminoff, too, is a Northerner, from the ancient town of Velikiy Ustyug. I'm glad. I like Northerners; they're the purest Russians, solid and strong.

Lina soon joined us. She was already in military uniform: khaki blouse and skirt, her own shoes (there were no boots her size).

More gossip until 1800 hours, when we started to load.

At first, the requisitioned *kolkhoz* horses refused to go into the cars, but, finally, their handlers, old collective farmers, working like demons, accomplished the seemingly impossible. Then Khaminoff ordered: "Into the cars! Women to the first sleeper! Officers to the staff car!"

Both were euphemisms. A "sleeper" was a freight car with sleeping tiers. So was the "staff car." Only Khaminoff, the commander, had a folding bed. I found a bunk near the door. It had been a long time since I shared a room with men. Dr. Chernoff and Dr. Mech got on upper tiers next to each other. Leningraders.

An old soldier, Stepan, had been appointed our staff orderly. We had been issued dry rations earlier in the afternoon, and Stepan somehow, from somewhere, materialized with a bucket of hot water. We ate dry biscuits, washing them down with hot water. No one had thought to bring tea. Khaminoff removed his jacket and shoes and sat smoking silently.

It was getting dark outside. We had a candle, but Khaminoff refused to allow us to light it. "We have no blackout screen," he pointed out. Dumb. We heard men walking and talking outside, but there was no locomotive.

I rolled up my peacoat for a pillow, but it took me a long time to fall asleep. For one thing, the bunk was hard. For another, I was getting depressed. Some very miserable people must have invented war.

We finally started to move after midnight, but a few hours later we were again pushed into a back siding, and our locomotive was requisitioned for a troop train. Young soldiers, bright faces, well dressed—a regular unit.

Yaroslavl. In this ancient Russian city northeast of Moscow we got stuck for several days. Khaminoff kept badgering the traffic officers, but he got nowhere. Troop trains had priority. He even sent a telegram to the War Medical Department in Moscow. It didn't matter. There was no response.

My sister and aunt lived in Yaroslavl, but they had no telephone, and we were not permitted to leave the immediate vicinity of the train. To relieve ourselves, we were only allowed to go behind some cars, which was embarrassing for our girls.

Khaminoff fumed. "Are we poor relatives? Don't they know how important medical service is? Bunglers!"

That was not important in any case. As a hospital we were useless. So far all we had was a list of equipment to which we were entitled, including an X-ray cabinet. In a horse-drawn hospital?

The horses were giving us a lot of trouble. They had to be exercised, and unloading and loading them took hours. The old *kolkhoz* farmers worked with dedication, but none of them seemed to be less than forty-five and some were much older. A few wore war medals.

Our food wasn't bad. There were no hot rations, but plenty of canned meat, bread, and tea. There was always hot water in our car and in the women's sleeper, and at least the days were beautiful, warm and clear.

A freight car jammed with Byelorussian refugees stood for a while next to us. The train had been bombed twice en route, and was filled with women, wailing children, old men. Emaciated mothers tried to nurse babies. Our commissar asked us not to speak to them, but of course we did.

"It's terrible, terrible . . . . The Fascists are burning everything, killing everybody . . . . There's no stopping them."

There was rumor that Smolensk had fallen. Impossible.

Our commissar, Shishkin, brought in daily communiqués from the station and read them in all the cars in a sad ritual. "I don't want any discussions, comrades," he'd say. What discussions? We didn't know what to think. Murmansk was mentioned, Riga, Borisov, Rovno, Zhitomir.

We were all depressed. Still life went on. The drill sergeant, for example, took our women out each morning for "field exercise"—marching to and fro. It was fun to watch, but the girls were quite serious about it and it was good for morale.

We all had become acquainted. None of the doctors, besides Khaminoff, impressed me. Our two Leningraders and Zvereff played cards all day. Shishkin had been wounded twice in the Finnish campaign and was a dedicated man, but he had little culture. Still he got along well with soldiers, listening to their complaints, comforting and advising them, writing letters for them. His usual refrain was: "No harmful conversation, comrades."

That was unnecessary. We had all learned to keep our thoughts to ourselves. During war the habit was useful. Idle talk was demoralizing.

Now and then I went for walks with Lina along the track. We were not permitted to go to the station: "We might get a locomotive at any time." But it didn't look hopeful. There were supply trains waiting, and they had priority.

I had a great deal of time to think, lying on my bunk. The drill sergeant didn't bother us, perhaps because we were officers. I thought mostly about surgery, trying to put my knowledge in order. I knew I would have much to learn in actual work, with human bodies as my school material.

On the morning of July 3, Lina, Tamara, and I sneaked away to the station when the commissar went to the party headquarters in town. The station was dirty and deserted. Everyone was outside, around a radio horn rigged to a telephone pole. Women with bundles, old men, children, a few soldiers. Excited voices: "Stalin, Stalin . . . " We held our breaths. What would he say? Our armies had gone on the offensive? A new agreement with America? Peace? Capitulation? The latter was impossible. Stalin never gave up.

The crowd was growing, but there was not a sound. Even the children had stopped whimpering. Then as the tension grew, there were some crackling noises from the horn, and then a dull guttural voice:

"Comrades . . . citizens . . . brothers and sisters . . . I am appealing to you, my friends . . . "

It was a tired voice, with a Caucasian accent, showing signs of obvious strain. Some old men in the crowd removed their hats. Women crossed themselves.

It was not a long speech, and not a cheerful one. Of course, war to the end. When the Germans advanced, everything had to be destroyed. Guerrilla war was to be waged behind the enemy lines. Long, hard, merciless war was the promise, and yet we could feel relief all around us. A bitter truth is better than ignorance. People had learned to trust that man.

The speech came to an end: "Our cause is just. Victory will be ours."

Everyone was waiting for something else. But there was nothing, not even music.

We walked back, thinking our thoughts. So much of our lives had gone by with Stalin. There were things we could not understand and forgive, but there had been others as well. The country had risen from shambles. Plants and factories had sprung up like mushrooms. Volunteers, boys and girls, worked days and nights, like maniacs. It was a hard, hungry time. But we didn't really care. We were building our future.

Then arrests, stupid trials, deportations started. It was bewildering. I never believed there could be so many traitors among us. But even that couldn't stop the country's march. We lived amid a crazy mixture of fear, despair, and excitement.

Who was that man? Perhaps he understood Russia better than Marxist theoreticians? A *Georgian*? But then Hitler was an Austrian, Napoleon, a Corsican, Alexander the Great, a Macedonian. I could not forget those old women crossing themselves in the crowd.

The girls kept asking questions: "Why did he say this or that? Did you hear his teeth chatter when he drank water?" What could I say? We simply had to trust him. At least he knew how to rule. It would have been better without that guttural accent, but that was a mere detail.

There was a new saying around: "This war will even everything up." Yes, things would be different. If we could only get to the front quicker!

Coming back to the train, we were greeted with good news: our first hot meal. Chapliuk, our cook, had got hold of some firewood and rigged up his pots in a hole in the ground. The result: hot soup, canned meat, and millet.

All conversation was about Stalin's speech. He didn't try to encourage us, and yet the feeling of despair had evaporated. Our commissar was particularly relieved. He came back smiling—the first smile on his face I had ever seen. His work had been difficult: answering questions to which he had no answers.

At 1500 hours Khaminoff came back from the station. There was absolutely no chance for us to move, he said, not for a few days.

I accosted him: "Boris Prokopievich, let Lina and me go to town. My sister lives here."

"Ask the commissar." It was becoming a refrain.

Shishkin wrinkled his brow: an important decision. But Stalin's speech must have mellowed him. "I don't know . . . and what if we are ordered to leave? How could we take care of the wounded without a head surgeon?"

Khaminoff cut in. "What wounded? There are four troop trains ahead of us waiting for locomotives."

Finally I got a pass to go to town for two hours—without Lina. Shishkin displayed Solomon-like wisdom. "At least one surgeon must be on duty," he said.

I dressed carefully, put on my "pips." No one would know I was a doctor; I had no medical insignia. I tightened my belt, blew out my chest. I never knew I had that kind of vanity, but apparently there is a rooster in every man. I even liked soldiers saluting me. Stupid.

I love Yaroslavl, the cradle of Mother Russia, a very old and beautiful Russian town, for Moscow once was a mere village in the Yaroslav-Suzdal principality. After Cherepovets and Arkhangelsk this is the town I know best.

My sister Maria and my aunt Natalia Fedorovna live here. I love my sister. She is thirty-six, unmarried, utterly apolitical. I call her an old virgin. She always protests. "No, anything but virgin!" But I think she is putting us on. She is a general practitioner. Our mother was a midwife, working in the same village for twenty-five years. We inherited from her a desire to help people. Maria is intelligent, a good physician, but too dry and reserved—and stubborn. Mother had her troubles with her.

Natalia Fedorovna, Aunt Natasha, is different. Her father

was an impoverished nobleman who died shortly after the revolution. Aunt Natasha accepted the revolution immediately and passionately. She fell in love with my mother's brother during the Civil War and followed him to the front. They had a son. After the war they settled in Yaroslavl. Uncle Pavel was an old Bolshevik, very active in the party work. And then, in 1938, he was arrested and sent away.

I came to see Aunt Natasha three days after the disaster. Maria lived with them; they helped her to get an education. The apartment was a mess. Friends warned my aunt: "Better go away." For a while people would have nothing to do with her. Then an old friend got her a job as a typist in an office. There were few educated women around, and she was not merely educated but intelligent.

Now she was the head secretary at the Regional Office of Economic Planning. She and Maria lived together.

She recovered from her misfortune, and her son was already in the Institute. And she had never lost her faith in the Revolution. Ideals are a great sustaining force.

I thought about this as I rode in a streetcar past the ancient cathedral, one of the most beautiful in Russia. It had been turned into a state museum and looked shabby. Churches are like people; once the spirit is removed from them they are empty shells.

Yaroslavl hadn't changed much. There was an ancient serenity about it. The only difference was the many men in uniforms, a few on crutches: Yaroslavl was an important base hospital area.

Would I find them at home? I approached the small house with the little tower. There was a goat tied to the fence. A goat? Had they moved?

And then: "Ni-i-i-ikolai!"

Maria. Hugs and kisses.

"Where have you come from? Why didn't you cable us? And why the uniform? You had a deferment card."

"You know me better than that, Maria."

She laughed. "Of course. Patriot. Let me look at you. The uniform looks good on you—except for that belt."

"Where's Aunt Natasha?"

"At work. She comes home at midnight. No Sundays, no holidays. Go in. I'll run over to the neighbors and call her."

Left alone, I sat on the comfortable old divan, looking at the familiar photographs on the wall. There were a few small things from the old apartment, small decorations in a general aura of austerity, almost of poverty.

Maria returned. She looked thin, tired, and older since I had seen her last. A plain, pleasant Russian face.

"She'll be right over! Are you hungry? We have some mushroom soup."

I declined. I knew what every scrap of food meant.

We talked. I told Maria about our hospital and the way we got stuck in Yaroslavl. She reproached me for not letting them know sooner.

Presently Aunt Natasha arrived—energetic, plump, handsome, surprisingly young looking.

"My darling! Let me look at you!" she said.

I stood up and saluted. She laughed. "Stop it! There's not a military streak in you!"

I think there is: my innate sense of discipline and order.

Maria made tea and served it in the familiar cups with blue flowers. There was even sugar and black bread.

Of course, conversation centered on the speech by Stalin, generally an unmentioned name in that house. Uncle Pavel, like many old Bolsheviks who knew Lenin, had disliked him from the first.

Maria kept guardedly silent, but not Aunt Natasha: "I can't forgive him. Getting rid of all those old Bolsheviks, Civil War heroes. Who is going to run the war now? No wonder there's such a mess. 'Brothers, sisters'! Ridiculous!"

That was Aunt Natasha: direct, uncompromising. I could see Maria fidget. I also felt uneasy.

Suddenly she said, "You know, Kolia . . . I have joined the Party!"

I was flabbergasted.

"Two days ago they accepted me as a candidate."

I was still bewildered. "But why?"

She became serious, thoughtful: "Party membership means something special now. It's a challenge. You'll see, the Party will see us through the war. It's the bone structure of our society. It has been decimated by that man, but it's bigger than any one man. They say the Fascists shoot all Communists they capture. This is why anyone who can must join today."

I felt even more uneasy. Was she hinting at my lack of courage? I had never thought of joining, though probably I would have been accepted. I had always been a good worker; my "family background" was good—peasants, always poor.

Then why hadn't I joined? Did I believe in the revolution? Yes. I knew what it had given to me and Maria and millions of little people like us. But I had always been a loner, treasuring my freedom. Yes, even the freedom to remain silent. And I didn't think that the secretary of the Regional Party Committee knew better than I what is good for our people. An intellectual snob. Maybe.

But during the war shouldn't everyone stand up and be counted? I had to think about that.

Meanwhile, Aunt Natasha talked about her work. Most men had gone to the army, and she practically had to run the office by herself. There were enormous difficulties. Women and children had to be trained to take men's jobs in factories and in the fields. She spoke like a true Communist. "We must . . . we will . . . we will see this through."

Her son, Serezha, was undergoing military training at his institute.

Maria had not yet been mobilized. She had been assigned to the blood transfusion center—war work but without military allotment. There were already shortages, and prices were soaring.

"Never mind. We'll get by. There can't be two deaths, and one is unavoidable": an old Russian saying. Fatalism, with underlying courage.

They asked me guardedly about Alla. Neither Maria nor Aunt Natasha ever liked her; they thought her capricious, spoiled. They never showed it openly, but I always felt it.

"That's all over. Finished. Forever," I said.

Forever. Yes, the war had cut my last connection with my past. Alla's photograph was at the bottom of my suitcase; I couldn't even remember how she looked. The woman I thought I would love all my life!

Was there something wrong with me? Some emotional deficiency? Perhaps it is best for a surgeon to be emotionally detached. I would soon know.

The last goodbyes. They were crying as I ran toward the streetcar stop.

When I returned, I got a surprise. An old locomotive had been hitched up to our train, belching clouds of black smoke.

Lina, almost hysterical, rushed toward me with the news. "Where have you been?! We are leaving! For the front! Quick! Get in!"

To the front. Thank God! And I almost missed my war.

AUGUST 4, 1941

We are approaching the front. Before us looms a dark cloud—or a dense pall of smoke. A steady sound of artillery fire, for the second day. A continuous booming around the clock.

We are moving westward.

Our orders: "By 1800 hours on August 4 you are to set up a hospital near Roslavl to recieve the wounded from front line medical battalions."

Our train: twenty-two sturdy carts, each pulled by two horses. We left the town of Zhizdra six days ago, and we are in a hurry. We have a little over an hour to meet the deadline.

The "staff cart" heads the procession. Khaminoff walks beside it. I know that he has varicose veins and is suffering. He hears the firing growing nearer and nearer, but he has to be in front. A commander. Our commissar is in the rear, running and shouting, seeing that no cart falls behind. A good man, but excitable.

Our horses are bearing up well even though the carts are heavy and we have covered over 110 miles in six days. At least our peasant drivers are experienced men. All the axles are greased, and the wheels are periodically doused with water to cool them down.

Now we are a true hospital. In Zhizdra we received all our surgical and hospital equipment. All of it was brand new, in wooden boxes—linen, bandages, medicines. We are ready.

As Head of the Surgical Department I also received a thick little book, *The Unified Surgical Doctrine*. Published by the Red Army Medical Department, it contained exact instructions for all surgical procedures. At first I was puzzled and even irked. What—no initiative? Everything covered by precise rules? But when I recalled that many doctors had been hastily mobilized, and that some of them were not surgeons, I had to admit the need for rules.

Russian military medical history is not brilliant. During the rule of the czars, the percentage of soldiers dying of wounds was appalling. "Evacuation" was the dominant principle: patch them up, load them into peasant carts, and send them back. There was a minimum of front-line surgery, only amputations when absolutely necessary (if gas gangrene developed later, well, too bad). There were always more *moujiks* to fill the ranks. The attitude of Peter the Great was typical: in one of his orders he decreed that medical personnel be kept out of soldiers' sight—"So that these scum would not remind men of death."

But this time, theoretically at least, we are ready. The Military Surgeon General, Professor Burdenko, had devised precise procedures for all emergencies, and these procedures had been tested during the clashes we had had with the Japanese in Mongolia and Manchuria and during the Finnish war, when the percentage of the wounded successfully treated and saved was quite satisfactory.

In practice, who knows? This is a different war, involving millions of soldiers, thousands of doctors who have never done any surgery, and young nurses who have had no battlefield experience.

Then, too, the war news has been bad. We are retreating all along the front—if there is such a thing as a "front." The communiqués stress the enemy's losses—millions. Then why are Germans still advancing with such apparent ease? Where do they get the fresh troops?

During the last month we have seen many troop trains going to the front—young, eager men, well dressed (our supply services have done a tremendous job). But they say we have few tanks, few planes; so much was lost during the first weeks of the war. How could we have been caught so much by surprise? Had we no intelligence service? Someone must have blundered. Who? We can only guess.

Of course no one discusses such matters. Even those who dislike and dread Stalin have learned to trust him. Propaganda? Yes and no. He has succeeded in transforming the country, though often by savage methods. We have built mighty industries out of nothing. Our men are brave. They have always been brave. Suicidal Russian courage, some call it. But why are we retreating? Why don't we attack?

It is best not to think about these things. We just follow orders, blindly, uncompromisingly; history will judge later.

We are moving toward the war. And the war is moving toward us. Our armies are still retreating, and we are anxious to get into action. Those weeks of doing nothing, of being shoved around from station to station, were most unpleasant.

Once, three weeks ago, we were bombed by a single German plane. It dropped two small bombs. We had no losses, but there was panic. I remember lying down, in accordance with instruction, face to the ground. But some others ran into a nearby forest. We lost a day gathering them together again.

Was I frightened? I think so, even though I did not feel any conscious fear. And I was not hysterical afterward, as were some of our men. Oddly enough, our girls stood up better. None of them developed hysterics. Well, at least we have had a taste of war: our "baptism by fire."

The men walk beside the carts; even the drivers walk to save their horses' strength. Only those women whose shoes have given out and whose feet are bleeding ride. Some of the girls walk barefoot. We still have not received small-size boots, but they have been promised.

I walk beside the surgical carts. My team is all here: Lina, Liza, Tamara, Zoya. Good girls, all of them, though slightly afraid of the approaching action. Who can blame them?

We have been following small country dirt roads to avoid German bombers and to leave the highway clear for motor traffic. On those back roads we were quite unaware of the war until we heard firing. We did not even hear any communiqués. Our radio is out of order, and Commissar Shishkin could not get any news. Or perhaps he did not try to—he is responsible for our morale, and it has not been too high, anyway.

The introduction of commissars into the army has been widely criticized, but during the Civil War, when many Red Army commanders were old officers who did not sympathize with the Revolution, they were necessary, and I think that they serve a useful purpose even now. We have two political officers: Zvereff, the second in command, and Shishkin. Zvereff is responsible for overall political education, and Shishkin for the morale of every person in the unit. His duties resemble those of the old army's chaplains—with one difference. All political officers and commissars fight in the first ranks; they say that Germans shoot all of them out of hand.

We have become accustomed to walking. At the end of the day we fall down on the ground, exhausted, then wake up at night, shivering. The nights are quite cold here, in the Smolensk province, and we wrap ourselves up in everything we can get. Every night Chapliuk cooks some soup, and we have water for tea, but often we are too tired to eat. The food is not too bad, but a bit monotonous.

Well, this is war. No time to think about feet or stomachs. The sound of firing is growing all the time, and the nervousness is spreading. There are grumbling voices: "Where the hell does he think he's leading us? . . . Can't you see? Straight to the Fascists. . . .

A home-grown Soussanin* . . . And where are those officers who are supposed to meet us? . . . Probably running away like rabbits."

Here and there we see groups of soldiers and detachments, not only rear-echelon men, but guns and ammunition trucks. But no wounded. Khaminoff sent men off to gather news. Reports are contradictory: "There's fighting in Roslavl . . . . The Germans broke through, going ahead like mad. . . . Roslavl's burning."

It is almost eight o'clock, and it is growing dark. We are hopelessly late. We approach a village, and here we have to turn onto the Warsaw highway. It is on this highway, somewhere near Roslavl, that representatives of the Army Medical Service are to meet us and give us further instructions.

Near a copse of trees, soldiers are fixing their field guns, the muzzles turned toward the sound of artillery firing. They do not speak to us—too busy. They just look at us in a puzzled way. Horses, carts, women. A gypsy caravan?

We turn north and approach the highway. The firing is very close. Someone says that he hears machine guns, but all I hear is a steady roar. From the highway we hear the sound of motor traffic—trucks, maybe tanks, a steady stream.

A road sign: "Roslavl—5 kilometers."

Our heavy carts climb the steep highway slope with difficulty, but finally we are lined up along the road.

"Are you all here? Forwa-a-ard!"

We move for about a hundred yards, and there is a halt. I can just make out a light military passenger car. The headlights, mere slits on the painted glass, pick out a group: Khaminoff, Zvereff, and some officer, not from our hospital. As I move up to get closer, I hear voices.

"Show me your orders and your map."

I see Khaminoff bring them out of his map case. A quick look. There! "Turn around and get out of here—at once."

---

*Soussanin was a Russian national hero. In the beginning of the eighteenth century, acting as a guide, he led a Polish detachment into a trackless forest where they all perished.—Trans.

A momentary pause.

"What are you waiting for? Issue the orders."

Zvereff: "And what about our orders?"

"I am ordering you. Colonel Tikhonoff of the army rear command. You can mention my name to your superiors. Clear?"

"Yes, Comrade Colonel."

Khaminoff gives the orders, and the carts begin to turn around. We get up on them. Overloading? Who cares? Fear does funny things. The drivers snap the reins, and we start off; it is easy going along the paved road, and we maintain full speed, covering seven and a half miles without a halt. Not a wheel broke, not a pack fell off.

The colonel was left standing on the highway. Probably laughing at our sudden mobility.

Finally, crossing the Oster River, we turn into a thin forest and stop there, exhausted.

No soup, no tea. Not even bread and sugar. Everyone collapses on the ground. Sleep. Blessed sleep.

LATE AUGUST, 1941

We are retreating farther and farther east.

Today's communiqué: Smolensk has been "evacuated." There is fighting near Kiev. Uman and Bielaya Tserkov are mentioned.

Our hospital retreats with us.

After we turned away from Roslavl, we had a day's rest in a former agricultural college. Roslavl had been taken by the Germans just after we had turned back.

We stop at Sukhinichi, where we've been ordered to set up our hospital. We've even received a large motor truck with a driver. Moving past the railway station and oil tanks surrounded by poplar trees, we finally approach a line of large barracks. Khaminoff gets off the truck. We join him.

"Look, Nikolai Mikhailovich . . . a perfect place . . . Our orders say to take any empty buildings . . . "

Suddenly: Bo-o-om! And immediately again: B-o-o-m! And then much closer: Bo-o-om!

Everyone jumps out of the truck. (Our carts are still behind us.) I crouch and instinctively draw in my head.

There are no more explosions, just a sound of a departing plane and several belated anti-aircraft gun bursts. Then, quiet and the sun. Peace.

We all get up, confused and a bit ashamed.

"Where the hell did they come from?" someone asks.

There is a small smoking crater near an oil tank. We were not the target, so the panic was unnecessary.

We inspect the place: two lines of twelve squat barracks, empty, not a stick of furniture inside.

"We can take a thousand wounded here."

"Yes, but look at our neighbors: the station and oil storage tanks."

"We must not expose the wounded to unnecessary risks."

Khaminoff brings out his map. We all study it. A couple of miles away we spot the village of Alneri. "A direct road from here," someone notices.

"All right. Let's take a look at it. Get in," says Khaminoff.

We arrive in Alneri, take one look, and make a decision. This is our place—close enough from the railroad not to be isolated but far enough away from such tempting targets.

The village sits in a narrow ravine on both banks of a small river. Small neat houses, clean and pretty, clustered together. At the far end of the village stands a primary school in a large apple orchard. There are a few old barns and a squat brick building. Next to it is the village club, in a former church building. The caretaker explains: "This was a landlord's estate. During the

Revolution they burned and looted it. Then they built the club. The orchard is so old that it produces no fruit."

The school, empty—vacations—is composed of four large classrooms and a small office. In one classroom—a group of small desks. On a blackboard—a round face: two eyes, nose, mouth, and two devil's horns. Probably some teacher.

We organize ourselves. The classrooms we'll reserve for bed cases. Lighter cases we'll handle in tents under the apple trees. The dressing station also will be in a tent. Dining tent and kitchen are also to be in the trees. We set up a bathhouse near the river, the staff quarters in a house nearby. All the rest of the personnel are billeted in the village.

It does not take long. Almost at once we begin to unload. At first the caretaker protests, but when we show him the requisition order, he helps us. He's a good old man and a former soldier from World War I. He was gassed near Riga.

We sit around waiting for the carts to come up.

EARLY SEPTEMBER, 1941

We have received our first wounded. We are working; we are finally in this war. My God, how difficult it all turns out to be. And we are only a GLR—a "hospital for the lightly wounded."

All my dreams about complicated surgery, for which I have been preparing in my mind, have evaporated. Khaminoff was relieved. "You're much too young to handle serious cases, Chief Surgeon," he said with a smile.

That is my official title now. I think Khaminoff was irked when they assigned it to me. A chief, indeed—so young and inexperienced. His attitude is understandable. Khaminoff if also a chief, so in effect we are addressed in the same way. But of course he is my superior.

Our hospital is a part of a Field Evacuation Area. Each army has one. The main feature is the Reception Center, where all the wounded are processed, sorted, and sent to different hospitals. Our area has three of them; ours is located at Sukhinichi, and the hospitals are in neighboring villages. The wounded are brought in from the front in cars; some of them are sent to the rear in hospital trains, and others are sent to the hospitals to be treated, ready for evacuation.

That's what happens most of the time. We, however, have been assigned a special task. Our wounded are not going anywhere, except back to their units.

Before the war there were no special military hospitals for light cases; they were the product of the first war months. Our losses were large; replacements were slow to arrive; and in the general chaos men with light injuries were often sent beyond the Urals along with the seriously wounded. The chaos was too great. and the High Command put a stop to it. All lightly wounded were to be treated locally, patched up as quickly as possible, and returned to their units. There was to be no pampering; military discipline was to be maintained. Morale-building political education was to be administered, and there was to be no drinking or loitering.

So we are a GLR. Originally our unit was designed to accommodate 200 bed cases. But then we got our new orders: "reorganize PPG-2266 to GLR to accommodate up to 1,000 light wounded." Our base in Alneri has been approved. All recuperating cases are to be transferred to Sukhinichi, to the barracks near the oil tanks. There they are to be taken over by drill sergeants and political instructors, eventually to be returned to the front.

We sort all our wounded in the school corridor, where they are registered and given anti-tetanus injections. Then they are taken to the bathhouse and the delousing station that we have set up at the edge of the river. Only then do they get to our "dining room" in the garden under a canvas canopy. One corner of the dressing station—three tables in a tent—is screened off for our "operating theater." We do some minor surgery, after all.

Just as we finished getting everything ready, we had visitors—a very resplendent officer, the Chief of the Evacuation Area, accompanied by a very nonmilitary-looking army surgeon. We had already stuffed mattresses with straw and put clean sheets on the beds.

"Take it all off! No pampering of the men—this is not a health resort! Just straw! And watch for lice! We don't want a single louse here!" I knew I was in the army then—for real!

The doctor politely pointed out to us that we had no special place where the wounded could undress, and that our reception section in the corridor was too small. But he made no suggestion as to how we could expand the school building. They finally left in a small military car.

We sat in the former school office and waited for our first cases. We had been warned that they were coming "very soon." Suddenly a young nurse burst in, calling "They're here!"

Outside, filled to capacity, were three 1½-ton trucks with red crosses on the green canvas. The wounded were sitting on benches and on the floor. The medics helped them out, led them into the schoolhouse, and seated them.

There they were—the defenders of the Motherland. The first thing we noticed was that all of them were utterly exhausted—hollow cheeks, unshaven, dirty. The majority were wearing only shirts—no greatcoats. Some had canvas bags, others nothing. Many had gas mask cases but no masks. There were cutaway sleeves and trouser legs, fresh bandages, slings, makeshift walking canes. Most were middle-aged men, reservists.

Some fell asleep at once, leaning against walls or on the floor.

"Tired, Comrades?"

"You'd get tired too," one said. "The whole day moving from place to place . . . some organization."

"We were already in a train. . . . But then:—Get out!—Inspection! Why the hell can't they send us back into the rear where we could be treated properly?"

The man was angry, but it was understandable. Having gone through hell, he had had the good fortune to suffer a slight wound. Nearly a hero, he's suddenly thrown back into the mill.

"We'll treat you here, comrades," we said.

"You're kidding. Just behind the front? They'll bomb this place to hell in a couple of days!"

"What do they care? That would save them a lot of bother."

Our first patients. And now we are a real hospital, complete with paper work and routine. The nurse who accompanied each group hands over all the appropriate documents, military cards, tags. Everyone has to be registered and listed. No document may be returned to a man—the order is strictly enforced. They might run away and try to get on some hospital train going to the rear.

As soon as ten men are registered, they are taken to the bathhouse near the river. The bathhouse is small, and men—emaciated, exhausted—wait outside on the benches, naked. All their things are taken away to be deloused; they are issued clean undergarments. There is plenty of hot and cold water, but soap and sponges are in short supply.

After the trip to the bathhouse, the general atmosphere is better. There are smiles and even jokes.

"Thanks, Comrade Doctor, for the bath. Haven't washed myself since the beginning of the war. Thought I'd get to Berlin stinking dirty."

"What about lice, men?"

"Sure, as many as you want. Government issue."

Our delousing station works slowly. Those who have had their bath sit outside in fresh undershirts and long underwear. There is some grumbling.

"We're hungry. Take us in as we are."

Fortunately it is warm. There is a large and growing heap of clothes near the delousing hut. How are we going to redistribute them? Well, that's not my problem.

In the dining room the soldiers are different again. For them it is the first hot soup they've had in many hours, even days. The food and the fresh undergarments make them cheerful.

"Just like Saturday night after a week in the fields. What about a little alcohol?"

No drinking is allowed.

Their wounds generally do not disturb them too much. To

wash, to eat, to rest—those are their main preoccupations.

Of course all bandaging must be checked, and the dressing station works full blast. The tables are not used. Men sit on benches. Medical histories must be filled in: a slow procedure even though all the available doctors work on it.

According to the rules of military surgery, there is no needless wound dressing, just inspection and registration. But sometimes bandages slip or become soggy. When men specifically ask for redressing, we treat them.

They're all simple injuries; there's no surgery. All we have to do is keep the wound clean and it will heal by itself, but this is my first encounter with war injuries, and it is interesting.

Our specialty has rapidly become flesh wounds, small shell fragments under the skin. The rules say: small fragments up to ¼ inch in size need not be removed. Larger fragments are different. They must be removed to prevent infection from setting in. All such wounds must be cut open and cleaned. We do not listen to the wounded men's descriptions. Some tend to exaggerate, others to minimize the extent of their injuries.

It's only minor surgery, but even that has its problems. I've had to learn the hard way.

One of my first patients was a man with a no-exit hip wound. Soft tissues. The entrance wound was about ½ inch in diameter. I examined it, dictated my diagnosis: no surgery required.

"Comrade Doctor, there's a piece right here—moving under the skin. Maybe it's better to cut it out?"

I felt the skin. "You're right, Comrade. Tatiana Georgievna, get the table ready. Local anesthesia."

The man was listening and became nervous: "What's that—local freezing? Oh, no, I won't allow it. I've seen what happens in medical battalions. They use local stuff and then cut them to pieces."

One must always consider the patient's mental condition. Generally, local anesthesia is not recommended under battlefield conditions. Men often are too emotionally disturbed and keyed up to respond to it.

"All right, sit here and wait," I said. "We'll finish with the light cases first."

In an hour all wound debridement was finished. It grew darker. Finally it was time for my first bit of military surgery.

"Tamara, general anesthesia. Tatiana, cover the table with a sterile sheet."

Our man removed his underpants. His teeth were chattering. He was pale. "Please . . . be careful . . . I'm afraid," he said.

"Don't worry, Soldier. Lie down."

Tamara knows her business. Everything was ready—a mask, a chloroethyl spray, a wound spreader, a tongue depressor. She smeared vaseline around his mouth and asked a medic to hold down the man's arms.

We put the mask on the man and aimed the chloroethyl spray at it.

"Start counting!"

"One . . . two . . . I'm choking!"

"Keep counting!"

The man jumped up, tore off his mask, face red, eyes wild. Gasping.

"I can't, Doctor, . . . can't! I'm choking!"

We calmed him down, put him back on the table, and secured him with belts.

"A stronger spray, Tamara."

Another attempt, another failure. The belts restrained him, but he jerked his head out of the mask. Such a humiliating struggle.

Other wounded soldiers crowded around the tent. "Operation . . . operation . . . " The word was out. Khaminoff came in, put on a white gown. He looked very unpleasant.

"Try ether. The man is too excited," he said.

We tightened the belts. Ether acts slowly, takes five or ten minutes. The man became excited again and mumbled something—the appropriate obscenities.

Finally he quieted down. I found the shell fragment, pressed the skin with a scalpel, but the damned thing was dull, wouldn't cut. The soldier started struggling again, screaming.

"Tamara, devil take you! Chloroform!"

Khaminoff ambled up to me, whispered: "Look, Nikolai Mikhailovich . . . it's been so long . . . you'd better do it yourself."

I felt my cheeks flush with shame.

"Lina Nikolaevna, put on sterile gloves. Give me chloroform."

While they prepared chloroform, I could hear voices outside.

"What do you think this is—a movie theater? Go back to your places." It was Kolia Kansky.

And there was a sarcastic voice: "Doctors! Cutting him up like a pig's carcass . . . "

Our patient kept muttering something. The ether had had no effect. Finally everything was ready. I began to drop chloroform, considered a dangerous anesthetic and not recommended. I had no experience with it at all, but I continued. We had to put him under. I remember thinking "And now his heart is going to stop . . . God forbid." There was no way out, of course. I had to go on.

"He has relaxed his muscles," Lina said, finally.

Thank God, I thought, and said "Go ahead, Lina Nikolaevna." Lina made an incision, putting clamps on all the small blood vessels. But we were losing time. I couldn't find the fragment; my hands were shaking. Then I saw it, a very small piece of metal. We removed it. Then the final haemostasis, iodine under the skin, a bandage. The end.

"Stay with him, Tamara. He may start vomiting. He could choke himself."

The wounded outside went away: there was no real scandal. People love scandals, even if they are not malicious. Khaminoff walked away without saying a word. Only we, the surgical staff, stayed around, discussing our first operation. What went wrong? Chloroethyl did not work because of the man's overexcitement; it happens in civilian cases as well. Also, we decided, our mask was too small; we would get a larger one, perhaps even cover the patient's face with a towel. And use more ether. At last we knew that chloroform could be effective.

All in all a humiliating experience, especially with such a simple case. Some beginning.

LATE SEPTEMBER, 1941

We've been working near Sukhinichi for over a month. The front has stabilized. More than that: we have retaken Elnya—a small town, but a big symbol. We, too, can hit back! For two weeks we have been able to hear gunfire, and all our wounded come from the Elnya sector. On the day we captured the town, everyone became excited, happy, absolutely different. That is what victory means, even a minor one.

Down south things are not going well. Kiev seems to be lost; the news hits us hard. Odessa is holding, deep behind the German lines. Leningrad, too, is holding well. Generally the communiqués do not sound too alarming. England is with us, and Roosevelt seems to sympathize with us. It's good not to be alone.

I live with Khaminoff in a small house. We are fairly comfortable. He is a good man, Khaminoff, and a good physician. He likes to play the superior, he likes power, he likes flattery, but all within reason—he's an intelligent man. He can be argued against, and he treats me well.

We are now very busy. This morning we had 1,150 cases on our list, though only 420 were here, in Alneri. The rest are in our "recovery battalion" in the large barracks in Sukhinichi.

Besides the school, the club, and our tents, we have constructed several dugouts, accommodating fifty men each. Yesterday the dugouts got us in trouble. The commissar general of the army came in and raised hell with us because many of the men were lying on the straw in the dugouts. He was right, of course, but what about those orders "not to pamper the men"?

EARLY OCTOBER, 1941

We are moving.

Yesterday we received orders to liquidate the Alneri hospital and to move to Sukhinichi—into the barracks occupied by our recovery battalion. I'm sorry to leave this place; here I had my first military surgery experience. I have become fast and sure and calm. There are no more hysterics—in fact, I'm perhaps a bit too sure. Still, this *is* war. One must make quick decisions, and so far all my operations have gone off as well as could be expected. Mistakes? Yes, a few, but none too bad.

We have already transferred most of our patients to Sukhinichi or sent them back to their units. Only about a hundred men are still in Alneri, all lying on mattresses with clean sheets, in clothes that have been washed and deloused. It's good to catch hell once in a while.

Our hospital in Sukhinichi will be a joy. The barracks, solidly constructed, were built only two years ago to house a large factory training school. There are baths, kitchens, and dining rooms. We can easily accommodate over 1,000 cases in comfort. At the moment we have about 750. I fought for one building and got it for surgery, dressing station, water therapy, and physiotherapy. The operating theater is a little jewel, with perfect aseptic conditions. We can even do major surgery, if that becomes necessary.

We ride with Khaminoff in a light one-horse carriage to the new hospital. Khaminoff likes to drive horses. "I had a carriage like this in Ustyug—only better, of course." He likes to boast a little, too; it's an innocent enough weakness.

The latest war news is the subject of constant discussion. "Hard fighting all along the front!" Communiqués describe the heroic exploits of soldiers, sacrificing their lives to save comrades. That's always been in our Russian blood—the suicidal streak. At least, our sector of the front seems to be quiet. In fact, it is a beautiful, peaceful morning. On the hill, our barracks settlement—buildings among poplar trees—looks as pretty as an architect's drawing.

Arriving at Sukhinichi, we drive into the yard. Khaminoff goes to see his supply people, I to my surgery building to see how Kolia Kansky, the sanitary instructor, is installing the autoclave.

Before I reach the building, I hear shouts: "Planes! Planes!"

I stop and look up. A steady loud hum—a sound I've not heard before. People pour out of the barracks: soldiers, nurses, doctors.

Chernoff yells hysterically: "Hey, you! In the white gowns! Take shelter! In the trenches!"

Here it is. For real. In the west, against the sun, I see a whole formation of planes heading straight for us. It's a good thing that we have enough slit trenches to accommodate everybody and that the barracks are not close together.

Chaos.

I yell, "Doctors, Nurses! Don't take cover until all the wounded are taken care of! See that all the barracks are empty!"

Of course no one can hear me. The planes are coming straight at us. Behind our barracks an anti-aircraft battery opens up—all guns at once. White puffs appear in the sky, but far away from the planes.

The gun muzzles swing up, firing steadily. The three leading planes peel off, seem to stand still for a moment, and then dive down—straight at the battery.

"Dive bombers!" Kolia Kansky shouts. He is standing beside me on the porch of our building.

He's right. They're the first I've seen.

Three tremendous plumes of earth rise and then settle slowly—right over the battery, it seems. Deafening sounds blend together: the roar of the planes, the whistling of the bombs, the crash of the explosions. The word *hell* crosses my mind.

A memory: We students are going through a psychiatric ward. "Violent cases." A large room, small barred windows. Semidarkness. Half-naked and naked women. No, just bodies. Lots of them. Weird poses, awkward gestures, cries. Disheveled hair, mad eyes. Nothing human. Hell.

The plumes of earth settle completely. The gunners, brave men obviously, have their guns raised vertically, still firing at another trio of diving bombers.

Roaring . . . whistling . . . explosions. This time, a clear miss.

The planes pass over us toward the station. The yard is empty. Everyone is in the slit trenches, lying face down. I feel like hiding, like running away. Kolia looks at me. Am I scared? No, stunned. But it is stupid to stand up like this.

"Let's sit down on the steps, Kolia. They're made of bricks."
As if that would make any difference.

We sit down, watching the planes. More bombs fall.

They're bombing the station. There is no direct danger any more. And yet, there is a strange emptiness in the head.

"Junkers 88's," Kolia says. I look at him. No, he doesn't look scared.

The barracks seem to be intact, except that all the windows have been blown out and there's a lot of dust in the air. The bombs missed both us and the battery. There can't be any injuries or there would be screaming. To make sure we walk around the barracks.

From there it is about half a mile to the railroad station, which lies below us. The tracks are jammed with burning cars, and it's a mess.

The anti-aircraft guns still fire like crazy at the planes, which peel off, drop their bombs, and fly off toward the town. The station is wrapped in smoke and dust, and as we watch we hear more explosions. But these are different.

"They must have hit a munitions train. . . . Those are shells bursting." Kolia Kansky knows something about war from the Finnish campaign.

The planes drop a few bombs over the town, nearly two miles away. Geysers of earth rise like weird flowers. The sound reaches us late, faintly. The town itself is small and green, and the picture we see is almost surrealistic.

All at once the planes fly off, one trailing a narrow ribbon of black smoke, and it becomes quiet. We see the burning railway cars and hear infrequent explosions of shells, but that's all.

"Come on, Kolia. Let's check on the damage," I say. Fortunately, there is not much damage except window glass. One bomb fell fairly close. A wall of one of the buildings collapsed, but no one was inside. The battery seems to be intact.

"It's good all our patients are walking cases," Kolia says. "Let's check the trenches."

The trenches are filled with people, who now are just stand-

ing up, talking. There's even some laughter, but it's tense, un-
natural.

"Well, soldiers, how did you like the German presents?" I
asked with forced bravado.

I notice respect in their eyes. Then I realize I'm still in my
white gown. A hero! Actually I'd been too much taken by surprise
to take cover.

"All right, Comrade Doctor. We're old hands at this,"
someone says.

Three men have been hit by flying glass. I send them to the
dressing station with Kansky.

Suddenly the anti-aircraft guns begin firing again. Immediately there are more cries: "They are coming back! . . . To the
trenches!"

This time both Kolia and I jump into a trench.

The sequence is repeated four times—at intervals of about
fifteen minutes. After the second raid, panic starts. Some of the
wounded run off toward Alneri, and there is no way of stopping
them.

During the third raid two of the barracks buildings are hit,
and Khaminoff issues orders to load up and move back to Alneri.
We leave most of our equipment behind, but five of our men were
slightly wounded.

I think I preserved my calm, but I am very glad to get out.

EARLY OCTOBER, 1941

Our garden in Alneri resembles a gypsy camp again. It's buz-
zing like a beehive. The Germans. Encirclement. According to
some soldiers, we had better start getting out. Of course no one
believes them. How can they know? Panic.

Then, toward five in the afternoon, a young officer in a
military car brings new orders for us to start pulling back to

Kozelsk, Peremyshl, Kaluga. The Germans have broken through near Kirov. There appears to be no immediate danger, but we are instructed not to lose time. "All walking wounded are to be formed into marching companies. Those who can't walk are to be taken on carts. No one is to be left behind."

Even before Khaminoff can give the orders to load, a small boy comes running in, breathless.

"Who's the head doctor here?" he asks.

Khaminoff says, "I'm the head. What do you want?"

"A hospital train has been bombed."

"Where?"

"Near the switch station, a mile away. They're screaming something awful."

Khaminoff tells me to take Kolia Kansky, Tamara, and four medics. We load several stretchers and first aid kits into the truck. The boy gets into the cab, between the driver and me.

In ten minutes we are there: a rye field.

There's the railway line and a few shrubs alongside it. On the track stand five smoking, burned-out cars; a few more cars lie on their sides, huge red crosses on their tops; there are several black, smoking bomb craters. The sharp smell of burned paint and thin smoke is in the air. So is a chorus of weak voices: "Oh . . . Oh . . . Water . . . Water . . . Help, for the love of Christ . . . Help . . . "

All over the field we pick out sprawling figures. At first they look like so many corpses, but then we see some are stirring, moving their heads, trying to turn over. As they see our truck, the cries become louder: "Medics! . . . Here . . . Here! . . . Wa-a-ater!"

How many of them are there? A hundred? Two hundred? How many of them are still alive? What can just a few men do? What does it matter. We must do *something*. We must get them some water first, but we did not bring any.

I turn to the driver. "Go back," I say. "Bring water barrels, medics, nurses, bandages, splints. But first see the chief. Tell him what you've seen here."

The truck drives off. We walk toward the cars. Those who have crawled away can wait. But these . . .

The scene is so horrible we are shocked into silence. In twisted, smoking cars, men lie squashed, crushed, broken. No, not men—corpses, burned bodies, black cooked blood, smoldering bandages, and shattered wooden splints. There is an unbearable stench of roasted flesh and burned paint.

The embankment is not high, and the cars simply jumped the rails, most falling on their sides. No one could have survived in any of them. The locomotive is standing alone, about a thousand feet away.

Scattered about near the cars, there are many motionless bodies. Some dead, some simply unconscious. Farther away, all over the fields, are those who were able to crawl away. Now they are crying, calling us, sitting up, moaning, weeping. Still farther away there are other figures; these, too, are shouting something, but we can't hear their words.

What to do? Whom to help first? It is getting late, and soon the dusk will be gathering. Some reconnaissance planes fly overhead, and there are sounds of explosions in the direction of Sukhinichi.

First of all, we decide to gather everyone together, so that they can eventually be taken away. For a staging area we choose a place near the railway track on level ground, where the highway is reasonably close at hand.

Kansky and I stand on the piece of ground we've selected.

"Co-o-omrades! All those who can move, come here!" we shout. "We'll take you to the hospital!"

I send two men to help any who can move. With Kansky, Tamara, and two stretcher bearers, I start to visit those we can—perhaps—help.

Walking along the railway track that separates the dead from those still alive, I try not to look at the smoldering cars. It is too horrible. I had heard that we had captured a secret order to the Luftwaffe to seek and destroy hospital trains. "Psychological warfare." It must be true.

A young man. A smashed skull. He probably just fell off the train. No pulse. No breath. Dead. We go on. Another "skull case"—unconscious this time, still breathing.

"Take him back."

We walk on. A man with a twisted, broken plaster cast. Some blood has oozed out. His eyes are open.

"Alive?"

"Y-y-e-es . . . Wa-a-a-ter . . . "

"Tamara, morphine. Kolia, get him to our assembly place."

I bend over a man lying on his side. Both legs are in Kramer's splints to the knees. Blood drips from his stomach.

"Doctor . . . I got hit in the belly . . . during the bombing . . . I crawled out, but I can't move any farther."

He hardly needed to tell me. Morphine. This one will need abdominal surgery—when and if he survives. For now we have to leave him here. The law of military surgery: "The amount of given help should be regulated in accordance with the situation." Meaning: If there are many cases, skip those who require too much time. First help those who can be helped quickly and have a fair chance of recovery. Cruel laws, but necessary.

We walk on. A few are alive, but in deep shock. Many are dead. I can see those who can crawl moving toward our assembly point, slowly, painfully. Some are being helped by my men. Kansky and Tamara inject morphine, quickly patch up open wounds. Some who are still alive are clearly beyond help, and there we spend no time. God himself would not be able to save them, and our supply of bandages is limited.

Suddenly I hear a call: "Nikolai Mikhailovich! Look . . . cars!"

I stand up. Wonderful! Three Red Cross trucks and an *Emka**—from the Evacuation Area, I think. I run forward, waving my arms. Here. *Here!* The head Evacuation Area surgeon, A. A. Bocharoff, and several unfamiliar doctors get out of the small car. Medics jump down from the trucks. Stretchers, bandages.

I report. They listen silently, nodding. Bocharoff offers some praise—grudgingly, it seems: "Well done. The comrades from other PPGs will take the most difficult cases."

---

*Slang for a light passenger car manufactured in the Soviet Union before World War II.—Trans.

Then he issues orders. Brief, precise, exhaustive. He's a great man—a real surgeon and a real leader.

It is amazing what fear can do. A sergeant lies prone with splints on both legs. He has no strength to move a finger; his hand grips some grass. Fair pulse, but fast. We turn him over. Bulging eyes. Wild. Hoarse whisper: "Take me away ... quick ... He'll be back . . . He'll kill all of us."

I try to calm him with morphine directly into the vein. He becomes limp, closes his eyes.

"How could you crawl so far in your condition?" I ask.

"I don't know. . . . In the train I couldn't even move a foot." He is four hundred yards from the train.

About 20 percent of the living men had suffered new wounds during the bombing. Many of those who had been alive were killed and burned to death. Some are wearing hospital pajamas, others shirts; almost all are barefoot; almost all of them have lost their documents.

Our own truck comes back carrying water, Chernoff, Shishkin, and a few medics. They say Khaminoff did not permit any women doctors to come; they are waiting in Alneri to take care of those whom we will send there.

Almost all the cases are serious. The few walking ones seem to have straggled away. Everyone else has been collected. The comparatively light cases go to Alneri; others are to go to other hospitals. We leave the dead where they are—it's shameful, but we have no time. I suppose the peasants from neighboring villages will bury them tomorrow. Their next of kin will never know what happened to their loved ones.

In four trips our truck brings almost a hundred cases into our hospital, and it all happens just when we have been ordered to move. Khaminoff grumbles sarcastically: "Couldn't you bring more? Okay, okay. Don't get mad."

I was ready to explode; I could barely control myself. I should have ripped into him. Instead, I said: "I'll work on this contingent. Some men must be operated on. Get Chernoff or somebody else to take care of the walking cases."

In the dressing tent we work like mad, sorting, listing. Some forty of the men need immediate surgical attention, and three doctors—Lina, Nina, Liza—work at it. I do surgery; Tamara administers anesthesia.

Well, we have them—real wounded. We have no time to redress all wounds. No time. They put a young soldier with a broken shoulder bone on the table. He has lost much blood and needs a transfusion, but we have no blood or plasma.

"We'll have to take off your arm, Comrade," I say.

"Oh, no, Doctor! What would I do without an arm? Depend on my wife for my bread?"

"I'm sorry, but there is nothing else to do. Your arm is dead; the arteries are cut. It is getting blue. Try to move your fingers."

He tries. It seems to him that he can, but he cannot. We cannot afford to lose any more time. The final argument: "With an arm like this we can't move you. You will develop gangrene on the way. We will have to leave you behind—in the local hospital."

"Leave me to the Germans?"

"What else can we do?"

"All right, cut away, goddamn you."

My first military amputation. Tourniquet. Deep incisions along the bone with a large amputation knife, a horrible looking thing the first time you see it. The arm falls off along the fracture. Kansky holds the bone with pincers while I saw it off. I tie up main vessels and cut the nerve.

"Loosen the tourniquet."

The blood bursts from the small vessels. I use forceps and tie them off. It takes time, but I can't help it. Unless the vessels are tied off, he might bleed to death before anyone notices it. That's all. Tight bandage. I remove my gloves, fill out the card. He is still unconscious. They put the shirt on his inert body.

"Cut off the sleeve so that they notice if he starts bleeding."

I push the card into his shirt pocket and button it up. This way he can be identified—in case.

They carry him out. The first cripple of my manufacture.

Lina is working on the cases not requiring immediate surgery, especially on the large wounds and bone injuries most likely to develop gangrene. The simplest treatment involves cutting all wounds open. My white gown is smeared with blood; I look like a careless butcher.

We work like a well-oiled machine. "On the table. Tighten the belts. Tamara, morphine. Chloroethyl. Tania, get another table ready. Take him away. Next."

At two o'clock in the morning, Khaminoff starts badgering us. "Come on, come on, wrap it up. The walking cases are ready to go, and all the carts are loaded."

I am flabbergasted. "And what about our new cases here?" I say.

"Zvereff and Shishkin went out to collect peasant carts, if they can find them. We are doing all we can. But one can't jump over one's own head."

I become tense. "Look Chief, not a single cart leaves here until everyone of these men is taken care of. If necessary, we must abandon all our equipment." I will not budge.

He senses it. "All right, but hurry up," he says.

Khaminoff can be hard. I have already heard him say, "All untransportable cases are to go to the local hospital." This might be regulation procedure, but it is too cruel. The regular German units might not touch them, but after them will come the SS and the Gestapo murder squads. Thank God, all our cases are transportable.

I walk out to watch the departure of our walking cases.

The night is warm and fairly light. A mob of men. Muffled voices. Now and then a lighted match—followed by cries: "Hey! Put it out! Tired of life?"

Near the gate, three loaded carts stand ready. Seated on one, surrounded by first aid kits, Nina nods. Chernoff is running around. It is not an easy task to be responsible for such a mob. I check on the equipment that is going along—stretchers, bandage material, crutches, medicines. Four medics are going along, too. Everything seems to be in order, and yet I know that in an emergency *something* will come up missing.

Khaminoff walks out onto the school porch. "Detachment, attention! Line up—four men abreast!" he shouts.

The crowd stirs. "Why this lining up?" I ask Khaminoff in a whisper.

"It is just to check them out. Later, of course, they'll march as best they can."

In the early gray dawn we're confronted by a bizarre scene: men in greatcoats, in shirts, in sweaters, hospital robes. Cut-away sleeves and trouser legs. Walking sticks, crutches. Men without boots, with legs in plaster casts. All line up four abreast. All are trained soldiers, about six hundred men.

It is a heartbreaking scene. It is nearly 25 miles to Kozelsk. And who knows if there will be any transport there? How many of them will make it?

THE FOLLOWING MORNING

By six o'clock in the morning we have completed our work. In all we have processed fifty-three men, at least half of whom are unconscious or delirious. There have been seventeen operations, three amputations.

We pack up. The conscious watch us with alarm. Are we going to leave them behind? They needn't worry. Khaminoff has promised that if worse comes to worst, we will abandon our equipment before we abandon our patients.

I watch the girls work. Pack well, Darlings. Who knows how far we are going back. The Germans have been dropping leaflets: "Moscow is doomed. Surrender." They must be crazy. If anything, the propaganda works in reverse, makes us fight harder.

At seven o'clock Zvereff and Shishkin come back with peasant carts—almost fifty of them! They are quite small, and each is pulled by one skinny horse. All are driven by old men in their seventies or eighties.

We load up. All our serious cases seem to be all right. Gangrene starts with sharp pains, and no one is complaining. Probably they all are afraid that if they do, they'll be left behind.

I never thought we had so much stuff! Blankets, linen, pillows, mattresses. We were ready to accomodate one thousand cases. Water therapy, physiotherapy. All this has gone to hell now. Once again we are a horse-drawn hospital.

At nine o'clock the procession starts off.

Khaminoff yells, from the porch, "Forward march! Go!"

I think, "Go with God."

By ten o'clock Khaminoff, myself, and Tikhomiroff still have not left. Deciding to leave nothing behind, we've spent the time loading the last odds and ends into our truck.

It's a clear, fresh morning. Khaminoff and I sit on a bale of hay under an apple tree. Some yellow leaves flutter down. It is Autumn. Strange, I do not feel tired, just lightheaded—and sad, as if something has come to an end.

"It's the reaction to overexcitement," Khaminoff tells me. "You won't be able to sleep for a while. Want a drink? Just to relax?"

I know he has a bottle in his pocket, but I decline the offer. I have never learned to drink.

Tikhomiroff joins us, having checked out everything. Nothing at all has been left behind. A soldier brings in our personal stuff from our old billets. It was not a bad place.

I have grown to like Khaminoff. He's an interesting man, and a good doctor. So what if his weakness is drink. If he takes a swig at night now and then, it's always within reason. I've never seen him drunk.

A group of German bombers passes overhead, going east. Sukhinichi does not interest them any longer. Both the station and the town have been burned out.

"Look at that one! It's ours!" A sudden shout.

We jump up, scan the sky. Eight bombers head east, not fast, not high, in tight formation. Going to work: to bomb stations, roads, bridges—even, maybe, hospital trains. And then there's our own, dear, snub-nosed *Yastrebok*,* heading straight at them. Alone! Firing tracer bullets, he passes over them. If only one German would start to smoke! But they fly on as though nothing has happened. The *Yastrebok* turns around and goes in for another pass, firing again. The Germans are fighting back. Eight of them.

"Fly away! What can you do alone? Fly away!" We shout as if we think he can hear us.

Another wide circle and another attack. Eight German bombers fire at him. He passes over them, makes another circle, gaining altitude, and then dives upon them.

"Look out! He's going to ram them!"

Our flyers have been ramming German bombers since the first day of the war. But this one does not make it. Before he reaches them, he bursts into a ball of flame, then hurtles down, trailing black smoke.

He crashes somewhere beyond the horizon. No parachute.

We stand there, shattered, tears in our eyes.

The Germans fly away, in tight formation, like eight irons, pressing the sky before them.

"Damn you, bastards." No one speaks a word. But we all feel it.

Khaminoff, Tikhomiroff, and I walk through the garden in silence. Pieces of bloodstained bandages, rags, boards, and bricks litter the kitchen area. I think of that single man in the sky. "The madness of the brave," Maxim Gorky called it in his *Song of the Falcon*. But that was not madness; that was desperation. Probably he could no longer bear to look at our poor, tortured Russia. Probably he could find no more strength to live.

"That's the way Hitler is going to lose this war," Khaminoff says finally as we approach our truck.

A strange remark. But somehow we all feel this way: the Russian people will never stop fighting, not in another year, not in five years, not in ten years.

Literally, "little hawk." I-16 attack interceptor.—Trans.

LATER THAT DAY

Our truck developed mechanical trouble, and we have been sitting in Alneri until almost seven o'clock in the evening. Finally we are leaving.

Khaminoff sits in the cabin next to the driver. Tikhomiroff and I are in the back of the truck, our legs dangling, under a green canopy with a large red cross on top. It does not protect us at all. The Germans ignore such humanitarian niceties. However, throughout the day squadrons of German bombers have been flying over us heading east and paying no attention to Alneri. A bad sign. It means that their troops are advancing or about to advance.

As the truck lurches along a bumpy road, I have a bit of time for thinking. For a month and a half I've had no time to myself at all, only four or five hours each night for sleeping.

Have I done everything right? No. I should have gone along with my wounded instead of riding in comfort like this. I am thinking about that pilot—one against eight. Attacking against impossible odds. That is the way we must wage this war.

And what about my surgical performance? Have I lived up to my responsibility? And are we really prepared medically for a war of this magnitude?

Historically, Russian medical services have always lagged behind. The Crimean campaign . . . Professor Pirogoff, "the father of Russian surgery." Doctors in dirty military jackets probed all wounds to remove bullets. The results were disastrous. Almost all cases with injured bones died of infection. And of course nearly all amputees.

The Turkish war of 1878. A new theory: touch the wounds as little as possible. The results were slightly better. By then we knew of Pasteur and Lister.

The Russo-Japanese war. The Russian disgrace. Only the most pressing surgery. The goal was evacuation, evacuation of all cases. The result—gangrene.

World War I. The corrupt Czar's system could not organize military surgery. They performed only the most pressing field surgery, and then, evacuation. Gangrene took a tremendous toll.

Nearly all abdominal wounds were fatal. And yet, in the West, particularly in France, things were different. All serious cases were operated on at once, during the first few hours. And the results were remarkably successful.

During the Civil War there was practically no field surgery. Fronts were changing every day. All one could hope for was evacuation of walking cases. Doctors worked honestly, even though they often cursed the Bolsheviks.

Since then, there has been a great improvement. The present Medical Service of the Red Army is a far cry from our dismal past. We have enough personnel, enough equipment. It is up to us surgeons to prove our worth.

It is dark now, and sad pictures pass through my mind. Suffering, dying men. Mangled bodies. Now we are retreating again. Terrible. And what has happened to those men we sent away during the night? Have they been evacuated safely? Perhaps Kozelsk has been bombed out. It is so far to Kaluga. And what about Kaluga? Could the Germans get that far? I remember the soldiers' stories about the first weeks of the war. Could that happen again? After Elnya, after Odessa, after the Leningrad defense? No, impossible. Our front is too secure.

We arrive in Kozelsk at eleven at night. A small, dark town with squat houses in the typically Russian style. The smoking ruins of the bombed-out railway station—an incredible mess of burned-out cars, twisted rails, pieces of brick, lumber. Everything is dead.

Finally we find the station commandant, an absolutely exhausted man, smoke-stained, hoarse. He can hardly speak.

"It is all over. Two hours ago we sent out our last train . . . No, we could not load everyone . . . No room, no time . . . I think they'll be all right. . . . They passed the bridge over the Upa. . . . The road to Tula is still intact. I don't think they would bomb them at night . . . The Evacuation Center? I don't know . . . There were so many different officers . . . hundreds, all giving orders."

I remember an Uzbek soldier who told me that they have a saying in the Karakum desert: "A happy country produces poets and artists, an unhappy one, dust and many supervisors."

We leave for Peremyshl.* We must find our wounded, our horse-drawn PPG. Of course, I should have been with them, but it's too late to develop a guilt complex.

Tikhomiroff and I are peering into the dark. In the West we see flashes of gunfire. Now they seem to be all around us—even ahead of us. A parachute drop? There have been rumors about such drops.

We finally catch up with our hospital in the large village of Kamenka. They have stopped there for the night. We almost passed them without knowing it.

"Well, how was it?" we ask.

They report that our walking wounded and our horse train united in Kozelsk, near the station. It was almost six o'clock in the evening. It was a terrible mess—crowds of wounded and no trains. Our people got hold of some freight cars, threw everything out of them, and formed two trains for the most serious cases. They loaded them like sardines in cans. All those who could walk were sent out on foot. Just in time, too. There was a massive air raid immediately afterward, and the station was completely destroyed.

No one knows for sure how many cases are still with us. All the seriously wounded were given their documents. We have all the documents of the walking wounded, but what good are they? Many men might have strayed without any documents.

OCTOBER 6, 1941

This morning I walked outside and discovered it had snowed. And last night it was so warm. Now it is cold, gray, overcast.

Our cook, Chapliuk, has managed to conjure up some soup. They are passing out dry rations to long, silent lines—the wounded

---

*Not to be confused with a large city by this name in Western Ukraine, lost during the first days of the war.—Trans.

and medical personnel together. That is not correct. The wounded should have priority, but no one seems to care.

At ten o'clock we leave, the walking wounded in front. No one talks about lining up. The men are tired and angry. No one even counts them. Obviously, many have strayed or managed to get into trains with the serious cases—without orders or documents.

Behind us, an obvious disaster. One has only to look around to see soldiers, in groups and alone, all walking east. They have no arms, and half of them have no overcoats or helmets. Deserters? They refuse to answer any questions. Some carry gas-mask bags filled with bread, spoons, knives, cups. Defeated, dispirited men. A miserable sight.

But there is fighting somewhere, because we hear a steady sound of gunfire. Some men must still be fighting. And dying.

Our caravan stretches for two miles. The carts are overloaded; everyone has to walk. Even our fat pharmacist is walking. She says that during the night her stores have been raided by men looking for alcohol. Now she demands that all her boxes and cans be kept next to her. She is wearing a military helmet and some impossible goat fur coat—a comical figure.

I am properly equipped now. I have traded my peacoat for a long cavalry overcoat. I have a helmet, a duffle bag, a cape-tent, and a real officer's leather belt. I even have a map case, but no maps. Everyone is trying to get rid of things. We even got two horses with saddles. It is odd, but men prefer to walk on foot when they're retreating. Khaminoff gave me one of the horses, and since lunchtime I've been riding. It's a large red mare, stubborn and temperamental. All I lack is spurs.

Toward evening, we enter Kaluga. We are to spend the night here and try to find some people from our Evacuation Area.

Khaminoff and I are billeted in a small house. A woman brings out some milk and straw for us. She refuses to take money.

"Is it possible that the Germans will come here? We have such a fine army, they told us. How could you let them go to the very heart of Russia?"

Listening to her questions, I wish we'd spent the night outside.

OCTOBER 7, 1941

Next morning we succeed in turning over our wounded to the Evacuation Center in Kaluga. Some of them seem to be well on the way to recovery—the long hike seems to have done them good. We turn over 220 men and the documents for over 350. What has happened to the rest? They say that 470 men were loaded into trains in Kozelsk. Some men probably got into the trains on their own—without any documents. For the most part, our consciences are clear.

The most frightening thing is that the Germans seem to be driving straight for Moscow. And Moscow is the symbol of Russia, its very heart. Of course Field Marshal Koutuzov said in 1812: "The loss of Moscow is not the loss of Russia." And Napoleon found that out.

All this is true, but my very soul is aching.

I have given my horse to Kansky. Now I understand why people prefer going on foot. My backside is so sore I can hardly walk.

In the evening we receive the order to move our entire hospital group toward Moscow. There we will get a new assignment. Our 28th Army, in all probability, has ceased to exist. They say that some of our divisions are mere numbers; some have only a few hundred men. In any event, a Russian division, fully manned, is much smaller than a German, so counting the opposing forces by the number of divisions is all wrong.

We have permission to use the old Kaluga highway, but our truck has broken down completely. It is our fate to be a horse-drawn unit. "He who was born to crawl, cannot fly," Maxim Gorky said in *Song of the Falcon*. He was right.

We retreat.

OCTOBER 11, 1941

For three days now we've been following the old Kaluga road.

Built by Catherine the Great, it is a broad highway, lined with birches on both sides. They are ancient trees, but still strong, each one a beauty. Not all the leaves have fallen, and when the sun shines through them, it is beautiful. A dreamlike Russian landscape.

Our life style is simple. We spend our nights in villages. They are half empty: all the men are gone, and even the young girls and women have been mobilized to build trenches around Moscow.

I have lost my map case somewhere and put my bag and helmet on one of the carts. Now I look like a defeated soldier, unshaven and dirty. Apathy.

Khaminoff bears up well. He walks in front, "the personal example of leadership." Sometimes we speak to him. With me he is quite frank. He blames Stalin for trusting Hitler, but he feels that his leadership is extremely important now—he has become a symbol to our soldiers. And he is absolutely sure that the Germans can never win this war. Not even if they go all the way to the Urals. "The more they swallow, the weaker they become. Even now they have to garrison half of Europe to keep people under their control, and Russia is not Europe. Our partisans have trackless forests to hide in. And when the winter comes, the Germans will be in real trouble."

I, too, cannot admit that we can be defeated. It's impossible. But then, what about France? A great nation, a first-class army.

We can only hope, since we no longer pray. And yet the Orthodox Church is still a sustaining force for many people; it has joined the government in calling for us to resist the invaders. They say the Patriarch has spoken to Stalin. Stalin was a theological student once. Perhaps he understands our people better than we do.

OCTOBER 16, 1941

Today we enter Moscow. Our valiant PPG-2266 will parade across the capital of our Motherland, going east.

We enter through the Kaluga gate, follow the great Kaluga street, and turn right. It is best to avoid the center of the city. We look grotesque. Bedraggled men and weary women in soldier's overcoats walk beside squeaking old carts loaded with God knows what—hardly an inspiring sight.

Near the gate we meet a detachment of civilian volunteers going to the front. A long column, four abreast, in clean new overcoats and helmets. Middle-aged men, some even old. The faces of intellectuals, workers, artisans, deferred from active service because of age, stomach ulcers, eye defects, tuberculosis, flat feet. Young girls with Red Cross arm bands and first aid kits walk beside each company. Young, fresh faces, some very pretty.

Could they save the capital? Doubtful. But then we have seen real soldiers—these are only reserves. And what about the Red Guards during the Civil War? They were probably even less impressive, and yet they defeated all the White Armies and the crack units of fourteen foreign countries. Lenin said, "Men who know what they are fighting for cannot be defeated."

It is strange to see Moscow like this. Strange and a little frightening. There is a sense of quiet panic in the air. People are loading their belongings onto carts, wheelbarrows, baby carriages. Bundled-up women leading bundled-up children, belongings on their backs. Stores are closed; the iron gratings are down. We travel by small streets in the southern suburbs. Perhaps things are different in the center, but here the atmosphere is depressing.

In the evening we listen to Scherbakoff, the secretary of the Moscow chapter of the Communist Party, speak on the radio. It is a good, strong speech. He says panic and demoralization have been created by a few people in responsible positions who have closed up their factories and offices and discharged workers. The Pary orders everyone to go back to his post—to show "personal responsibility." Panic-mongers are to be punished "without mercy." Good.

The speech has a sobering effect. There was not a word about the possible evacuation of Moscow. We all feel encouraged.

We leave Moscow by the Ryazan highway and move eastward toward Lubertzi. We'll spend the night there and wait for new orders.

DATE UNKNOWN

We arrive in Egorievsk, our new destination, nearly 100 miles east of Moscow. We are to establish our hospital here.

Our "holiday" is over. Thank God. It is easier when one is working.

Apparently our PPG-2266 has shown exemplary behavior during the retreat. We did not lose any equipment, and we evacuated all our cases. The fact that some walking cases strayed away is not ever mentioned—apparently that is normal. We did not abandon a single man to the enemy. It seems that other hospitals, even those with motor transport, have not done that well.

Now we are attached directly to "the Front," i.e., an army group. Our original 28th Army has been disbanded and absorbed by other armies. We have no idea what has happened to its head surgeon, Nikolaeff, and his staff. Have they been captured by the Germans or just lost in the shuffle? It's best not to ask too many questions.

Because of our "honorable performance" we have been upgraded into a "hospital for those with moderately serious injuries." As "the leading officers," we are brought to Egorievsk in a military truck to prepare the way for the hospital. Our cart trains will be here in two days. We are to take over a former hospital that occupied the building of a former technical school. I get a very small room all to myself, equipped with a radio receiver. It is wonderful to be able to listen to something besides rumors. I hear all communiqués and a lot of good music. One song moves me almost to tears: "The people's war—the holy war."

Khaminoff gets a large room, a combination living quarters and office. Lina and Liza share a small bedroom. All this comfort is fine, but it is not the main thing.

The main thing is even better—a solid three-story building with three hundred real beds. There are wound dressing rooms, an operation theater, bathrooms, and a large dining room. We are expanding our capacity to 100 additional beds and getting a shock ward and a gangrene ward set up.

We are not unduly hurried. Egorievsk is not on any main

highway, and apparently there is no overflow of the wounded.

DATE UNKNOWN

Heavy fighting near Moscow. No place to fall back to any farther. Zhukov has been appointed the commander of the Moscow front. In some places the Germans are less than 100 miles from the Kremlin, but Stalin and the government are still there. However, some ministries have been transferred to Kuibyshev on the Volga. In the South, the Germans are attacking in the Donets coal basin and in the Crimea.

Today we were to receive our first wounded. They are coming in a special hospital train. We have waited all day and all night, but the train has apparently been delayed on the way. We curse the railway.

Our reception and sorting departments are ready. We have corrected all our former errors.

Riaboff has set up his bathrooms and has mobilized a whole squad of local volunteer women with sponges. Liubov Vladimirovna Bykova has been appointed head surgery nurse. Liubochka, as we call her behind her back, is a complicated person, but she knows her work and is full of energy and initiative. She's had twenty years of experience as a doctor's assistant. I feel absolutely secure with her at my side. Besides, she is an intellectual and a woman of culture. One can learn things by listening to her.

Zoya Radionova, a girl from Bielozersk, is my operation room nurse. She's a little nervous, but fast and accurate. Tamara is our anesthetist. We have another one, Masha Poletova, a frail little blonde. She joined us in Sukhinichi. I have a first-class team with Lina as my assistant surgeon. Everything is ready. There is even a 500-watt lamp over the operating table!

It is surprising how well I work with Lina. We understand each other practically without words. And there is absolutely no reference to our intimate past. We are close friends, and that is all.

Khaminoff walks around in a new white gown, like a minister. He's full of authority, but I must admit that he has never lost his composure, even during our worst days.

At five o'clock in the morning, enormous Red Cross vans drive up to the hospital. We all run out. Everything goes quickly and smoothly: sorting, registering, hot tea, dressing wounds when necessary.

Here they are, the defenders of Moscow. They are tired and unnerved by their long train ride. Half of them are bed cases, but there are no splints. According to their cards, they have medium to light injuries. All were wounded 3 to 5 days ago.

And the way they are dressed! Each man has an overcoat, a cotton-padded uniform, a fur hat, boots, a sweater, and woolen undergarments. A country that can dress its soldiers like this has to win!

Most are middle-aged men, reservists.

"How are things at the front?" I ask.

One should not ask such questions. The wounded are always pessimistic. We know that by now. But this time the answers are different.

"The Germans are throwing everything at us . . . But we are holding."

Soldiers do not like big words.

"And our losses?"

"Not too bad. We're dug in."

Most of them are from fresh reinforcements, some from as far as Siberia. They had their first encounter with the enemy near Moscow and have not been demoralized by the summer retreats.

Altogether we receive 135 cases. All wounds have been treated in front-line medical units. There is no major surgery, but still plenty of work for us. We cut open all wounds, I operate on one radial artery, we remove bullets and shell fragments when possible, and so on throughout the day.

We finish at ten o'clock at night—with a feeling of satisfaction. Every case has been treated to the best of our ability. Our bit for the defense of Moscow.

MID-NOVEMBER, 1941

The November holidays are over.* There is very hard fighting around Moscow.

Stalin is a great man. He may be heartless and cruel, but he has a streak of genius. He held the usual Red Square parade and delivered a wonderful speech. The troops went straight to the front after marching past Lenin's mausoleum. It was so wonderful that I can find no words to express how I felt.

We all repeat his words: "The enemy is not as strong as they describe him . . . Half a year more, or a year, and Germany will collapse under the weight of her crimes." He mentioned our Russian national heroes. He has given us confidence, faith in ultimate victory.

I watched our wounded. Their faces showed their adoration of that man. No, he could not be replaced by anyone else. He has been built up as a symbol of Russia—the historical "father image" that has always inspired Russian soldiers in the past.

And all the time we listen to that wonderful song, "The Holy War." I shall remember it my whole life. When we win this war, our poets and composers must be specially honored. They give our people the strength to endure the unendurable.

We are learning a new method of treating bullet fracture. Arkady Alexeivich Bocharoff introduced it to us. He now comes in almost every day—we are becoming his favorite hospital.

It all started on the 6th of November. He came in just as Kansky and I were preparing a complicated metal construction for a plaster cast—so that plaster would not touch the wound.

"Let me do it, Nikolai Mikhailovich—the modern way," he said.

We watched him do it. First he made sure that the wound was thoroughly cleansed. Then he took bandage strips, dipped them in plaster and put them directly over the wound as if it were a closed fracture. It was a light, delicate cast. He took a chemical pencil, wrote the date on the cast, and drew a diagram of the fracture. Then he said, "That is the way to do it."

---

*November 7 and 8, the anniversary of the Revolution.—Trans.

Of course we began to question him, citing our misgivings, and he explained everything precisely and patiently. The blind cast method, he said, was revolutionizing the treatment of firearm fractures. It had been developed by Professor Yudin. Bocharoff was one of Yudin's pupils, and so was an authority on the subject.

I had two years of surgical experience, no surgery philosophy of my own, and inadequate textbook knowledge, so I was easy to convince. But Bocharoff claimed he was having trouble with the older, more experienced surgeons.

"They are not only conservative, but also ignorant," he complained.

I was momentarily flattered. I was certainly not conservative.

But I was ignorant. This method had been widely described in surgical publications after the Finnish war of 1940. Professor Pirogoff first used it as early as the nineteenth century. According to Yudin, the technique must combine three elements: a very thorough debridement of the wound, sulfa drugs, and then a blind plaster bandage over the wound. Bocharoff told us that abroad this was known as "the Russian method." And we had never heard of it!

The advantages are obvious. Bones are kept firmly in place, and the wounded can walk. But there are drawbacks as well. It requires a complete removal of all dead tissues and bone fragments—everything that might provide food for bacteria. There is no way of watching the possible development of septic processes under the plaster. It takes time, a precious commodity under war conditions. And, of course, only highly qualified surgeons can apply the method.

So we are experimenting, but only on simple leg fractures. Kansky is doing very well, and some of the nurses are learning the technique.

NOVEMBER, 1941

The Germans are trying to storm Moscow—to get into warm

quarters for the winter. We hear that their troops are lightly dressed. They say Hitler believes that will encourage his soldiers to fight harder. There are alarming headlines in *Pravda* again: "Moscow is in danger." The Germans are trying to surround it by driving from Kalinin and toward Tula.

We are working hard, but coping. We have already put on five closed plaster casts on shoulder fractures. This is a very complicated operation, involving much of the chest area as well.

We have received the second shipment of wounded. The men are optimistic. "We'll never surrender Moscow," they say, but I am worried.

NOVEMBER, 1941

Yesterday I heard an interesting story. They sent us a new group of medical personnel. They had all escaped from an encirclement by the Germans. Among them is an operating room nurse, Lyda Denisenko, a tall, thin, blonde, quite good looking. She became ill upon arrival. Every time she tries to walk, she becomes dizzy. She is a modest, very attractive girl.

She had been a third term student at the Pedagogical Institute in Smolensk, switched to a school for nurses during the Finnish war, and then graduated when the war was over. But she has been in this war from the very first day, and she has had her quota of trouble. Front-line medical units. Forests. Poor defenses. They worked day and night, but their facilities were limited, and the wounded were dying. In September they had to cross the Dnieper, where they lost all their equipment and many men. On October 4th the Germans broke through towards Vyazma. They were surrounded. They received the usual orders: "Try to escape, in small groups or individually." She and a girl friend wandered through the forests. They heard German voices. Then a group of Russian soldiers headed by a young lieutenant picked them up. Together they walked at night for thirty days trying to get out of the encirclement. They were cold, hungry, disoriented. The Germans were all around, and there were traitors in the villages. Some members of their little group were killed. Ragged and dispirited, they finally encountered some partisan guerrillas who led them to safety.

Lyda said that guerrillas were operating all over the occupied territory, and the Germans could only hold the main communication lines. Yes, there were traitors, but the local people hated them, and the guerrillas killed them whenever they captured them. They kept lists of those they did not capture so that eventually they could be brought to justice.

A brave girl, Lyda. No personal heroics, but she has saved her Young Communist League card and the triangles on her collar.* And chivalry is not dead. She said that the men had protected the two girls with their lives.

I asked Lyda about her father. She said he was the Secretary of the Communist Party in Smolensk. He was sent to Leningrad at the beginning of the war. She did not know what had become of him.

Speaking to this fine young woman, I felt greatly encouraged. Indeed, the farther the Germans go, the more enemies appear behind their backs. They have behaved like beasts, burning villages and killing people, but that has only increased the people's resistance. No, this is not France. Napoleon was the first conqueror who was defeated by the people—the Russian peasants who attacked his supply columns and trains and made him lose his whole army during his retreat from Moscow.

The last night communiqué: we recaptured Rostov, but lost Tikhvin. That isn't far from Cherepovets, but somehow I have no feeling of panic.

LATE NOVEMBER, 1941

Today we used the closed plaster cast method on a hip fracture. Our first one.

---

*Before the introduction of shoulder straps in the Soviet Army late in 1942, sergeants wore red triangles on their collars.—Trans.

The patient's name is Smagin. A regular army sergeant, he has fought from the first day of the war. Near Moscow a shell tore off his left arm and smashed his hip bone. He was brought in by plane. A very serious case. Bloodless lips, the temperature 40°C., and he is joking with nurses—a very strong fellow.

Actually, a leg amputation was clearly indicated, but Bocharoff himself put on the cast, leaving a long cut for pus drainage. I am really worried. There were clear signs of a septic condition.

When he came to, he was shivering and still joking. If a will to survive really works, this will be the experiment to prove it. Bocharoff promises that in a few days the man's temperature will come down. Hmm.

Lyda Denisenko is still too ill to work—a pity.

DECEMBER 12, 1941

Hurray, hurray, hurray! We are attacking!

The night communiqué: "a serious defeat of the Germans before Moscow."

We are told that on December 6th our troops stopped the Germans and went on the offensive. They liberated Solnechnogorsk, Istra, and a number of other towns. The Germans abandoned masses of heavy equipment, guns, and tanks. Several crack German divisions have been completely shattered.

Thank God! We did not surrender Moscow, and now we are driving the Germans back. And how!

The story is that Stalin and the High Command have been collecting fresh reserves, and they have not touched them even in the most critical days. They must have had nerves of steel.

We've received the first shipment of wounded since the offensive. They are jubilant, despite their suffering. Outside it is 27° C. below, but we've had not a single case of serious frostbite, even though, they say, many Germans are found frozen to death in their light overcoats. Good.

The whole morning I walk through the wards congratulating the men. We smile and joke. Their blood has contributed to this victory.

"What about a drop of vodka, Comrade Military Surgeon?"

I am all for it, but our orders are strict. A little wine only to critical cases. But we cannot do even that today—all the others would be offended.

Smagin is still running a high temperature, but he is in high spirits.

"Not in vain did I lose my arm!" he says. "Now, to get well quickly!"

And I think, "You might still lose your leg—even your life." We are treating him with the entire arsenal of Yudin's school. But he hasn't shown much improvement. And how would we know if a gangrene process started under that cast!

Our political officers, Zvereff and Shishkin, walk around all smiles, speaking to the men, trading jokes. This is a great day for them. Fine men, both of them.

We are all thinking about the future. We must move west soon to keep up with the advancing troops. But so far, no orders.

Lyda Denisenko is feeling better—it is amazing what some good news can do. She came into the dressing station today, looking radiant. There is something very attractive about that girl. But she is still too weak to work.

DECEMBER 16, 1941

The news is great. The Germans are running. We have liberated Klin and Yasnaya Polyana, the homes of Tchaikovsky and Tolstoy. We are advancing on several fronts—on Taganrog, on Kalinin, and especially before Moscow. Tula was almost encircled, but never taken. They say that factory workers defended it. The historic arms-making center of Russia.

Zhukov's picture is in all the newspapers, along with pictures of several other generals.

The war is spreading. When the Japanese attacked the American fleet at Pearl Harbor, we were worried. Now the U.S., we thought, would be too occupied in the Pacific to pay much attention to the war in Europe. But the Germans are idiots, and Hitler is a moron. He declared war on the United States! They underestimated America in 1917, and they are doing it again. This is a war of machines. And the American industrial potential is enormous.

Khaminoff said, "Today the Germans have lost the war, no matter how long it continues."

With America on our side we simply can't lose—it's simple mathematics.

DECEMBER, 1941

I am depressed. I am a damned fool. An ignoramus. I should never have been the head of any surgery department. I am only good at dressing wounds, and some of the nurses are even better at that. I should have been working in some front-line regimental hospital. But they won't send me there. They think I am a surgeon.

"Bad, Nikolai Mikhailovich, very bad." That was all Bocharoff had to tell me. It would have been better had he slapped my face.

I have just returned from the autopsy, I am lying on my cot trying to figure out where I made the fatal error.

First of all, carelessness and too much self-assurance. Not enough attention given to individual cases. A routine approach.

Private Georgieff, 24. Wounded four days before. He had been treated properly before coming to us. His wound was properly cleansed and bandaged.

He arrived at 6 o'clock in the morning with a temperature of

38.2°C. "Satisfactory condition, no emergency," was my diagnosis. He wasn't brought to the dressing station until 2 o'clock in the afternoon.

They put him on the table. He was a large man with a black beard framing his pale face. When we removed the bandages he groaned. The wound appeared normal, but there was a swelling on the lower leg. I gave him the routine treatment: a fresh bandage, a splint, and into a ward.

We went on working. We had many cases, and we were in a hurry. One cannot hurry. No, one must hurry, but never relax vigilance.

My first error occurred later. In three hours a ward nurse asked Lina to come and take a look at Georgieff. "He is restless, moaning, trying to tear off the bandage," she said.

And I said, "Inject some morphine. He is just hysterical." Lina was busy, and I did not permit her to go.

In two more hours the nurse returned. "Georgieff is screaming, tossing about, asking for water," she said.

They brought him back. It had been less than six hours, and how everything had changed! I never thought that the process could develop so quickly. Muscles were bulging out; the skin was like a drum. But the main sign of gaseous gangrene, crepitation, was not present. I decided to operate. I did not realize that amputation was the only hope.

At eleven o'clock that night I looked at him. He was asleep. His pulse was 120, just as it had been before the operation. I decided that everything was in order and left for home at one o'clock in the morning, having asked the ward nurses to watch him. I cannot blame them. If I could not notice danger, how could they? Anesthetic and incisions had decreased the pain, since all pus had been drained. They called me back at six in the morning. A dying man. Unconscious. Almost no pulse. By eight o'clock he was dead.

Then Bocharoff came in. I told him everything. That's when he said, "Bad . . . very bad."

During the autopsy we found a few gas bubbles near the bone. How difficult it is to evaluate those things! An early amputation, a cripple. No amputation, a corpse.

For two years I worked under an experienced surgeon, under

strict supervision. But that was not real surgery; it was just an exercise.

Thousands of people die in the war. That is normal. But Georgieff did not have to die. Had he been under the care of an experienced surgeon, he could have lived.

Our autopsy man is Abram Touroff. He had been with Lyda Denisenko's unit when they were surrounded by the Germans. I met him today for the first time. A thorough, taciturn man—I liked him.

DECEMBER, 1941

We are about to relocate closer to the front.

At six in the morning I am listening to the first communiqué. A German Volkov group has been smashed. Another Red Army front has switched from defense to attack. Can it be the beginning of Leningrad's relief? That city has been completely blockaded. They say there is famine there, but the defenses hold very strongly.

Hospital trains are no longer bringing any wounded to us. Our entire hospital group is being prepared for relocation. I wish they would hurry; it would be sad to get into the "light cases" category again. (And what about Georgieff? No, I have not forgotten, but that error will not be repeated.)

At present we have two gangrene cases, Usmanoff and Nazaroff. Both are improving. I visit them first thing each morning.

We have had our trouble with them, plenty of it.

Usmanoff is a Turkmen from a desert village. We call him "Keer-vul." He speaks Russian poorly. They brought him in with a gaseous gangrene, temperature 39.8° C., in poor condition. He had a leg wound, improperly cleansed, a typical case—small bubbles of gas whenever I pressed the skin around the wound. We operated, cut out all injured tissues, found a small fragment, and removed it—a splinter from a shell. We inserted drainage tubes, organized a steady chloramine irrigation. And, of course, we gave plasma and blood transfusions. We were ready to amputate on four occasions, but the process did not seem to spread. I would have amputated, after Georgieff, but Bocharoff recommended that we wait. The man ran a high temperature for two weeks, and then we noticed a definite improvement. Wound dressings were painful, and he kept repeating: "keer-vul, keer-vul." We all have learned to love him. He has such a fine, kind face. Now he is ready for evacuation.

The second "lucky one" was Nazaroff. He came with a shoulder wound and a typical gangrene. But we have succeeded in arresting the infection. He is on the mend and will definitely recover.

Another gangrene case died an hour after coming to us. It was an obviously hopeless case, and therefore we could not blame ourselves.

And so, four gangrene cases and two fatalities. One must be charged to my carelessness. There is a cruel rule: "All cases with leg and arm wounds have the right to die only after amputation." Otherwise the surgeon has been careless.

Bocharoff's predictions about Smagin did not come true. His temperature remained high for two weeks after we put him on the cast. We listened to his jokes, but secretly we were worried—how not to miss the amputation deadline? We did all we could: special food, sulfa drugs, vitamins. And his high morale was a great help. Finally, on the third week the temperature went down and his blood composition improved.

Now he is out of danger. We are teaching him to walk with his heavy cast.

DECEMBER 31, 1941

We are going to the front.

We are driving westward in a brand new truck. We do not know our destination, but we know that we are advancing instead of retreating. Our hospital, with all our equipment, went by rail. Khaminoff, Kansky, I, and a few medics are riding in the truck, our mobile office. We must overtake the train and meet our hospital at our final destination, wherever that might be. We will be advised later.

We turned over all our cases for evacuation—Smagin, "Keer-vul," Nazaroff, and about thirty other bed cases. All in satisfactory condition and with full medical documentation.

It was sad to part with them. They had become our friends. Our hearts and our skills were in all of them. Yes, our skills. The majority of them will not go back to war, but all will be able to live useful lives. Every pair of hands is necessary. Newspapers are full of terrible stories of devastation in liberated towns and villages. Many of them have been burned to the ground.

We stop for the night at Kraskovo. We have a small room with a table, three chairs, and a portable radio.

We are going to celebrate the New Year here. We have half a liter of alcohol, a teakettle, some canned meat, bread, and a few tin cups.

We have just listened to the last hour's communiqué. Our men have liberated Kaluga. The same Kaluga where we had once sent our walking cases from Sukhinichi, thinking that it would never be taken.

We stand around the table. Khaminoff pours alcohol into cups and adds water "to taste." We wait for the Kremlin chimes, and then we hear them—those wonderful, beautiful, Kremlin chimes—the heartbeats of our country.

Khaminoff nods, and we raise our cups.

"Let's drink to victory, Comrades!"

"To victory in 1942!"

We drink. Alcohol burns my mouth, and I choke. I have never learned how to drink. It makes me sick. I gulp cold water to rinse my mouth.

We eat in silence listening to Kalinin's* New Year speech.

---

*M. Kalinin was the President of the Soviet Union during the war. —Trans.

Each of us is looking inside himself, remembering the past year, and our dear ones. I have no one to remember. No wife, no children. But I can see how dark Khaminoff's face has become. He has a wife and two daughters. They were visiting some relatives in Byelorussia and were caught there by the German advance. Will he ever see them again?

He reaches for his bag and brings out his own "private" bottle. "Let's have another drink, children," he says.

I can see tears in his eyes. One is rolling down his unshaven cheek. How many people are weeping in Russia this night?

JANUARY 8, 1942

Town of Podolsk, south of Moscow.

How long all these moves take! Will we again lose days and even weeks moving from place to place—even during the offensive?

Only yesterday we started to work again.

And what work! We have three upper floors of a large school building and are still assigned to moderately serious cases. The reception center of the Evacuation Area is on the ground floor. All cases are brought there and sorted out. Some are sent to light injury hospitals, some to special hospitals, and some upstairs to us.

During this week there have been changes. Now we have two surgical departments instead of one. The second one is under the direction of Dr. Z., the candidate of medical sciences whom I knew in Arkhangelsk. He was an assistant professor there in the surgical department, a neurosurgeon. An interesting man, he is a book lover of vast erudition. He smokes a pipe, even when performing operations. For some reason we called him "Blackbird."

And he was appointed the head surgeon, instead of me.

Bocharoff said, "He's had more experience, and is older than you. Your hospital will do some brain surgery, and he's a specialist. But he won't interfere with your work."

It's all right with me. Titles mean nothing to me, as long as I can do my own work.

Blackbird and I work in two 12-hour shifts. Each of us specially supervises 150 cases, even though during our shifts we are responsible for all our patients.

We are billeted in a former obstetrics clinic. Not bad. I sleep in a high delivery bed.

Today is my day shift. We run to the hospital with Lina and Lisa. Both are on my team. Also Zoya and Tamara. But Kansky has been taken away from me, and Blackbird got Lyda Denisenko as his head operating room nurse.

It is beastly cold. Good. The Germans must be frozen out. In our villages they freeze out cockroaches like this every winter.

Near the hospital building stand two 1½-ton trucks and an autobus. Medics are unloading the wounded. There are the usual groans, curses, entreaties.

"Faster . . . damn you . . . faster . . . take us in . . . oh . . . "

The reception room is located in a former school gym. We call it "the railway station." It accommodates up to 200 men. The center of the room is filled with stretchers. Other wounded sit on the floor along the walls and in the aisles. There is a registration table. I see a medic in a blood-stained gown. The room is overflowing with the cases. An exhausted, hirsute military doctor is walking among them, trying to sort them. A nurse and two medics are with him. There is a hum of voices, moans and groans, clouds of *makhorka** smoke, a stench of sweat and blood. The windows are boarded up. A small, naked light bulb hangs from the ceiling.

I approach the doctor and greet him cheerfully, "Good morning. How's the situation?"

He snaps at me. "Are you blind? If there is no evacuation train by noon, we'll be putting them on top of one another. This your shift? Take those, along that wall—they're yours. Take them. I'll order them to be carried upstairs or put on the stairway."

---

*Rough tobacco, government issue in the Red Army.—Trans.

Upstairs I find Blackbird, pipe in his mouth, sitting on the bench in the dressing station. Lyda Denisenko and another nurse are working. Lyda is still weak after her illness, and she looks exhausted. Blackbird looks at me with his dull eyes.

"We're exhausted," he says. "We've processed about fifty cases, and there are more to be looked at."

Fifty is not enough, but we never criticize one another. An unwritten rule.

"Come on, girls," I say.

We plunge into work. Lina and Liza work in the dressing station, and I check on the wards, marking those who can stand transportation for evacuation. We absolutely must create room for new cases. I mark them "sitting up," "lying down," "must be watched." I send some to have their wounds redressed, and I watch for possible gangrene. Bocharoff is already talking about Yudin plaster casts, but there is no time. We are swept along by a torrent of wounded men, a continuous space crisis. Each bed is at a premium.

None of our cases are very serious, but almost all are bed cases. Flesh wounds, leg, foot, and arm fractures. And not a single serious frostbite case. And this during the offensive, with no dugouts or trenches and with all villages burned to the ground by the retreating army. Our supply services are wonderful. And they say that the Germans are walking around in women's shawls stolen from peasants, with rags over their boots.

There are lice. I have not seen any, but the girls are complaining. We must absolutely delouse all clothing. During the Civil War, typhus killed more people than bullets.

Wound dressing. It takes two men to carry the case in and put him on the table. If this is the first radical dressing, the bandages are stuck to the wound. Removing them is very painful. One can use peroxide, but it takes too much time. It is simpler to remove them by single jerk, which usually brings a howl: "What are you doing, you bastard?! Use some water!" They are right, of course. Tamara is a master at appealing to masculine pride. "Just try to bear it a little, dear," she says. "It will be painful, but quick. After all, you're a man and a soldier."

Zoya is quick and accurate. She always works in a sterile gown and gloves. She maintains the highest standards.

Lyda Denisenko and another night nurse help for a few hours after the end of their shift until we order them home. All our girls are killing themselves.

I am doing all the surgery myself. Lina is good, but I am faster. We are opening simple wounds with local anesthesia, more complicated ones with general. We operate on about every fifth man. There is no time for radical debridement, but wound opening is necessary. So far, no gangrene cases. In the winter, the germs are less active.

About plastering. Under these conditions it is hardly practical. It takes too much time and delays evacuation. They can do that in Moscow hospitals. Yesterday we put on only four casts: three simple leg factures and one shoulder cast. With Kansky gone, I must do it myself.

We leave all skull cases for Blackbird—his specialty. But there are few of those.

We work like a precise mechanism:

"An empty table! Get a move on!"

"Lina, a leg splint!"

"Zoya, local anesthesia. Quick!"

"Tamara! Cloroethyl!"

"Liza, write: 'Kiriloff. Blind wound in left leg with a fractured tibia. Swelling. The entry wound: 3 x 0.8 mm. Surgery: incision 9 centimeters to the bone. Two bone pieces removed. Bullet not found. Kramer's splint. Evacuate lying down. Watch for infection.'—Next!"

Now and then, Liubov Vladimirovna, our head ward nurse, looks in, boiling with excitement. "Nikolai Mikhailovich!" she yells. "Reception wants us to take in eight more bed cases. We have no beds. They say they will bring them in anyway. What do I do?"

"How do I know? Put them on the floor or two in a bed."

"But that's terrible!"

"Yes, it is, but what else can you suggest?"

We work this way until four o'clock, when they bring in our dinner after feeding the wounded.

The night shift arrives at eight. We eat supper, clean up, and do some secondary wound dressing, usually until two in the morning. Only then we stagger home, dead tired but satisfied. No, we haven't done everything, but we've done everything that is absolutely necessary. Usually there is at least one evacuation train a day, sometimes two. After all, we are close to Moscow.

And in six more hours we are back at work, with the night shift working overtime to help us.

JANUARY 10, 1942

Am I really so stupid, and will I never learn? Such self-assurance and composure, and then, when it comes to a crunch—an idiotic lapse! I'm ready to cry. Such a depressing feeling. It will stay with me for the rest of my life.

Private Popkoff. Wounded right here in Podolsk during an air raid and brought to our reception ward ten minutes after being hit. (We don't notice those raids unless our windows are blown out. And the Germans rarely get through our anti-aircraft defenses these days. Even when they do get through, they drop their bombs haphazardly.) I was summoned right away, and even before approaching "the railway station" I heard hysterical yells: "Let me go! Let me go!"

The right trouser leg was ripped open and inside was a bloody mess of torn muscles. He couldn't understand anything and tried to get up. It was awful to see the leg bent at such a crazy angle near the hip. There was a puddle of blood on the stretcher even though a tourniquet had been applied. He was conscious, but hysterical. He had a strong pulse, but very slow.

They brought him to the dressing room on the run. As we undressed him, he became quieter, but his pulse became weaker and faster. I could see he was both hysterical and in shock. I called for morphine, heart stimulants, and hot water bottles. After half an hour, he showed all the symptoms of shock: he became quiet and kept shivering. We transfused half a liter of whole blood and a liter of a solution of glucose and alcohol, all into the vein. In an hour his blood pressure stabilized at 80-90. I had to do something. The tourniquet was still on. On the upper leg, he had an enormous wound, at least 20 centimeters. All the tissues had been shredded. The bone was shattered.

This, I thought, was my chance to prove myself. An absolutely fresh wound, with no chance of infection. Ideal conditions for an experiment with Yudin's technique. And we had some time on our hands—no patients waiting.

"We'll work over the wound and put plaster on it," I announced.

No one contradicted me. Of course not. A talented young surgeon, even Bocharoff praises him, they must have thought.

"Ether! Zoya, everything for a radical debridement. Lina, you will help me."

We administered ether. In a few minutes he was under.

Even then it was not too late to stop. But no, I started to operate according to the Yudin method. I cut out all loose tissues and removed all bone fragments. We put him on a sustentaculum, and I put on a perfect plaster cast with local splints.

When I began to put on his cast, his pulse was almost normal and he was breathing well. Obviously he had come out of shock. I felt jubilant. "This is the way to treat these kinds of fractures," I thought.

Finally everything was finished. "Tamara, remove the mask," I said. And then something strange—and terrible—happened. The man opened his eyes and suddenly became violent. He kicked with the broken leg and waved his arms. Three medics and all the doctors and nurses tried to hold him down, but it was hopeless. The soft plaster couldn't hold, turned into a blood-soaked rag. I tried to hold down the bone—impossible. I still can feel the way it turned under my fingers.

This paroxysm continued for about five minutes, and then he became quiet. I felt his pulse. None! We started transfusions. Hopeless. In ten minutes he was dead—a young man, handsome, with a well-developed, muscular body. A corpse of my making.

We stood around silently. No, I didn't think anything. I was stunned. Finally I said, "Take him out."

We have a special dark room on the ground floor. Our temporary morgue. It is never empty. Often soldiers are taken there directly from ambulances.

"All right. Clean up, and let's get back to work," I said.

In a few moments everything went on as before. Routine. Bandaging, cutting wounds open, putting on splints. I worked like an automaton, but in my brain there was a turmoil.

So that's what shock is. First erective, and then the real thing. Repeating? Under anesthesia he came out of the original shock. And then? A post-anesthesia shock? What difference does it all make? He is dead. And I killed him.

I should have stopped when we had completed all transfusions. We should have just kept him warm until he was completely out of shock and then amputated his leg. It was stupid to try to save a shattered leg like that. Criminal.

It makes no difference now. Except to Popkoff. He is dead, and the dead do not return.

JANUARY 15, 1942

No, the dead don't come back. And this captain will not come back either.

All those deaths. Suddenly they are following me like ghosts. Damn the war. And damn the hour when I decided to become a surgeon.

They brought him in today from the front line in an open car. Soldiers. They were trying to save "their captain," to get him into a "real" hospital. All that was sensible. Podolsk is only a forty-minute drive from the front.

And we did everything correctly this time. But the result was the same.

Our science is not worth a damn compared with the science that invents death. Cruelty, it seems, is stronger than mercy.

They brought two men in the same car. Both with abdominal wounds. The sergeant was dead in fifteen minutes. There was nothing we could do. He was a dying man.

But the captain was alive, and moaning softly. "Drink . . . water. . . . " Nervous hands. Very weak pulse. We took him immediately into the dressing station. Morphine, camphor, hot water bags. A small wound in the upper abdomen. Very painful. Obviously penetration into the abdominal cavity. A probability of injury to the inner organs.

His body was ice cold. It was 30° C. below outside.

"We'll never get him warm like that. Take him to the bathroom . . . to the iron stove."

We took him there and kept transfusing glucose and alcohol, drop by drop, for half an hour. He became quiet. His blood pressure was 70, and he seemed uninterested in anything.

He dozed off, then woke up.

"We must operate, Comrade Captain," I told him.

He nodded, indicating that he wanted to talk to me. I bent over him to listen.

"Operate . . . if you must . . . but I feel that I'll die . . . I'm a company commander . . . My boys have been on the front line since November . . . What men . . . marvels . . . Russians from Siberia . . . I'm sorry for them . . . Some hot-headed fool will waste them . . . I've been trying to protect them . . . like my own fingers. . . . "

We waited for three hours. He drifted off, then started talking again. About his family. Two children. A teacher in civilian life, his wife also a teacher.

"In my shirt pocket . . . with my documents . . . a snapshot . . . Please bring it in . . . I want to see them once again. . . . "

We found the documents and a snapshot. Two small boys. A woman with bangs, serious, very plain. He stroked the photograph, dropped it, and started groping for it. "Where? Where are they?"

Meanwhile, I'd been working on other cases, but I knew that we couldn't wait much longer. The outside control time for abdominal injuries is six hours. Then there is the imminent and catastrophic possibility of peritonitis. The wound was over the liver, a possible internal hemorrhage. We got everything ready for the operation.

"Tamara. Anesthesia."

A routine, uncomplicated, and quick laparotomy. Blood and food in abdominal cavity, but no fatal internal injuries. We cleaned and patched up everything, and removed a small shell fragment. We wiped away the blood with tampons, poured in some sulfa, and sewed up the incision. A good, efficient piece of surgery. Then suddenly: "No pulse!"

I felt for myself—no pulse. Only the artery in the neck still pulsated. Very shallow, weak breathing.

The captain was dying. A company commander. A teacher. A husband and father. What for? Why?

We did everything to save him. More blood. More glucose. I opened the artery and injected three ampules of whole blood, under pressure.

It was hopeless. A few minutes, and it was all over. There are no miracles.

The next morning a young lieutenant and three soldiers came in to take his body. They silently listened to my explanation. No, they did not believe that nothing could be done. Probably thought, "If we had only taken him to the right surgeon."

But in fact we had done everything properly, had maintained the highest standards. The problem of shock: it must be studied and studied. We know so little about it.

JANUARY 20, 1942

The front has moved forward, and the pressure is off. No more front line cases.

The entire hospital group is relocating to Kaluga. Bocharoff came to say goodbye. Looking at Lina like a cat looking at a piece of butter. Promised plenty of work at Kaluga.

"We are setting you up as a special hospital," he said.

"How many beds?"

He thought for a moment and said, "At least six hundred. Perhaps more."

Meanwhile we are cleaning up. Our "railway station" is empty: the reception people have moved to Kaluga. Most of our own cases have already been evacuated; others are ready to be sent back.

We don't work in shifts any longer. Everyone is catching up on sleep. Only one doctor and two nurses are on night duty.

I went to Moscow for one day, to the medical library, to read up on shock. But I didn't find any illuminating information. This is still an obscure area.

Moscow has changed. There is a sense of security in the air. The Ministries that had been evacuated to Kuibyshev are coming back.

JANUARY 23, 1942

This morning we got the orders: to pack up and relocate at once in Kaluga. They are sending two large autobuses and a 1½-ton truck to help us move. Also we are to use our horse carts. We sent our last cases to Moscow in a special train.

During the last few days we've been having trouble with Khaminoff—a drinking problem. In the morning he walks around sober and gloomy; by lunchtime he's cheerful, and toward evening, drunk. Very unpleasant. Zvereff and Shishkin are trying to protect him, but everyone notices it.

Tonight he is too drunk to supervise the loading up. So Zvereff, Shishkin, and Tikhomiroff are doing it for him. It has been decided that he will travel to Kaluga with our horse train.

The autobuses are large, but not designed for heavy loads. The operating room equipment goes on one, then some linen and blankets. Lina, Lisa, and I will go with it, and also Tamara and Kansky. Blackbird and his team and the commissar will go in the second. Chapliuk with his kitchen and some heavy stuff will go in the truck. All the rest will go in the horse carts. Zvereff will come, too. We can't depend on Khaminoff any longer.

They promise to issue food in Kaluga. We are to look for some solid building, just as we did in Podolsk.

Toward evening, we start. As soon as we leave Podolsk, we enter territory once occupied by the Germans. We want to see it, but our windows become frosted at once. It is bitterly cold, and we are trying to snatch a few hours of sleep, bundled up in hospital blankets.

At night we pass Maloyaroslavets. The town has been completely burned down; not a light is showing. The second bus falls behind and we lose it.

We arrive in Kaluga early in the morning of the 24th, completely frozen. How can soldiers fight in weather like this?

Kansky and I are looking at the city, trying to spot an empty building for our hospital. The truck with Chapliuk and Tikhomiroff join us. They know nothing about our second autobus. Must have passed it on the way without noticing it.

The long Station Street. Every building either burnt down or blown up. Here and there, German signs and abandoned German equipment. There isn't as much as in the newspaper photographs, but still there are some cannons, burnt-out tanks, and colossal troop-carriers with several rows of seats for soldiers. We saw them in newsreels when the Germans were conquering Europe.

Closer to the center, some buildings are still intact, and some are already occupied: boarded-up windows with stovepipes sticking out, belching smoke.

We even see some frozen German corpses that have not been buried. We find three of them in a narrow alley. Light jackets, bare frozen feet, very white faces, blond hair. I try to find in myself some feeling for these young men, but cannot. They got what they asked for.

In the center of town there are many buildings intact, but all of them are burned out. Glassless windows. Skeletons.

We like one of the buildings. The sign reads "Pedagogical College." We stop. All windows are blown out, but it has not been gutted by fire. We go inside. The first building we've seen that's been occupied by the Germans. Was this one used as a barracks? On the walls there are comical drawings, mostly obscene. Not badly drawn. Empty wine bottles with French labels. And next to them, heaps of frozen feces, on the floor. In several rooms the floors have been torn up, obviously for fuel. Heaps of rags—peasant blankets, women's garments. No furniture. Everything has been burned. One room was probably an office. Heaps of papers on the floor, among them, soldiers' "pay books"—probably those who were killed. Good paper, young, intelligent faces—"a cultured nation." Many people abroad counted on this culture, but then came Hitler, and these young, handsome men with neat haircuts turned into killers, thieves, and rapists. Perhaps those are only the SS men? No, everyone says that the regular soldiers act just as barbarically.

Yes, this building could do very well. We must start putting it in order at once. We board up the windows and light the stoves. They seem to be intact.

We send word to the Evacuation Area about our find and go to work. We find one room with windows still intact and some firewood—broken chairs. We build a fire in a tile stove, but it's hopeless. There's no draft, and the walls are frozen through. It will take a week to unfreeze them. We must start looking for temporary stoves with pipes. But where?

We are invited to a small house across the street by a wonderful Russian family, the first people we've met who have lived under German occupation. The old man was a bookkeeper in some office. He had graduated from the Derpt university with Burdenko, our Surgeon General. His wife, much younger, is a teacher. They have a daughter. They greet us as though we are their relatives and make us feel welcome in their simple wooden house. But it is cold inside; there is a single *bourjuika*.* They give us tea and some potato pancakes. They tell horrible stories about German atrocities. When they captured the local hospital, they shot all the doctors and threw the patients out to freeze to death. Every day they hanged partisans and communists from balconies. Hard to believe, but obviously true. The old man cried telling us all this.

We started planning. Obviously we will need workers, material, transport, cleaning women. So far there is no sign of the second autobus, and only the commissar has the right to mobilize local labor.

We spend the night with our new friends, sleeping on the floor, men and women together. It is amazing how under war conditions sex differences cease to exist. We are all comrades and co-workers.

JANUARY 24, 1942

This morning the head of the Evacuation Area came around and vetoed our choice. He said the building was too small, and it would take too long to put it into shape. We were ordered to take over the Evacuation Reception Center, along with the wounded there. The Center is moving closer to the railway station. "You'll find everything you need there until your own equipment comes in," he said. "Get going."

The place turned out to be nearby. A large three-story building, formerly part of a theological seminary and later of some technical school. Large, arched windows boarded up with plywood. Smoking pipes sticking out. It has an imposing entrance

---

Literally, "a bourgeois woman." A slang term for a small wood-burning stove.—Trans.

with a line of cars in front of it, unloading the wounded. A familiar scene: stretchers, splints sticking out of overcoats, seated figures with cut-away sleeves. Blood-stained bandages. Icicles on eyebrows and whiskers. Moans and groans.

We enter. A door with a tight spring closes with a bang. A large lobby with arched ceiling. Semidarkness. Smoke and humid haze. From the lobby to the right and left, two very wide corridors, also with arched ceilings. Along the walls, rows of stretchers with a narrow passage between them. Very cold. At the end of the corridors, two large oil drums with some smoking wood in them and black pipes leading to the windows. To the right and left, former classrooms, each with a smoking makeshift stove. Some of them contain beds without mattresses; in others, stretchers lie on bare floors. All the rooms are filled with wounded men, moaning and cursing.

Here and there we see figures wearing white gowns over their coats, with fur hats and felt boots.

"Medic! A helmet!"

A helmet? Yes, German helmets serve as bedpans. We see a nurse carrying two of them. She opens the door and splashes the contents out into the street.

We find the surgical station, a very large room filled with the same smoke and haze. A barrel stove with a long pipe leading outside through a hole in the plywood in the window. Piles of wood around the stove. Benches with the wounded sitting on them. Three tables. The wounds are bandaged without undressing the men. There are two nurses in fur hats, wearing white gowns over army coats. A doctor, dressed in the same manner, is at the table, filling out cards. The medics are wrapping up the splints. There is an autoclave behind a clothes rack with some army coats hanging on it. A rather dismal scene.

We speak to the doctor briefly and continue our inspection. Most of the wounded are on the ground floor. Water is being distributed in empty tin cans.

The second floor is almost empty. The windows are covered with plywood; there are stoves, but it is even colder here. The same smoke and haze. The third floor is not yet ready. There are no stoves, and soldiers from an engineering battalion are boarding up the windows. A young sergeant is in charge.

"We'll have it ready for you by tomorrow," he says. Eventually we'll fix the central heating, too. But later. The waterworks in the city have been wrecked by the Fascists."

By this time the second autobus arrives, bringing the commissar and Blackbird. They've been delayed by motor trouble.

We start looking for the head of the hospital. We finally find him. An exhausted, unshaven man with red-rimmed eyes, he greets us curtly.

"Glad to see you. We have orders to turn over the wounded to you by noon. By one o'clock we must start working in our new place."

He tells us that there are "about 200" cases here—skull, jaw, stomach, chest injuries, hip and leg fractures. The Evacuation Center will send us about 100 additional cases every day. Bed cases cannot be evacuated yet because the railway bridge at Alexin was blown up and is being repaired, but the walking wounded can cross the river on the ice. Wood can be obtained from the lumber mill, and water must be brought from the river. The plumbing is not yet working, but the kitchen is in operation, and the wounded have been fed.

"Well, good luck. The wounded say there is hard fighting all along the line. The Germans refuse to retreat any further."

I beg him, "Please don't send us any new cases today. Let us organize this place first. Only today."

"I can't promise you anything. The new place is probably even less organized than this one. You must understand."

We do, but that doesn't help us.

In another hour they pack up and depart. "It's all yours."

What to do first?

First, water and food. Then clean up this place. Then pick out hemorrhaging cases and those with possible wound infections for bandaging and surgery.

Khaminoff is not here; Blackbird seems to be lost, smoking his pipe; Shishkin is inexperienced in our work; so I assume command. I send out the girls to check on the wards and call in supply people, head nurses, and the pharmacist.

The situation is even worse than I thought. There are sheets, but no pillows. Soup cans, but no spoons. Our pharmacy is coming later by horse caravan. (My fault. I should have checked on this. Khaminoff should be courtmartialed for this!)

My girls report that the volunteer women are ready to leave, despite the food rations. They complain that conditions are too terrible.

I turn to Shishkin. "Comrade Commissar, this is your department. No one must be permitted to leave. Use any means. Threaten them with your revolver, if necessary."

"Don't worry. I'll stop them."

And he will. A good, dedicated man, Shishkin.

I order Tikhomiroff to get food supplies and Chapliuk to get the kitchen going.

Then we start to work. Fortunately our predecessors left enough wound dressing material, and we brought our own kits. But no fast or radical improvement. The volunteer women have been ordered to stay on, and Shishkin has even drafted some new ones. They are willing, but frightened and inexperienced.

The volunteers free our men to bring in firewood, water, and food supplies. Fortunately the kitchen is going, and Chapliuk is cooking some buckwheat soup. We begin to collect food cans and spoons. I send some men to go from house to house and beg for whatever they can get.

They bring water and firewood, but it is damp. The stoves are smoking but producing little heat. The walls are dripping. I send Shishkin with some men to break up some barns in the neighborhood. A direct, no-nonsense man, Shishkin knows how to organize those things.

Only then do we discuss our organization. We will work again in two shifts, just as we did in Podolsk. Blackbird and his team will relieve us in the evening. Meanwhile they go out to look for billets for all of us. Shishkin will help them.

Finally, we set up our dressing station. We put in seven tables. By three o'clock in the afternoon the station starts to function. But we don't know where to start: the whole building is filled with a gray, formless, moaning mass of suffering people. And the most terrible thing is that they keep bringing in new cases, even before we can check on those already here.

With difficulty we clear out one room in the ground floor for our reception ward, so that all new cases can be put there instead of being scattered all over the building. Riaboff is a good organizer.

I start my rounds to select the cases requiring urgent attention.

A sad situation. Much worse than in Podolsk.

The main victims of an offensive are the wounded. As the troops move on, they leave their wounded behind, in dugouts or peasant huts it they can find them, often without any immediate help. Front-line medical units are too busy to do anything beyond bandaging and patching up before they have to move on. The only surgery they perform is emergency amputation. Most of the cases here haven't had their wounds looked at for days. They wear blood-stained, dirty, stinking bandages. And all the men are exhausted, utterly exhausted. For six weeks now our armies have been attacking in bitter cold. Supply trains are slow to follow, all roads are snow-bound, and the men have been subsisting on dry bread and cold rations. Most villages have been burned down, and there is no way of getting warm. Yes, General Frost is tough on everybody, including our own men, despite their warm clothing. In fact, the Germans are in a better position. They have bases and strong points, and they fight for every village, every house. Then they set them on fire before retreating.

All our cases look old, unshaven, hairy. Most of them are men of 40 or 45, according to their cards. There are few young ones. The young have better resistance and can often walk; therefore they are evacuated first.

In the corridors and in some of the rooms men are lying on bare floors. There are iron bedsteads for only about half of them. German helmets are used as bedpans. Liubochka tells me: "You know, they are quite comfortable." A strange woman. She gets upset easily, but is enormously resilient in a crisis.

I pick the cases for immediate attention. Only about ten percent of them have had their wounds redressed since coming here. There are many skull cases; most are unconscious, some delirious. We must keep them as comfortable as we can—Blackbird will operate on them.

But generally our men are enormously courageous and patient. There are few complaints about food, old bandages, pains, cold, and smoke. Questions are usually about evacuation: "When are they going to send us back? Will we go like this, or will you treat us first?" I don't promise anything impossible but firmly tell them that we will help them all before evacuation.

There are some curses and insults. That must be expected and accepted. We discover that some men have had no water for two days.

The most serious cases are not those who curse or scream, but those who are silent: they have no strength to react to anything. We find a young man like that in a corner. Pale face, cracked, bloodless lips. A Dietrich splint, the food wrapped in dirty rags. The bandage is covered with dry, cracked blood. I read his card: "A shell fragment wound in right hip with a broken bone." He was wounded eight days ago and has not been operated on.

"Are you in pain, soldier?"

A crazy smile. "Na-a-a . . . I'd like a drink before I die . . . Some bread kvass . . . "

His neighbor says, "He's delirious, doctor. I told them about him before, but they paid no attention."

"To the surgery ward! Immediately!"

A classical gangrene case. And almost certainly too late to do anything. We will amputate, of course. I order everything prepared while I check on other emergency cases. It is almost impossible to determine who must be attended to first.

Back to my young soldier. I amputate his leg to the hip. Miraculously he does not die on the table. Will this be a miracle? "The gangrenous form of an anaerobic infection develops slower than other forms." I have read that somewhere. We shall see.

We work in fur hats with overcoats under our white gowns. And we don't undress or wash our men. It's too cold, there's no hot water, and not enough time. The aseptic conditions are frightening, but what can we do?

The stove in the dressing station burns better now, but the smoke makes our eyes water. The only ventilation is the hole in the plywood. And they say it is 20° C. below outside.

Just as I walk out into the corridor, Riaboff rushes up to me. "Nikolai Mikhailovich, they have just brought in eighteen bed cases in five cars. Where do we take them?"

"What do you mean, *where*? We've cleared a room for you."

"It's full. There's an empty room on the second floor with a stove. Shall I take them in there?"

So much for our reception procedure. A large building, and no room. I must send Shishkin upstairs to prod the soldiers working there. We must have that floor ready as quickly as possible.

A report from the kitchen: "The soup is ready."

Liubov Vladimirovna says, "What's the use? We have only twenty spoons. I sent two women to collect them from civilians outside, and they did not come back. And I have just one man."

I know I cannot yell at her. She's too sensitive. But this is clearly her fault. She should have thought of it sooner.

"I can't help you. Some soldiers must have their own spoons. And this is your department. The men must be fed."

I continue my rounds. Nearly all the men need urgent attention, but our facilities are pitifully limited. We can process only about ten cases in an hour. Suddenly Liza runs from the dressing station. "Nikolai Mikhailovich! An absolutely critical hemorrhaging case. Lina wants you to come at once."

Hemorrhage. Our worst enemy. I have had little experience with major arteries, just diagrams from medical textbooks. And this must be a critical case; Lina is a good surgeon.

The scene: On the table sits the wounded man. He is held by our head surgery medic, Igumnoff, by the armpits. The whole head is crudely bandaged. The bandages are soaked through

with blood, and saliva is dripping out of the place where there was
once a mouth. On the neck, running down, is a small trickle of
blood, dripping to the floor. Doctors and nurses are crowding
around.

"Put him down."

"He'll choke on his blood, Doctor."

For a moment I am lost. How to approach a case like this?

"Cut away the bandage."

While Tamara cuts away the stiff, blood-stained bandages, I
wrack my brain. There are two possibilities: tie up the bleeding
vessel in the wound, or tie up the artery outside the wound
through a special incision. The first is quicker, but difficult to do.
The second . . . well, I can only go by textbook diagrams, as I
remember them.

The bandage is removed. A terrible sight: in place of the right
cheek a yawning wound up to the eye. One can see the bones of
the upper jaw and the remnants of the lower. This hole is filled
with a mass of congealed blood and torn flesh through which there
flows fresh arterial blood. The right eye cannot close—no bone
support—and the lower eyelid is hanging loosely. The left eye is
closed by swelling, no way of telling whether it is injured. It is
terrible, incredibly difficult to look at that single, unclosing eye . . .
the expression of mortal anguish in it . . . I am trying not to look at
it.

"One moment, boy . . . one moment . . . "

How can I find the bleeding vessel in that mass of blood clots
and torn muscles? No, I must tie the artery in the neck. The blood
is flowing in a steady trickle. We must put him down. I won't be
able to do anything otherwise.

We put him down, slightly on the left side, and turn his head
farther to the left so that the blood will not penetrate the breathing
tract.

"Gloves! Iodine! Novocaine! Lancet! This will hurt, my boy . . .
Try to bear it." (Stupid words, considering the agony he must be
going through.)

We push a sterile sheet under him to maintain the minimum

of asepsis. It is dark. No electricity. The oil lamp is smoking. God, why this ordeal? No, it is easier to fight in trenches.

"Give me more light. Igumnoff, another lamp! Quickly!"

I find the pulse on the side of the neck not torn by the wound. Novocaine. Incision. Clamps. I am thinking, "We must keep this dry . . . I must not hurry . . . Hell, so little light . . . Here, the fascia . . . the masseter muscle . . . the parotid gland . . . here, the artery! The vein . . . There must be a nerve here somewhere . . . " I am almost calm now. My hands are steady. I put a ligature under the artery . . . a loose clamp. Let us see.

"Lina, start removing blood clots from the wound, carefully."

That is not simple, either. But Lina is good—sure and thorough. We remove the clots and wash out the wound with boiled water. A terrible open hole. Pieces of lower jaw, broken teeth, mangled tongue. The upper jaw is also injured, but not broken. And everything is covered with a film of dirt. Infection. But no fresh blood. Thank God. It has truly been a race against death.

"The operation is over. Don't worry, soldier, you won't have any more bleeding. And tomorrow, we'll patch you up properly."

The expression of the horrible eye becomes warmer; there are tears in it. I must attend to the eye later, place supporting ligature. The upper lid covers only half the eye.

Now we must feed him, considering all the loss of blood. Through a tube placed through the open wound, we pour in some buckwheat soup with butter, and almost a liter of sweet tea. That should keep him for a while. Only a temporary bandage today; we postpone the radical debridement until tomorrow. It's too dark, and we have no time. Other cases are waiting.

The night shift comes in. Blackbird works on his skulls, but we also continue working, until two o'clock in the morning. We can't sleep in the hospital; all heated rooms are taken by the wounded, but Shishkin has not been idle. He has our billets for us in various small houses along the street. He has the authority of the Party behind him, and there is no arguing with him when he knows that something must be done.

My landlady is an old woman, a wife of a local priest. A kind, intelligent woman. She tells me that her husband joined the local guerrillas while the Germans were approaching. Yes, "the holy war." No, she doesn't know whether he is dead or alive.

Thus ends our first working day in Kaluga. As we leave, the boy with the amputated leg is still alive. But there is little hope for him.

JANUARY 27, 1942

We relieve the night shift at seven o'clock. No breakfast yet, but Chapliuk promises to feed everybody by nine. During the night Blackbird operated on fourteen skull cases. Two died; five more are critical. He looks exhausted but stays on to help us. Lyda Denisenko tells me confidentially, "I think he is too nervous for this kind of work." Who isn't?

During the night they brought in 40 more bed cases. Tikhomiroff has succeeded in heating two more rooms on the second floor, and they have put them there. Fortunately all of them are in satisfactory condition, but many wounds require redressing. Five civilian women workers escaped during the night. Shishkin will confiscate their passports from now on.

At ten o'clock Khaminoff arrives in a small military car, bringing our pharmacy. "I noticed that you left it behind so I got a special car." Bastard. I don't even want to look at him, much less speak to him. He is absolutely sober and looks like a beaten dog. He promises to organize everything. He is an excellent organizer when sober, and we can only hope.

Again we work until two o'clock the next morning. Work? No, this is not work, but a desperate struggle to bring some order out of chaos. But the arrival of new parties of frozen, screaming wounded only compounds the chaos. Khaminoff is dashing to and fro, but so far he is unable to solve any of our problems. But our pharmacy and our kitchen have been put in order and are functioning properly.

My young leg amputee died. Today we had three more amputations. Gangrene. The first frostbite cases have made their appearance. We amputated two feet and will probably amputate many more.

We properly bandaged that soldier with the terrible cheek wound. He seems to be satisfactory. We have taught our junior nurse Shura Matashkova to feed him through a tube and instructed her to watch him. She's a quiet, kind girl.

In the evening our horse train arrives with all our equipment. Khaminoff supervises the unloading. He is dead sober and works like a demon. He will stay in the hospital throughout the night to try to organize things. Now we have enough linen for all the cases, and Khaminoff promises to get some beds from the Medical Depot.

JANUARY 30, 1942

During the 28th and 29th we succeeded in placing all our cases in beds and issued mattresses, sheets, and pillow cases. Khaminoff is still sober, and he works 20 hours a day. His next goal is central heating. Because of the smoke we all suffer eye irritation, but the wounded suffer more. We still cannot undress them because of the cold. And because of this, many beds have become infested with lice. Khaminoff is organizing a delousing chamber in the basement, and eventually we will have to treat all our linen there.

Now all the men are fed regularly three times a day, even though it is only buckwheat soup with salt pork and half a kilo of dark bread. We eat in the basement. The same food. But there is absolutely no glass available for our windows in any foreseeable future. We must use oil and kerosene lamps, but we have obtained more of them from the supply stores in town. Khaminoff knows how to get things moving. He spoke to me and promised not to touch a drink again.

The surgery department is still working poorly. During every 24 hours we can only process 80 to 90 cases, while at least 40 new ones are brought in every day. There have been three more deaths on my shift: a gangrene, a hemorrhage, and a chest wound case. But he was absolutely critical when he was brought in.

We don't perform any autopsies yet. Touroff is organizing his morgue in our basement. It will service all of Kaluga.

FEBRUARY 1, 1942

A miracle. They connected our central heating during the night. True, the radiators are merely warm, but we can throw out all those smoking stoves. It is still very cold, but already there is less smoke.

The communiqués have been mentioning liberated villages, but the wounded say that every house must be stormed and the Germans fight like wildcats, even when surrounded.

Last night our Communist Party members had a meeting in the basement. I sneaked in for a few minutes to listen. Khaminoff was severely criticized. I even felt sorry for him, and Shishkin tried to soft-pedal the accusations. But in fact one cannot excuse him. If it were not for his drinking, we would be in better shape today.

Bocharoff also appeared last night. He said he had been too busy organizing the Reception Center to come sooner. He promised to come more often from now on. I told him about all the fatalities I had had, and he said that the number was "within tolerable limits." Death—tolerable?

"You must organize plastering instead of sending your cases off in temporary splints. This is not the Crimean war," he said.

True, but how can we think of any radical procedures when there are still men who have not even been properly bandaged since coming here?

Central heating allows us to expand to new rooms and start washing the more serious cases from different wards. We have enough hot water, sponges, and civilian women workers, but they are inexperienced and sloppy. Some bandages get soggy, and the wounds must be redressed.

They are setting up a new operating theater on the third floor for face, head, and skull cases. They're even painting the walls. Blackbird will do his brain surgery there, assisted by Lyda Denisenko and Kansky. I'm a little envious. How can one compare legs and arms with the brain? But Bocharoff says that the main problem of military surgery is extremities. My specialty. I am getting to be quite good and fast at amputations.

FEBRUARY 4, 1942

Today we have a "great migration of nations." Nonetheless, Khaminoff is good. He has succeeded in prevailing upon them not to send us any new cases for a day, and we are properly sorting our cases according to injuries. Arm and leg cases go to the first floor, chests and abdomens to the second, and heads and skulls to the third. All skulls are either unconscious or violent and must be isolated. Paroxysms, convulsions, delirium, curses. However, many men curse us now and then. I am surprised that they don't curse us more. The vast majority of the wounded are patient and cooperative.

The great Russian people! Long-suffering and all-forgiving! Sounds pompous, but it is true. I am sure that no other people have such a limitless capacity for enduring suffering and forgiving those who are hurting them. Even about the Germans they say, "Well, they are people too . . . only thick-headed and poisoned by lies . . . It's not sugar for them either, this war. They all curse Hitler when we capture them."

FEBRUARY 5, 1942

Today Blackbird invited me to a ceremonious opening of his

neurosurgery theater. Fresh paint, even glass in the windows. But the room is small. His head nurse, Lyda Denisenko, is a remarkable girl. She has fully recovered and is dashing about like lightning. He also has Kansky. The best head medic of them all. In our dressing station we have Ivan Igumnoff, also a first-class man, but Kansky is truly an all-around assistant.

We have another difficult day. Three amputations, one death in our gangrene ward.

FEBRUARY 6, 1942

They have repaired the railway, and today we sent out our first hospital train for bed cases. That's good, because we were overflowing—over 700 men, many of them serious and a few critical. In my own wards alone there were 286 of them, 140 with Dietrich splints, and therefore unable to move at all.

Of course we could not evacuate all those we would like to send back. Perhaps it's just as well. We would never have been able to get them all ready. Everyone must be thoroughly checked over. They are not going far, probably only to Tula.

It was a very tough day. We checked all bandages, fixed splints, got documents ready, and dressed the men. All this on top of our regular work. Many men did not have warm clothing. Tikhomiroff had to raid the local supply depots. He brought all used things, nothing new, and some have not even been cleaned.

When we sent away the last truck, Liubov Vladimirovna, who was in overall charge, sank down on a bench, almost crying from sheer fatigue. And, of course, relief. She has been working for 18 hours a day ever since she joined us.

Our next goal is to redress all wounds and eliminate lice. We are all scratching ourselves. Imaginary itching—I personally have not seen a single louse on me. Our girls are constantly running with bundles of their clothing to our delousing chamber.

FEBRUARY 10, 1942

On February 7th we put the first blind plaster cast on a fractured leg. Since Kansky is upstairs, we did this work with Igumnoff, a very intelligent fellow. But we need a traction table. We will have to construct one ourselves.

On February 8th we got electricity.

"Now you have no excuses. You have water, heating, electricity, and in a few days you'll get a portable X-ray cabinet. So, deliver . . . produce." That is what Bocharoff told us when he saw our first electric light.

No excuses, of course, but still our "production" is far from satisfactory. From eight in the morning until two the next morning we are bandaging, operating, amputating, and also supplying the morgue with our production. And now we are putting on plaster casts as well, although only on a limited scale. And the effect is miserable. Many cases become more grave hour by hour. Every second hip or knee case develops infection, runs a high temperature, and must have a prolonged treatment before evacuation.

Infection will be our undoing. The men are so exhausted and weak that they have no natural resistance. And we cannot build them up because there isn't enough blood for transfusion, there's no time, and no proper food. The buckwheat soup with lard cannot replace a proper postoperative diet.

We now have a physiological laboratory in the care of an excellent—and pretty—specialist, Galia. But nearly all blood analyses are bad. We must do something, but what?

Anaerobic infection is not particularly prevalent with us, if one considers the gravity of most of our cases. In fact, it is "within tolerable limits" according to Bocharoff. So much so that he has the idea that gangrene is our specialty. He has ordered us to set up a special anaerobic ward for 20 beds, with a special dressing station.

Each day they bring in 3 to 4 cases from other hospitals. Gaseous gangrene. In poor condition, mostly because of someone's carelessness. We are amputating every day. And every day we have one, two, and sometimes three deaths. Some production.

FEBRUARY 12, 1942

Today Igumnoff, myself, and our ironsmith have been trying to construct a traction table. It is essential to have one for plaster casts. Finally we have created a makeshift contraption. Not very elegant, but serviceable.

For the last three weeks we have been working like mad. Every day for 18 hours, or even 20. If anyone had told me that this was possible, I would not have believed it. I just don't know when our girls sleep. They are usually already there when I come in.

We set up another face-wound ward. That young man with the torn-out cheek is doing well. The swelling has gone down, and his left eye has opened. He even tries to talk. But so far only Shura Matashkova can understand him.

Our women are remarkable. When we win this war, it must be said that they contributed enormously. Without them we would not have survived. They say that in all factories and farms girls of 12 to 15 work 18 hours a day replacing men. We have some aviation units with women flyers and in all partisan units behind the German lines, women fight along with men. All this must be a surprise for German planners who consider women as mere breeding machines.

FEBRUARY 20, 1942

Today we received new orders: not to evacuate any cases in temporary wood splints. I don't know what we're going to do. I have put Igumnoff only on plaster, and he is trying to teach two volunteer girls from the town.

Yudin must have experimented with men under perfect conditions, but with us things are bad. No, terrible. Fully half of all gangrene cases die, and of our hip cases, two of every three.

Every time I come into the ward I get sick. I look at them and know that half of them are doomed.

In our main wards, on the first floor, things are also sad. They are about a hundred untransportable cases with hip and knee fractures. Many of them develop infection, slowly but surely. What we can do for them short of amputation, I don't know.

Those knee joints. Petroff, Bocharoff, and Yudin tell us that blind plaster casts perform miracles. If there is any sign of pus arthritis, all that must be done is arthrotomy, opening of joint antra, and then a blind plaster cast. We followed this routine in more than ten cases, and they are growing progressively more critical.

FEBRUARY 23, 1942

The Red Army Day, our own holiday. The morning communiqué is written in a major key: orders of the day, congratulations, hints of an early victory.

In the morning we put on two high plaster casts. Igumnoff now has a civilian volunteer, Marusia, a bright, pretty girl who seems to have a real talent for plaster work. If I could only believe in this plaster cast method!

Almost every morning now I wake up depressed and sluggish. Lack of sleep? Overwork? I don't know. This morning I feel particularly gloomy, but as soon as I get to work the feeling evaporates. We are too busy to feel or think anything.

At eleven o'clock some superior officers come into our dressing station: the commissar general of the Evacuation Area, Khaminoff, Zvereff. They are wearing new uniforms and medals. When superiors appear, it usually means trouble. I am in an apron, my hands in plaster. We exchange greetings, and then Khaminoff brings out a small leather box and speaks pompously. "Comrade Military Surgeon, Third Class. The Evacuation Area is awarding you this special commemorative watch in appreciation of your good work during the winter offensive."

I am stunned. Me? What for? For the one half of all gangrene cases who die and for all those cases operated on who develop infection?

I mumble, "Thank you."

Khaminoff corrects me with a smile. "You should say, 'I serve the Soviet Union.' All right, Amosoff, carry on. Good luck."

They leave and everyone examines my new watch. A very fine watch with 16 jewels and with an engraved inscription. Very timely, too. My own watch stopped dead a few days earlier.

Everyone congratulates me. It's all very nice—if only my cases did not die so often and the front were moving forward faster, I might have felt really happy.

I go back to work. At noon they bring in a very tall young man, blond, snub-nosed, round-faced, with a plywood splint on the left forearm.

We seat him and remove his bandages. He winces. "Please be careful, comrades . . . I've been waiting so long for treatment . . . such pain."

I examine the wound. Yes, he has good reasons for pain. A shell fragment wound, a bone fracture. Infection. Large swelling. The skin is taut, and there are even gas bubbles in one place. Gaseous gangrene. Classical. And needless—pure carelessness. But the process has not advanced above the elbow. That means it is not very dangerous. A radical debridement should help, and an amputation would help without a doubt.

"When were you hit?"

"Four days ago."

"What's your profession?"

"A veterinary assistant surgeon."

"Well, colleague, why didn't you insist on their attending to you in the medical battalion? This should not have happened."

"I know . . . but they were terribly busy . . . I let more serious cases go ahead . . . and then there was a car going to Kaluga, and I thought it was best to go to a real hospital . . . but we got stuck on the way. All roads are snowbound. But all's well that ends well."

And I think, "A good man. Obvious euphoria, he talks too

much. It's good that he got here in time." I look at his card. The temperature—39.7°C! A very fast pulse, but normal blood pressure.

"We'll operate right away. And don't worry. Just radical debridement. No amputation. I hope that won't be necessary. You were lucky to get here today. Another day might have been dangerous."

He nods and smiles.

"Thanks, Doctor."

"Tamara!"

"Tamara has gone to the blood center for plasma. But I'll be ready in a second."

Zoya. A good girl, but not as good as Tamara. Proper anesthesia is important. I must do the radical muscle separation and cleaning up. That will take time. Wait, why not use the Kullenkamf method. Novocaine into the nerves of the scalenus plexus. A complete local anesthesia for over an hour: one can work carefully, without rushing. I saw it used in Cherepovets on about five cases of phlegmon in the arm, and it worked perfectly. Why not start using it in military surgery?

"Zoya, we shall use a local anesthesia. Two percent novocaine solution. Use a ten-milliliter syringe. Yes, fill it up."

Lina and Liza come over to look. We seat the man in an upright position, according to all the rules, with the arm pulled down and back and the head turned right. I ask Igumnoff to fix the position.

"It will hurt a little, but only for a second."

The syringe is ready. Gloves, iodine, long needle. I insert it into the hollow of the shoulder blade. The man winces, but then smiles. A bit of novocaine, and then I push the needle deeper. Pull back the plunger. No blood, no air. It means I have missed all vessels and the lung. Perfect. Now there is quite a crowd around. Nurses and medics. A new method.

I inject two cc's and again check for blood and air. I wait for about twenty seconds and inject three more cc's. Suddenly the man sways, and I almost lose the syringe.

"Hold him!"

What is that—a fainting spell? Why?

I pull the needle out. Igumnoff now holds him firmly because he has become absolutely limp.

"No pulse!" There is alarm in Zoya's voice.

"Put him on the table! Quick, Ivan!"

Igumnoff lifts him up and puts him on the table. He is limp, lifeless.

"Caffeine! Artificial respiration! Wait—let me!"

I start working. Arms over head, on stomach; once, twice, three times. I feel the pulse. None. Rare, shallow breathing spasms.

"Open the vein in the groin! Lina, quickly! He's dying!"

I press my ear to his chest. Nothing. Dead? But why? How could this happen?

Just then Bocharoff comes in. One look and he understands everything. He takes over. Bocharoff starts pumping blood into the groin vein. One ampule, two . . . Then he presses the stethoscope to the man's heart, and straightens up.

"Stop it. He's dead."

Dead silence for a second. Then to me:

"What did you use?"

"Novocaine."

Bocharoff turns and walks toward the door. Then turns to me.

"You'll tell me later. Carry on."

Here we are. Five minutes ago, a strong, young man. And now, a corpse on the table. I just killed a man.

I have become used to deaths. They no longer shock me. They are a part of my work. But this is different. This man had no reason to die. None whatever. With any other form of anesthesia, he would have been alive, and would eventually have recovered. There is no doubt about that. And in all probability with both arms intact. His case was not even dangerous.

What am I doing anyway? What is my record? Wounds heal by themselves. When they don't—men die. And I am just walking around trying to look erudite and important. How many people have I actually saved? *How many?*

"How many what, Nikolai Mikhailovich?"

Apparently I spoke the last two words aloud.

"Oh, nothing . . . I am a bit tired . . . I'd like to go out for some air—for ten minutes. You carry on."

In our corridor there is a place where we leave our winter clothing. My overcoat and felt boots are there.

I remove my white gown. I think, "I must end all this. I can't keep on killing people . . . our soldiers . . . "

On the table near the door there is a large open box with morphine ampules. It is open because we use morphine quite often. There are also syringes and needles in an antiseptic solution. I turn my back toward the others, take a handful of ampules, and drop them into my pocket. I pick up a syringe and a needle. I doubt that anyone notices, because all of them are trying not to look at me. They are getting ready to take the dead man down and to get on to the next case.

I walk out into the corridor, put on my overcoat and fur hat, remove my shoes, and put my oversize felt boots on. I push the syringe and ampules into one of them. Just in time. I see Lina walking toward me, her face pale and strained.

"Please . . . no sympathy."

"What did you take from the table?"

"Nothing. And it is none of your business. Leave me alone, and go back to work!"

I walk away.

"Nikolai!"

She never calls me that now. Not since that last day in Cherepovets. It is always "Nikolai Mikhailovich" or "Comrade Doctor." I call her Lina, but then I address all our girls by their first names, except Liubov Vladimirovna.

"Nikolai!"

I do not answer. She falls behind and then turns and walks away. I do not have to account to Lina or anyone else for what I am doing. I am still head surgeon of our department.

The street . . . so this is how the town looks in the sun? I haven't seen it since that day when we arrived here. It is dark when we go to work and dark when we go "home." And we eat in the basement dining room. No windows.

It's a beautiful day. Frost, but not cold, and already a spring sun. There are even children running around . . . with toboggans . . . Children! I haven't seen children since Egorievsk. When we came to Kaluga there were none of them. Life goes on.

Enough of sentiment.

I turn into the first small courtyard. It is completely deserted. I remove my felt boot. Damn it, several ampules are broken. I shake out the glass pieces and retrieve those that are intact. One . . . two . . . three . . . seven. Not enough. Go back for more? No, Lina must have gone to Khaminoff already. I'll use these. Not a fatal dose. Scared? No, but there is no way of getting more, and I cannot wait. I can't face it any longer. I'm at the end of my rope. At least I'll sleep—long, long sleep . . .

I break ampules one after another and fill the syringe. Six and a half cc's . . . No, this isn't enough to kill me. But then, maybe in my weakened condition . . .

Two minutes and it's all finished. I rub out the bubble under the skin and throw away the syringe. Now I must rush home. It would be ridiculous if I collapsed in the street. At home I'll just go to sleep. Tired. No one will question it.

How interesting this German troop carrier looks in the sunlight. Children have already taken it over. A majestic machine. So much iron. There is glass in many windows now. Quite a few people in the street . . . It's warm—must be a little below zero . . . Women have already taken off their shawls. And the most amazing thing—children. They say schools are already open . . . but it is a holiday today. . . .

This is the place where I live. A small house next to a wrecked church. Alexandra Stepanovna opens the door. She is surprised to see me.

"Has something happened, Nikolai Mikhailovich?"

"No, nothing. I've just got a couple of hours off. Thank you."

Nothing. It's true, I feel nothing. I'm not even drowsy. A small room—table, two chairs, a couch. A dark icon in the corner with a small altar light burning . . . Where does she get the oil? Such a strange woman . . . very religious, but admires Stalin . . . "He will save Russia . . . " Mental images race through my mind . . . He is on the bench . . . We remove the splint and dry bandages . . . It hurts . . . the wound . . . swelling . . . "Tamara . . . " Perhaps if Tamara had been there? No, I myself chose novocaine and administered it . . . And then he collapsed . . . What was wrong? What difference does it make now? I killed a man. With my own hands.

I remove my felt boots, overcoat, and fur hat and lie down. I unbutton my collar and throw an old shawl over my feet. Alexandra Stepanovna gave it to me the first day I came here. I wear foot wraps instead of stockings, and they are not very clean; I haven't changed them for a week . . . I begin to imagine the scene . . . people coming . . . sad and distressed.

I close my eyes. The scenes of the operating theater appear again, but they begin to change . . . Tamara has not gone away. She is helping me . . . What nonsense. I don't want any visions . . . But no . . . Igumnoff is putting on a plaster cast . . . Marusia is helping him . . . The gangrene ward . . . Five men in beds—without legs . . . They all look at me, hating me for turning them into cripples . . . And now they will say: "And he murdered that young soldier, too. Butcher."

Sleep, sleep. I don't want any dreams. Like Hamlet.

And where is my watch?

Oh yes, there, on the table . . . a good watch . . . They awarded it to me and not to Blackbird . . . Well, they just don't know me, that's all.

Thank God, the mental pictures begin to blur. And the icon lamp is flickering. Maybe he did not die? Maybe it was all a dream? Maybe I'll get up now, dress, and go to the hospital? We must put a plaster cast on Selezneff today.

No, it was all true. He died. Well, never mind. It was not my fault. I wanted to save his arm.

I feel that I am falling into some dark hole . . . trying to get hold of something . . . my fingers slip . . . Down, down. No hope. Darkness.

I wake up. Dark windows. Only the small, flickering light before the dark icon. Is it night? Morning? Someone is sitting at the edge of my bed, at my feet.

"Who is there . . . who?"

"It's me. Don't get excited. It's Bocharoff."

"Oh . . . sorry . . . I thought . . . "

"How do you feel?"

"All right . . . a bit of nausea . . . I must have eaten something . . . I didn't feel well, and I came home . . . and fell asleep."

A short silence.

"You're a hothead, Nikolai. That's good. There are too many lukewarm people around . . . No, no, don't tell me—I know everything. Your Lina saw you take morphine . . . No, I don't know why he died. In some people—very rarely—there is a complete novocaine sensitivity. There is no way of telling it. And such deaths—stupid deaths—will occur again and again in your lifetime. No surgeon can escape them."

He is speaking softly, evenly, as though trying to hypnotize me. I understand every word. But I accept it all with indifference, as if it didn't concern me. He tells me about terrible cases in his own practice. There is no branch of medicine where the doctor's guilt is so obvious as in surgery and gynecology.

". . . Once a famous opera diva was gaining weight. She tried everything, without success. Her career was at stake. Besides, she had just acquired a new husband, and she needed her figure. She came to Sergei Sergeievich Yudin. He loves artists—he's a bit of an actor himself. 'Oh certainly—we can remove this excess fat from the stomach . . . Just a faint scar along the skin fold . . .' He set a date for the operation. She came in. They talked a bit, joked. He put her on the table . . . spinal cord anesthesia . . . She was sitting up, and suddenly she collapsed, and in five minutes she was dead. Her husband was waiting downstairs with flowers . . . Yudin had used this method thousands of times—always successfully. They never found the reason. Yudin went out hunting. He always goes hunting when his patients begin to die. 'A bad stretch,' he calls it."

"And I have had nothing but bad stretches."

I feel his hand on my arm.

"Nonsense. You're doing well. Believe me. I'm watching many surgeons. You've just become exhausted during the last few weeks. Your nerves snapped. You must get more sleep—at least an extra hour a night. Don't worry, your work won't suffer."

I retch. I do not vomit, but Bocharoff notices it.

"Get dressed and come with me. My carriage is waiting outside, and I have an extra cot."

He took me to his place. A fine little apartment—neat, warm, cozy. For some reason he wants to pump my stomach, but I can't swallow the rubber tube. Then he uses the old "restaurant method." Makes me drink three cups of tea, then puts me over a wash basin and inserts his two fingers deep into my mouth, to the uvula. I vomit, long and copiously, and immediately feel better.

"Wonderful," he says. "Now go to sleep, and tomorrow you'll be as fresh as a young cucumber. And no one will ask you anything. I told them about the novocaine reaction and also that I wanted you to work with me tonight on a report to the Medical Department."

I fall asleep on his couch, deeply and peacefully, like a saint.

That was the end of one of the worst days of my life.

The next morning we both went to watch the autopsy. Touroff was grim and precise. "Yes, gaseous gangrene. Localized. No needle marks on either the artery or vein. The pleura is also intact. Shall I mark it 'anaphylactic reaction to novocaine'?"

Bocharoff said yes, and personally signed the report.

That day was a turning point for me.

END OF FEBRUARY, 1942

The wounded are coming just as before, even more than before, but somehow I am coping better. More experience and better facilities. And, fewer nerves. Now I do not stay later than midnight. What I lose in time I more than make up for in added efficiency. I have ordered my team to do the same.

Our January and February records are not too good. We treated 1,560 serious cases. 427 were operated on, and 113 died. And only 20 were doomed when they were brought in. Others could have been saved had we had more time and skill. And had our science been better.

I have worked out a detailed analysis of fatalities in connection with leg and arm wounds, and I have shown it to Bocharoff. In about half of all cases errors were made that affected the outcome. Most of them occurred because we did not amputate quickly enough. But amputations are hardly the solution.

I have been working with Touroff in his basement morgue for about an hour each evening. They bring him up to twenty corpses a day, from all over Kaluga, and he works on two tables for fourteen hours a day performing detailed autopsies. Here one can learn all the medical errors and then try to avoid them in one's own practice. A fine man, Touroff, gentle and sensitive. He tells me that he writes poetry. He sleeps in a little basement room next to his corpses. He looks like an operatic devil—tall, bony, hairy. Our girls try to avoid him in the dining room.

He has three sons. Two of them were killed near Kiev. He certainly knows what this war is all about.

Blackbird is sick from overwork and temporarily I am heading both surgical departments. I have never had any neurosurgical experience. Bocharoff comes in every day and does some brain surgery, with my assistance. But now I am doing skulls on my own as well. All skull cases go through the X-ray and are examined by the eye specialist and neuropathologist, Dr. Weinstein, before they come to us. Of course there are specific problems here as well, but they seem to me simpler than ours with hips and knees.

The attitude is different, too. A man has been wounded in the head, his brain has been damaged, he is unconscious, and if he dies—well, he was beyond salvation. But with us it's a simple leg wound, so why should a man die? It's obviously the surgeon's fault.

But in fact the brain is an extraordinarily durable organ. Even infection does not develop there as quickly as in stomach or joint injuries. There are, of course, meningitis and encephalitis cases, but they are not frequent. In fact, neurosurgeons have been playing gods for no good reason—our work is often more difficult.

Our military neurosurgery doctrine is quite simple. Routine

trephination—bite off the bone around the wound, cut through the brain pachymeninx, remove haematomae and bone fragments, and that is practically all. Even chasing metal fragments and bullets is not recommended: they become quickly covered by connective tissue, and do not cause any future trouble. Not that I am quite convinced of this, but who am I to contradict the experts?

Lyda Denisenko is a tremendous help. She has been working with Blackbird and she has learned a great deal. An excellent operating room nurse, and a charming woman. I catch myself admiring her. Do others notice it? I don't think so. It's surprising how the pressure of work inhibits all emotions. We all walk around like squeezed lemons.

MARCH 10, 1942

Men in our wards continue to die. Now we have electricity, hot and cold water, heating, X-ray cabinet, laboratory, and a physiotherapy room. Lice have become very infrequent visitors. Food is quite ample. Our antiseptic conditions are perfect, and we keep accurate case histories and case diaries.

And all this has not improved our survival record. If anything, the crisis is growing. The torrent of wounded is not slackening; in fact, it has grown, even though the front seems to have stabilized.

We are working steadily and accurately. Our work day is shorter—from eight in the morning until eleven at night or midnight, and yet our productivity has increased. Wound treatments, operations, plaster casts.

Those plaster casts! I'm not at all impressed with this "miracle of military surgery."

Our worst bottleneck is knee joints. They are torturing us. They contribute greatly to our bad record. The Yudin doctrine is simple: in all cases of pus arthritis, cut open the joint, put on plaster, and all will be well.

Like hell it will. The wounded continue to run a high fever, they lose weight, become anemic, and then, quite often, the gravest sepsis develops, and unless you amputate at once, there is a good chance of a fatal outcome. And it is this "at once" that is so hard to determine, even though we cut "windows" in the plaster casts.

The picture: out of all cases with serious knee injuries about thirty per cent die, about thirty per cent are saved by amputation, and only about forty percent with plaster casts survive with some hope of eventual recovery. But, of course, no knee will ever bend.

One day I buttonholed Bocharoff. "Look at the figures, please. Where is that famous magic effect? This is a disaster."

"But Yudin—"

"I know, he's a genius, but his method does not fit our conditions. Our men are gravely injured, exhausted, emaciated, with practically zero natural resistance. It is impossible to have only every third man eventually walk on his own legs. We must look for some new method."

"Do you have anything in mind?"

"No, but I'd like to experiment."

As my superior, Bocharoff had the right to order me to continue working along the approved lines. But that is the beauty of Bocharoff. He never imposes his authority, never stops anyone from exercising initiative. He even said once, "All great discoveries have been made by people breaking rules."

But for some reason he stopped coming to our hospital. Was he offended?

MARCH 26, 1942

Knees have become an obsession for me. I'm sure that the pus process cannot be arrested as long as there remains joint cavity. And before it is filled, infection often destroys cartilage and inner coating. Plaster cannot help, and the danger is that it makes it difficult to detect the developing sepsis.

I would like to discuss it with Bocharoff, but he is still shunning us. Is he trying to escape responsibility? Unlikely. He is an excellent man, and a true friend. He proved it during that night I spent in his apartment. He really "covered up" for me that time. He told everyone that we were working together on some reports.

I have designed a new operation. A variation on an economic knee joint resection with the retention of ligaments. I have worked it out on corpses in Touroff's morgue.

On March 22nd, we performed the first new operation. Perhaps it is not new at all, since it is so obvious. But I am not interested in glory and priorities, only in results. Now I am watching this case like a hawk.

Alexander Bilibin, 24. We all call him Sasha. He was wounded at the end of·February, and at that time the wound was cut open and cleaned. He came to us five days after having been hit. He had developed pus arthritis, so we performed arthrotomy and put on plaster, but there developed an acute danger of sepsis. He could be saved by amputation, but he begged me not to do it. "My girl is waiting for me. We're going to get married. It would be better for me to die than come home on one leg." I offered to try the new operation. "I cannot guarantee results, Sasha. I have hopes, but that is all." For some reason all those boys trust me. With all those corpses and cripples to my credit. "Yes, yes, please, Nikolai Mikhailovich! Please try! I beg you. Please."

I made up my mind. If this Sasha dies, I will leave this hospital. No matter where. To some regimental dressing station or medical battalion. Anywhere.

Bocharoff finally came two days after the operation. Well, Sasha is certainly not dying from my surgery, but he runs a high temperature, and it is much too early to feel relieved.

Of course I told Bocharoff everything that happened during his absence (he said he was away on an inspection trip.) He listened very patiently, even though, I feel, still skeptically. I drew diagrams. I do not think he is convinced, but there is no negative reaction. We examine Sasha together, then return to our dressing station and check carefully on all past figures concerning knee joints.

Bocharoff listened patiently, pulling at his little beard and looking at Lina roguishly with his gray, bulging eyes. (He actually likes Lina. And, though it is stupid to feel this way, that is vaguely unpleasant to me.)

And then he says, "Well . . . carry on."

An approval? Not quite. But it's enough to give me the green light.

MARCH 31, 1942

The end of March. Our record for the month: We processed 2,300 cases in our hospital, 860 of them in my own wards. We put on some 500 blind plaster casts and operated on 340 cases in my own department. Fifty-four of them died.

No, we are not out of the crisis. But I feel encouraged. This is an obvious improvement. Knock on wood.

APRIL 10, 1942

Sasha Bilibin is still running a high temperature. The plaster cast has become soggy underneath, but his general condition is quite satisfactory. And, most important, he has a good appetite. It is too early to shout "Hurray!" but I feel tremendously encouraged.

During the last two weeks we have performed nine more knee resections. Bocharoff personally witnessed one operation and, I think, was impressed. Not a word of criticism from him.

Until yesterday I felt triumphant: the terrible problem of knees had been solved! And this morning, a fatality. We operated on an absolutely exhausted middle-aged man last night, and this morning he was dead. Apparently my technique is not good for extremely serious cases. Only an amputation could have saved that exhausted soldier.

END OF APRIL, 1942

We got orders to evacuate all our transportable cases and generally put our house in order. We don't know what this means, but we think it may be a new offensive.

We all expect the war to end during the coming summer. This is nothing like those terrible first months of the war when the Germans seemed to move at will. Today, it is a different Red Army, and different Germans. They have tasted defeat—the first defeat since Hitler came to power.

They say that all armament factories that were evacuated beyond the Ural now work at full capacity. Tanks, guns, and airplanes are coming in a steady stream. Even we can feel it. No more German air raids—our anti-aircraft defenses seem to be almost impregnable. Moscow was only very slightly damaged even though at one time the Germans were only a few kilometers away.

During the last few days we sent away all our "old guard." Generally joint resection has proved itself. Sasha is already walking. Others are still running fever, but not very high, not much pus, and good appetites.

Our hip cases are less encouraging. I don't feel convinced that many of them will avoid eventual amputations.

We said goodbye to our gaseous gangrene cases and others with infections. Many of them are already walking on crutches and have put on their uniforms—with trouser legs pinned up.

Sasha almost cried when he bid me goodbye.

"I'll write to you when we get married. I can't tell you how grateful I am. Natasha will write to you, too."

Such love. He writes her every day. Reminds me of Alla and myself. How far away all that seems now! I wonder what has happened to her?

Yesterday we brought some cases downstairs to our evacuation room. They had to wait there for transportation to the station, fully dressed. Among them was a leg amputee, Semen Surin, 29, a very quiet, patient man. We took his leg off becuase of the threatening sepsis. A hip wound. I thought a long time before that amputation—it seemed to me to be a 50-50 case—and finally I decided to amputate. His general condition was not too good, and the danger was considerable.

He went around his ward upstairs bidding goodbye to the nurses. "Forgive me if I have caused you trouble." He even thanked me for the operation. "It didn't hurt much, Doctor."

When they put out the lights in the evening, he covered himself with a blanket and cut his throat ear to ear with a knife. At first no one understood. They just heard some gurgling noise. By the time they put on the light, called the nurse, and took him upstairs to the operating theater, it was too late. The knife was sharp—he had cut not merely the trachea, but the artery as well. The wound looked terrible, obscene. It takes a lot of courage and willpower to cut one's own throat that way.

It was a small kitchen knife. Of course we always take away all sharp objects from the wounded. One of our civilian volunteer workers must have brought it to him. But of course no one has confessed.

Among his things we found a letter from his wife: "I am sorry, but I can't live with a husband who has no leg."

Was it my fault? Could we have saved his leg? Amputation is always tempting under war conditions. It's clean, final, and even safe, in most cases. It is much more difficult to treat a case. Amputation takes twenty minutes; proper treatment takes weeks, and there is always a danger of infection and death. But we must find some way of saving legs and arms. It is no good to hide behind authorities such as Yudin. One must search for one's own solution.

END OF JANUARY, 1943

Once again we are a mobile field hospital, and once again we are in a train. Carts, horses, and all.

Somewhere I have lost two large notebooks with my notes covering the last nine months. I don't want to forget, so I'll try to review briefly the events covered in my missing notebooks.

The spring saw very hard fighting on our front, but no spectacular advances, only liquidation of German pockets in front of Moscow. We had a steady torrent of wounded—in one day there were nineteen hospital trains coming to Kaluga, to different hospitals. But this time we were ready. All cases were sorted, washed, put in beds with mattresses and sheets, and given clean linen. All wounds were treated and all operations performed immediately.

The men were different, too. They were better fed and better treated in front-line medical battalions. They said that they had more guns, more tanks, more planes.

And then something strange and frightening began. Instead of our troops rolling to Berlin, the Germans broke through all along the southern front, crossed the Don Cossack country, and finally reached the Volga at Stalingrad and the northern Caucasus as far as the oil fields of Mozdok. This was so unexpected and tragic that we were all stunned.

Apparently this took the high command by surprise, too. At the end of July, Stalin issued an order of the day. I have never heard anything like it. A merciless struggle against cowards, panic-mongers, and all those who feel that our country is large and that we can fall back indefinitely. "Not a step back—the country is ashamed of its army." I do not remember the exact words, but that was the meaning.

Stalin's words had an effect. The German advance ground to a halt at Stalingrad and in the Caucasus. In Stalingrad they fought street by street, house by house. And the Germans could not cross the Volga or reach the Baku oil fields.

All these events left us on the sidelines. We were too far north. But here, too, our troops kept attacking—probably to prevent the Germans from shifting any troops south.

As the winter approached, things changed dramatically. It was the repetition of the Moscow battle, but on even a larger scale. At the end of November they announced a tremendous victory. Our armies broke through north and south of Stalingrad and trapped 330,000 crack German troops. In the Caucasus, too, the Germans retreated quickly. It was a rout. "A holiday in our streets," as Stalin called it. Victory upon victory, great territories liberated, tremendous amounts of booty, thousands upon thousands of prisoners.

There have been many changes for us, as well. My knee surgery methods were accepted, if not approved. I was even invited to Moscow for a surgical conference and spoke for two hours. I didn't convince everybody, but we continued to use my method in our hospital with good results.

After knees, I concentrated on hips. First of all, I spoke to Bocharoff.

"Let's discuss what to do with our hip cases."

"There's nothing to discuss."

"Yes, there is. Our present methods are wrong. The results are miserable. A plaster cast works only when the general condition of the patient is good."

After a long argument he permitted me to try treating hip cases by traction, but only as an experiment. And the results were striking. So much so that Bocharoff fully approved it. I was overjoyed. Not all legs could be saved, but many amputations were averted.

Some other changes were painful to me.

The most painful was the departure of Bocharoff. He was appointed chief surgeon of an army group. I begged him to take me with him. He tried, but he couldn't do it. I almost cried when I saw him off.

Both our political officers, Zvereff and Shishkin, were transferred to front-line units. Liza became ill and was sent home. Tamara also collapsed from overwork and was demobilized. Zoya became engaged to some officer and was transferred. We got replacements, fine girls all, but I was sorry to see my old friends go. From our entire Cherepovets contingent only Lina, Kansky, Chapliuk and I were still with PPG-2266. Also some medics and drivers.

Khaminoff is gone, too. In September he went on another alcoholic binge, and this time he was courtmartialed. They accused him of misappropriating some hospital funds. He got ten years, but the sentence was commuted, and he was sent to the front instead. I was sorry to see him go. He was a good administrator, when sober, and a good physician. Our parting was sad, even though we had drifted apart after our arrival in Kaluga.

He was replaced by Dr. L., a military surgeon second class, an eye specialist from Moscow. He is courteous and well brought up, but he lacks Khaminoff's drive.

The new commissar, a former political instructor in one of the Moscow hospitals, is a martinet and disciplinarian. Our girls started to hate him at once—mostly because of his insistence on discipline and his night checks. For some reason he appointed himself guardian of their morals. All the new nurses were young and pretty, and there was no dearth of young men in Kaluga. Although they worked hard, there was a bit of flirting going on, but no promiscuity. At least I had never noticed any.

During the summer I wrote a dissertation and passed the examination for the title of Candidate of Sciences. I presented my dissertation to the First Moscow Medical Institute, but before I could defend it, our Kaluga period came to an abrupt end.

In the middle of January we got our orders: to wrap up our Kaluga operation and get ready to depart to the front. We were to become a mobile unit again. Our staff: 5 doctors, 4 head nurses, 12 nurses and 18 male medics. Also horse drivers and handlers. We had to lose many good people who were assigned to other units.

They took Igumnoff. "You won't be putting on any plaster

casts where you're going, and we need him here." But fortunately Lina and Kansky stayed with us. Also Lyda Denisenko and Blackbird—still the head surgeon.

We received a large truck, Zis-5, 22 brand new carts, entirely new equipment and medical supplies, and we succeeded in taking some of our own equipment from Kaluga. Just before New Year's we were loaded into a train and on our way.

We had no idea of our final destination. We reached Michurinsk and suddenly turned west toward Orel, with frequent stops, often in open, snow-covered fields.

We passed through recently liberated territory, torn-up ground, burned-down villages. Often we were stranded in demolished stations. Nearly all railroad buildings were blown up. In some dugout or snow-bound freight car there would be a tired, unshaven telegraph operator—our only connection with the outside world. From him we would get the latest communiqués. Our troops continued driving the Germans back from the Volga and out of the Caucasus.

We learned about the termination of the battle of Stalingrad on a frosty morning when our train was standing in an open field near Eletz. It was a long wait, and we all got out to get some fresh air. It was a beautiful, sunny day. Military traffic was moving along the highway flanking the railway track. One vehicle halted momentarily, and a smiling young officer shouted to us, "Paulus capitulated! With his entire army!"

We danced in the snow, rolled on the ground, laughing and crying from sheer happiness like a bunch of children.

FEBRUARY 6, 1943

We have stopped at the station called Russky Brod.

"Get ready to unload!"

At last. Outside it is 20° C. below. All along the railway tracks there are mountains of boxes: shell cases, barrels of herring and salt beef, sacks of grain. There is a village in the distance—a few houses on a bare, snow-covered hill. Between the houses are piles of supplies and military vehicles. No civilians. In a ravine, an anti-aircraft battery.

For half an hour we are shifted to and fro until we finally come to a stop. The station commandant appears from nowhere, bristling with importance.

"Get out, get out! Throw everything out! You can sort it out later! We need this track! Quick!" he shouts.

We quickly unload, and the empty train moves away. A Red Cross car drives in, and a middle-aged officer wearing a white camouflage gown over his overcoat gets out.

"PPG-2266? At last! I am the head of the Army Evacuation Area."

He looks at our stuff piled along the track, and bursts out laughing.

"Haven't you brought a piano?"

Among our things there are two large wardrobes and a desk with a desk lamp on it. They look incongruous.

Our head tries to explain. "Those are necessary things, Comrade. We—"

"Never mind! That's your affair. Now here are your orders. Our troops are advancing, but with serious losses. Load up at once and be ready to move. You must set up your hospital and receive the wounded today. Wait for further instructions."

He drives away. While our drivers are hitching up, four Red Cross 1½-ton trucks arrive, seemingly from nowhere. A young captain jumps down from one.

"Load up—quickly! Never mind the horses! Get the most important equipment and people. We will take you to a village, just liberated, where you will relieve a medical battalion!"

We throw everything we can into the trucks and get in. The captain explains, "It's only 18 kilometers. We'll unload you there and come back for the rest of your stuff. It won't take any time at all!"

But in fact it takes a lot of time, because the captain does not know the way. It is beginning to grow dark when we finally find our destination—the village of Pokrovskoye.

Here we are at the front. For a soldier the front line is his foxhole. For a hospital, 5 to 10 kilometers farther back. That is our psychology.

The village has been completely burned down. Only a half-wrecked school and a church remain. This is where the medical battalion is working. We see cars coming and the wounded being unloaded on the snow.

And we cursed these people for sending us improperly treated cases!

The harried head doctor of the battalion tells us that there is a village—Ugolnaya—about three miles farther along the road.

"There is nothing you can do here. But there are many wounded at Ugolnaya—from our division. And there are many houses intact there. They threw the Fritzes out before they could burn the place down."

Here it is—the real war.

LATER

We arrive in Ugolnaya late at night, frozen to the bone.

In the moonlight we see houses scattered around under huge, naked linden trees. Some seem to be intact, but not all. There are many bare brick chimneys rising from the snow. There are some army vehicles parked here and there.

Our trucks stop in front of the first house. We enter it. A single oil lamp illuminates a nightmarish scene. Everywhere, on the large Russian oven*, on the benches, and on the floor, lie wound-

---

*Traditionally in Russian peasant huts a brick oven occupied a large part of the room, and its flat top was used by the entire family for sleeping.—Trans.

ed men. Tobacco smoke, stench of blood, freezing cold. Moans, delirium. Horrified, we slam the door shut. In the next house we see the same scene, but finally we find a medic. He tells us that the entire village is crammed with the wounded and that there are only two nurses and three medics from the medical battalion in attendance. Some houses are still occupied by some rear-echelon supply people, but they are getting ready to depart.

"All we can do is give them water, when we can. Most barns and other service buildings have been broken down for firewood. There are some dead lying there among the live ones. Now that you are here, we are leaving."

We walk from house to house. We find some half-empty ones and finally "requisition" a large peasant cottage by moving the wounded into neighboring houses.

Here we unload. It is already 11 o'clock. The house is large and well warmed by an iron stove. We are dead tired, cold, and hungry, and we lie together on the floor. There is nothing we can do tonight.

FEBRUARY 7, 1943

At first dawn I wake up our supply officer and we go out to reconnoiter. Only now do we realize how close we are to the front. In the frosty morning air we can clearly hear not only artillery salvos but machine-gun bursts.

There are about 100 houses in the village, about 70 of them still intact. Between the houses are foxholes and trenches half covered by snow. The village stands about two miles from the highway and is connected with it by a narrow snowbound road. The trucks that brought us here have departed. The only large building in the village, a former school, is gutted out.

All the better houses, about twenty of them, are occupied by some rear-echelon military, but some cars are being loaded, ready to depart. Our Chapliuk is a marvel. He has already rigged up his kitchen between some trenches.

The rest of the houses are crammed with wounded, and small groups of them are wandering around, on crutches and with arms in slings, looking for shelter and food.

By this time the rest of our people wake up. The house where we slept became icy toward morning. Our first problem is to set up a dressing station. Let our supply people worry about food.

Finally we find a large peasant house with a large front room and, behind the stove, a small isolated corner. We bring in the minimum of equipment and set up two tables, one for wound dressing, another for surgical equipment. Kansky is setting up the autoclave in the anteroom. By noon our dressing station is ready.

But before starting to function as a surgical unit we have to feed the wounded. Blackbird and I decide to divide the village into two departments and to receive the wounded. "To receive" means simply to send the nurses from house to house for a head count. They counted 320 cases in 28 houses. Chapliuk has cooked the gruel, but doesn't know how to distribute it. We left our food cans behind at Russky Brod. We start to distribute it in old helmets and water pails, and it is not until afternoon that we feed everyone—dry bread and cold gruel.

Manpower is our bottleneck. In Kaluga we drafted civilian women to help, but here there are no civilians. We have only 18 medics in our PPG, and 8 of them are coming with our horse carts. And all the men we have are collecting firewood. Without heat all our wounded would freeze. We even force some walking wounded to help, but obviously that is no solution.

In the afternoon a snowstorm starts, and it looks as if all roads may become impassable.

While they are setting up our dressing station, I look into the neighboring peasant huts. Absolutely horrifying scenes. All the wounded must be urgently attended to. They are lying in makeshift bandages put on by front-line medics. No way of knowing how many might be developing gangrene. Those who can move are attending to the stoves. Very dangerous. A fire would lead to a terrible tragedy, but there is no other way.

During the day we operate on only four cases. One is a chest wound. Two walking wounded actually drag him in. He is gasping for breath and has almost no pulse. We put him on the table and remove the bandage. It is horrible. The entire right side of the chest is a terrible open wound . . . broken ribs . . . gray, pulsating lungs. We clean the wound and remove broken pieces of ribs, but we cannot close the wound. We just apply a tampon, put on a tight bandage, and take him into the next hut. He hasn't a ghost of a chance, of course. In fact, we should not have wasted two hours on him.

The three other cases are amputations. Two legs to the hip, and one to the knee.

By nightfall our train arrives, all 22 carts, but there is no point in continuing our work. By midnight we call a halt. We assign several huts to each medic, ordering them to sleep there, and we doctors and nurses collapse on the floor of our dressing station, pell-mell.

The girls have spent a nightmarish day. Each was assigned 3 or 4 huts. Until dark they tried to feed their charges, listening to entreaties, reproaches, hysterics, curses. They needed water, warmth, the most primitive medical help, and we could not provide anything. One man threatened to toss a hand grenade at Anna Suchkova. Tacia has been bringing water up all day from a wrecked well with a pail, tying together several belts and scarves. All of them wept many times during the day, cursing superiors, doctors, and the very hour when they had decided to become military nurses.

FEBRUARY 8, 1943

Only four men, including my chest case, died during the

night. I expected more. We had to take them into an empty dugout. It will be difficult to bury them. The frozen ground is granite hard.

In the morning we hold a quick conference. Blackbird and I will take turns, one working in our surgery, another making rounds of the huts, picking out the most critical cases.

From the early dawn new cases begin to arrive! Some are brought by horses directly from regiments; others struggle in on foot. I attempt to organize the sorting. We clear out one hut for this, but in an hour it is full, and walking cases are again wandering all over the place, looking for shelter.

First of all we must organize the surgery and dressing station. None of the available huts is large enough, so we set up a large tent with an iron stove. It takes far too much time. The ground is too hard to hold the stakes; we have to drill holes and freeze the stakes in.

By nightfall we finish with the tent, set up seven tables, and warm the place up.

We hold another conference. For the first time we become really terrified. We remember our first day in Kaluga as a paradise.

The situation: almost 500 unattended wounded in 40 huts, dirty and poorly heated. Most of them lying on floors. True, all have been fed, but the food was cold—it's a long way from the kitchen, over snow drifts. There is very little water and no question of using it for washing. All the nurses are dirty, exhausted, absolutely miserable. They say that the wounded are cursing them, insulting them.

We, too, curse everyone, including ourselves. We should have set up our tent surgery the first night instead of sleeping. We should have insisted on our entire unit being brought here together. We should have been preparing ourselves for front-line conditions instead of resting during slack periods in Kaluga.

Yes, "should have, should have . . . "

And it is the wounded who pay for everything. Out of eight operations during the day, three amputations. Should have been five, but I have taken a long chance on two. The reports from the huts: "many gangrene suspects." Of course. Many bandages have not been changed for days. There are no prospects for early evacuation—the roads are becoming snowbound. Fortunately we have enough food, if only dry rations and buckwheat, and fodder for our horses.

We are now attached to the 48th Army. It is a brand new one. Perhaps that is why there is all this disorder.

Tonight nurses and medics will take turns visiting all the huts, at least once every two or three hours.

We again sleep on the floor, huddled up together for warmth. But our commissar is clearing out one small hut for our women. He's still worrying about our girls' morals. Stupid.

FEBRUARY 9, 1943

Our surgery is in operation at the first light of dawn.

Blackbird and one head nurse go from hut to hut selecting the most critical cases for immediate surgery. Our commander has organized horse transport for them. We have also formed "the recovery battalion"—light walking cases. They can't help much, but they are trying to relieve our manpower shortage. Bessonoff is in charge there. He is a former skull case, medically demobilized, who has volunteered to work in our hospital. A middle-aged, taciturn man, a bit odd, I think.

The cases are unloaded outside our tent on stretchers, and we take them in one by one. We do not undress them—only as much as is necessary to get to the wound. We find grime and lice. But Lyda Denisenko stands by the instrument table in a spotless white gown and surgical gloves. A remarkable girl.

We also have a mobile surgical team: Lina and one of our senior medics. Loaded down with bandages, splints, and antiseptics, they visit huts and redress wounds whenever absolutely necessary. This is against all aseptic rules, but there is nothing we can do.

By now every hut has been visited by a doctor at least once. Chapliuk and our supply people have organized fairly regular distribution of hot gruel, and each hut is supplied with firewood. But the wounded must attend to their stoves themselves. Each medic has from 3 to 5 huts to look after. They work without relief, sleeping with the wounded.

The special hut for our women has been set up, but some of our girls are too exhausted to go there. They snatch catnaps wherever they can.

Fortunately there are few new cases. Either the front has moved forward, or the roads have become impassable. We still hear artillery fire, but no machine guns.

We work like mad the whole day, but the results are not good. Forty operations, including 14 amputations. Bessonoff takes the severed arms and legs out and dumps them into a trench. It's butchery, but what else can we do? (Strange: I don't know what they do with them in city hospitals. Bury them?) Our dugout morgue is also filling up. Eleven corpses, by the last count, all frozen stiff.

FEBRUARY 10, 1943

Today it's my turn to work in the "wards" while Blackbird handles the surgery. He is getting very nervous and very exhausted. He has trouble sleeping at night. We hear him tossing and mumbling.

I don't start my rounds until ten o'clock, having spent the entire morning checking and sorting new cases brought in during the night. Fortunately none of them are critical.

In each hut I find the same scene. All the inner walls have been broken up for firewood, and I enter directly into the hut, bringing clouds of frosty haze with me. Smoke and stench. I can hardly see after the bright sunlight outside.

"Hey, you—close the door, damn you!"

I close it. Gradually my eyes become accustomed to the semi-darkness. There is a single window, no glass, stuffed with frozen hay for warmth.

"Ah . . . a doctor . . . at last."

On the floor, wall to wall, the seriously wounded, with wooden splints. Those who could move have grabbed the best places—on the stove and on benches.

"Get your medical cards ready," I say.

Grumbling. "That's all they're doing, going around and checking. What about evacuation? How long are you going to torture us? What about some proper food instead of dry bread and cold swill? And the lice—they are eating us alive."

I try to speak evenly and calmly, "Those are your own lice, comrades. We didn't bring any with us. Yes, the food is bad, but it will be better. And you will be evacuated in due time. Show me your cards."

I check the cards and try to spot any possible gangrene. The nurse is taking temperatures and fixing bandages. In the first three huts I find eight cases requiring wound debridement and surgery. Suddenly Bessonoff bursts in. "Nikolai Mikhailovich! Some officers! They want you right away!"

There is a small military car with snow chains in front of our surgery tent. Inside the tent are the commissar, Blackbird, doctors, and nurses. And also the inspector-general of the Evacuation Area—a military surgeon, second class. Rather short and stocky. Round face. Handlebar moustache á la Marshal Budenny.* Boiling with indignation.

"What is this?" he yells. "What kind of hospital do you call this? Why is there no proper sorting procedure? And why are men being treated in huts? And the wounded are lying on floors and wearing overcoats in surgery?! This is a madhouse, not a hospital!"

Of course, he is right. But honestly I cannot see how we could

---

*Marshal S. Budenny, a hero of the Civil War. He wore a long handlebar moustache.—Trans.

have done better. However, this moustachioed man seems to be constructive. After giving us hell, he cools off.

"Very well, comrades, let's plan together. First of all, don't count on any help. You must solve all your problems on your own. We have nothing to promise you. We ourselves have nothing but promises from above."

We know this situation very well. So we remain silent.

"You must set up two separate departments. One for registration, reception, and treatment of lighter cases. Another, the main surgical. No more bandaging in huts. Create the minimum aseptic conditions. Undress all men before surgery. You must organize evacuation of the lighter cases to Russky Brod. Take them yourselves. Use your horses to take them to the highway and then stop all empty vehicles going back. If they refuse, take down their numbers." He smiles. "That would frighten them. Eventually you can start off the walking cases on foot. Give them dry rations for two days. Most of them will be picked up on the way. You'd be surprised how much you can do yourselves with a bit of organization."

I begin to like this man.

"Now, who is going to head the reception department? You, doctor, as the younger one?"

Me. I knew it. I look so young and insignificant.

"I am a surgeon, Comrade."

"That's exactly what we need. You'll do all the simpler surgery on the spot. Set up a special tent for that purpose. Get a move on. We've got the German on the run, so let's show a bit of enthusiasm. Clear?"

What can one say to that?

"Yes, Comrade."

"I'm depending on you."

"I serve the Soviet Union."

He gives a few more orders, and then he and the commander go away to eat at Chapliuk's "restaurant." And we go to work. It is surprising what a bit of encouragement can do.

We mobilize all our forces. We set up a large tent before dark.

We even put a sign over the entrance: "Reception-Sorting Dept., PPG-2266." Next to it we set up a smaller tent with two surgical tables. We put iron stoves in both and bring in some firewood.

By the time "Budenny" drives away, the entire village is in motion. Kansky draws a rough plan, marking all usable buildings, and we divide them: 25 for me and 35 for Blackbird and his team. Meanwhile, the nurses prepare lists of the cases in accordance with the seriousness of injuries.

However, it takes the whole next day to redistribute the wounded and to bring some order into our work.

All new arrivals come to us first. We register them, and then Lina and I examine them. Serious cases (skulls, chests, stomachs, and hips) we send over to Blackbird, but all others we treat ourselves, including minor surgery and wound dressing. We also feed them and give them hot tea. "Liubochka" has organized it to perfection. Our stoves work well, too, and we can maintain sufficient warmth.

Our commander organizes our living quarters in two clean huts, quite warm. The food isn't bad at all.

FEBRUARY 15, 1943

Today we hit our absolute capacity—800 cases. We have even repaired the burned-out school, which is known as "White House." We cannot absorb any more cases, and still there is no organized evacuation.

Lice. Everywhere. We try to combat this menace, but without success. We have one portable delousing chamber, but it cannot service more than 5 to 6 huts a day. We have developed another method. A Russian stove. When it is sufficiently hot, we remove all the coals and put lousy garments there, closing it tight. In two hours all the insects die. However, all this does not help, because we cannot change the old straw in all the huts, and in a few days lice reappear again.

FEBRUARY 16, 1943

The torrent of wounded has slackened. The front has moved forward, and it has become difficult to bring in bed cases. Walking cases continue to arrive, up to 100 a day. But we have developed a method of handling them. We register and examine them, redress the wounds when necessary, feed them, give them dry rations, form into groups and send them away on foot to Russky Brod. Those who come in the evening sleep in our sorting tent and leave in the morning. No protests—all want to get as far to the rear as possible. It is more difficult to detain those who really should not be walking.

Every morning a group of pilgrims forms in front of our tent with arms in slings, splints, bandaged heads, canes, and makeshift crutches. The main problem for them is to get to the highway, two miles away. There some of them are picked up by military vehicles, but not all. Our drivers are not too softhearted when it comes to the wounded.

In our department things have become satisfactory. The main problem, manpower, has almost been resolved. Our recovery battalion now numbers almost 50 men. They are hardly efficient workers but they are trying.

FEBRUARY 20, 1943

By February 20th the number of the wounded has reached 900. All huts are crammed to capacity. The conditions are deplorable; many of the wounded are lying on floors. This is a real crisis. Walking cases walk away, but bed cases become walking cases very slowly.

We found it impossible to organize evacuation to Russky Brod in our carts. Our horses have become thin; we have nothing but straw to feed them. But our commander had a brilliant idea. We set up a tent on the highway and took some bed cases there in charge of a nurse. We placed a sergeant with a machine gun on the road to stop all cars going to Russky Brod. As one party is evacuated, we send more. By this method we have sent up to 50 men away. Of course we don't send the more serious cases, but those who are fully transportable.

FEBRUARY 23, 1943

We celebrated Red Army Day, February 23rd, in our tent, almost pleasantly. In our department we have only about 100 wounded, since they are the first to be evacuated, and that is no problem at all. Chapliuk baked a fruit pie from canned fruit, and someone had a bottle of red wine. We ate well and read aloud some of Simonoff's poems.* Lina has a thin little book of his. Then we discussed our affairs. Generally we all felt that the commander and the commissar had been doing very well.

But in our surgical department things have been far from satisfactory, even though the commander has been trying to help Blackbird all he could. I've had almost no contact with him, which is very abnormal. We met two or three times a week to discuss administrative problems but that's all. I don't know whose fault it was. We knew that mortality in his department was alarmingly high—two, three, and sometimes five deaths a day. I knew what that meant to a surgeon. On several occasions I wanted to go and speak to him, offer him advice. But I was afraid he would be offended. He has had so much more experience than I, but most of that experience was under normal peacetime conditions. Mine had been mostly under wartime stress.

---

*K. Simonoff, Soviet writer and poet. His poems were enormously popular during the war.—Trans.

FEBRUARY 25, 1943

Today everything was resolved without my interference.

This morning the commander called me and ordered me to take over the surgical department, leaving Lina in charge of my own department. He said that Blackbird and his assistant, Nadya, had been transferred to the Army Evacuation Area. "For health reasons."

Perhaps I should have refused or at least protested, but I did not. In fact, I agreed readily. I only asked, "Why?"

He gave the standard answer: "He couldn't handle the work."

Perhaps I should have gone and spoken to him? But what could I tell him? That I had not been intriguing against him? That would have been stupid.

In two hours he and Nadya left in one of the carts for our highway evacuation tent to wait for transportation to Russky Brod. He left without saying goodbye to any of us. It was quite unpleasant.

The same evening I learned a few details. The whole thing was simple. The man was completely exhausted by inhumanly hard work under terrible conditions. His cases kept dying, and to a surgeon of his reputation that was unbearable. On many occasions he became hysterical, and finally he quarrelled with all the members of his team.

It was harder to judge his surgical mistakes. Kansky and Lyda told me that there had been some unnecessary fatalities during operations in their opinion. But no war-time surgeon is free from such tragedies.

So once again I am the head surgeon of PPG-2266.

FEBRUARY 26, 1943

I start my new work in the morning. I have a fine team—Lyda

Denisenko, the head nurse, Masha Poletova, Shura Filina, Vera Tarasenko. They all wear trousers under their white gowns to protect themselves from cold and lice. Kolia Kansky is the best head medic we have, and we have two stretcher-bearers. I still have Bessonoff and a few men from our recovery battalion.

I deliver a short speech. "Comrades. From now on every case is to be undressed to his linen before coming to the operating theater. Set up a special corner for major surgery—two tables—and screen it off with clean sheets. Aseptic conditions must be improved. After I make my rounds, we'll do some of the important surgery."

In the huts the conditions have improved. No one lies on the floor. The straw is covered with sheets and pillows. But all the wounded are lying in their own clothes. The cases have been sorted out. Chests occupy two huts; skulls, one; stomachs, one; gaseous gangrene, two. All the other huts are occupied by "extremities" (hips, joints, serious leg injuries). All huts are completely lice-bound. To eliminate lice we must wash everyone, redress all wounds, and disinfect the huts. And all the cases are so serious that it is impossible even to think of such a radical procedure. Many of them would not survive it.

The extremity cases are in especially frightening condition. Compared to them, chests, skulls and stomachs are better off. All the really serious cases have already died. The sepsis in those cases develops quickly, with deaths, as a rule, occurring on the tenth or twelfth day. The extremities are different. The infection might take a month or two to fully develop. And in most cases it is developing.

Extremities are my specialty. The tactic is obvious: amputation. It goes back to the time of the Crimean war. Some of these men are so weak that they might not even survive amputation, but there is no way out. It is their last chance. If some of them could have been evacuated by air to our old Kaluga hospital, their legs and arms might have been saved. But not under our conditions, and not under the conditions that exist at Russky Brod. So our only aim should be saving lives, wherever possible.

The wounded receive my visit with a sense of alarm—a new doctor, and a young one. That is normal. There is never any real contact under such conditions. Not with 200-odd cases in 22 huts.

By lunch time, when I finish my rounds, I have a clear picture of our situation. It is much worse than in Kaluga a year ago.

We redressed some "quiet" wounds on the spot. After two o'clock, we started our surgery. For today we have selected five of the most critical cases, all hips and joints. We do four radical hip amputations, and one knee operation with a plaster cast. In a few cases, we drained pus from the pleural cavity. Those seem to be doomed. Among all our stomach cases, only one was operated on by a front-line medical battalion. This means that all really serious cases have already died here. According to our calculations, the percentage of wounds properly attended to by front-line units does not exceed fifteen. But how can we blame them? What about ourselves?

I return to my billet feeling very sad. My easy life has come to an end. Even the communiqué describing new victories does not help. We know the price of these victories.

FEBRUARY 27, 1943

Early in the morning I started amputations, absolutely appalled by this butchery. But there was no way out. Many men with fractured hips have been lying in high splints for up to three weeks and were barely alive.

Of last night's amputees, one died and others are still critical. The sepsis has progressed to the point that the simplest amputation becomes a mortal trauma.

Around eleven o'clock, Dr. Nadya, Blackbird's assistant, runs in, quite pale. She's wearing her overcoat and fur hat.

"Quick!" she says. "We brought Dr. Z. back! He's bleeding! An accident!"

Lyda and I were operating on a knee joint.

This takes us by surprise. We thought he was at Russky Brod. Accident? What accident?

"Nina, go and take a look! Take some bandages and things. I'll be free in a few minutes."

In five minutes Nina returns, rather calm.

"Nothing serious. A severed vein in the neck. Nadya is bandaging it."

In a few more minutes the picture becomes clear. Because he was not wounded and had no transfer papers, no one would pick him up. They spent a whole day yesterday waiting there, and this morning Nadya insisted on their coming back to get the necessary papers. Before arriving in Ugolnaya, Blackbird had cut his vein with his razor. Now, he absolutely refuses to see me or anyone else.

"Inject morphine. Let him calm down and sleep."

I remembered myself in Kaluga a year ago. I could understand Blackbird. A complete work failure, a dishonorable dismissal, extreme fatigue, accumulation of despair. And personal conflicts with his coworkers to boot.

Poor surgeons! But—if one considers all this soberly—self-pity is an unforgivable weakness. Millions of people are today in much worse situations. It is difficult to watch people die, but it is more difficult to do the dying. One must keep oneself in check and do one's work, the best one knows how. Without sentiment and self-indulgence.

The report is that Blackbird has fallen asleep. His condition is not dangerous. A long sleep should fix him up. He is a good surgeon, and he will find his place. Of course, in Kaluga I had Bocharoff. Well, he has Nadya, a very devoted friend. More than merely devoted, and more than a friend. They have been together for many years.

We operate all day long. I cut off eight more legs. Terrible. I have never heard of such surgical "productivity." In fact, I should have done three more amputations, but I just hadn't the heart. Most likely I'll have to do them later on. There are no miracles.

Yes, we'll leave quite a cemetery at Ugolnaya. Over 100 corpses so far, crammed into three mass graves. Two of them have filled up with snow, and some soldiers from the recovery battalion put crudely made crosses over them. Of course, whenever possible we collect their documents, but not all of them have papers.

We don't know exactly how many men have gone through our meat-grinder. After we started proper registration, we processed 1,220 cases, but there were at least 600 before that who went unregistered. Terrible fatality figures when one considers that there were many light wounded, many walking ones. But even those figures don't tell the whole story. Many others will still die. Very many. I hope that medical services in other armies on our front are better organized than we are.

And this is merely the beginning of our ordeal! There is no end of the war in sight, even though the outcome is no longer in doubt. But it is our soldiers who are dousing the dreadful Nazi fire that is threatening the whole world, with their blood. And not only soldiers. Millions of civilians have been butchered by the Fascists. How many millions? Only history will give the answer.

MARCH 1, 1943

Our hospital chief called us together in the morning.

"New orders," he said. "We are to relocate by our own transport to the village of Verkhnaya Sosna. Set up the hospital by March 2nd. Evacuate all the wounded to Russky Brod."

We were stunned.

"Tell them to go to hell!"

"Absolutely unrealistic! What about our untransportable cases?"

"All I know is that I have our orders," he said.

Nonsense.

Of course, we could not even begin any relocation. During the night a blizzard blocked all the roads with snow, even the main highway. Whole transport columns are frozen fast, and one can reach the highway from our place only on foot over huge snow-drifts.

We continue active surgery. I have performed several more amputations. That, I think, is all for a while. Out of those on whom we operated during the first two days, six died—two after my knee resection. A warning: one must not be stingy with amputations. Stingy? Several other cases are on the borderline. We are doing all we can—treating them, transfusions—we take blood from our own personnel.

The patience of our soldiers is incredible. That is the strength of our people. There have been many beautiful songs written during this war. I often think of the one that goes:

> There they come—
> The laboring people,
> The fighting people,
> Ready for suffering,
> Ready for sorrow,
> Ready to fight to the death.

Suffering and sorrow have been a part of our national life for centuries. In war, and in peace. We know how to die. That is important knowledge, since death is the only thing that no one can contest and no medicine can cure.

Philosophy.

MARCH 5, 1943

The roads are beginning to come to life. "The Studebakers"* have started to move. We have cleared our road to the main high-

---

*A great number of Studebaker cars were a part of the lend-lease agreement. They were highly appreciated in the Red Army.—Trans.

way and started to evacuate our serious cases. We must unload as quickly as possible. We are going to be forced to move.

MARCH 6, 1943

A reserve army regiment has arrived at Ugolnaya, and they are pressuring us to get out. But they are helping us with their horses. Every morning we load a dozen sleighs with straw and put the wounded in sleeping bags or wrap them in blankets. We send a nurse with a first aid kit to accompany each party until they are picked up on the highway.

Blackbird and Doctor Nadya finally left for the Army Medical Center. For me his departure has been a sort of emotional trauma. I should not have agreed to take his place without seeing him first and talking to him. Of course the extremity cases had been badly neglected by him, and many soldiers died because of his negligence or lack of experience. But a part of the responsibility is mine. I should have tried to share my experience with him. But I did nothing because of my stupid pride.

MARCH 8, 1943

On the 8th we get new orders: "Relocate to the village of Kuban, set up the hospital, and receive the wounded." Again, "by our own transport." And we have only seven horses; the others have died. True, we have a large motor truck, but it can't take us all.

Nevertheless, we have to obey orders. With the help of the reserve regiment we have taken some 200 of the wounded to the highway for evacuation to Russky Brod. We have about 100 cases left, 18 of them absolutely untransportable. We will have to leave them behind in care of the regimental medics, who will also take the rest of the wounded to the highway. Still, we will be at least two days late. Who wrote those orders that cannot possibly be carried out? It must be easy to fight a war on paper.

The winter stays on. We have had blizzards almost every day.

MARCH 10, 1943

The great migration is beginning. It's a fine, frosty morning. Near our staff tent our "infantry column" has assembled: all those who can walk, and also four carts loaded with our most necessary property. All nurses and medics who could be freed are ready to go on foot. They have duffle bags and dry rations for two days, and they are ready. The major, Bykova, Chapliuk, I, and three more people will go tomorrow in our truck. It is loaded with kitchen equipment and food supplies. The weather might interrupt all communications at that time. One can live without wound dressings, but not without food.

"Column . . . forward march."

The major is smiling. "Looks like an Arctic expedition."

They start off, slowly, over the deep snow. Our people. There is a warm feeling inside me as I watch them. "Ready for suffering . . . ready for sorrow . . . " Ready for everything.

The rest of the day and most of the night we spend checking all the wounded who will stay behind. Fortunately none of them is really critical.

The next morning we leave. Our 3-ton Zis-5 truck is not new, but our driver, Fedya, is young and experienced. And still it took us two days to reach Kuban. In many spots the roads were almost impassable.

MARCH 19, 1943

Our hurry proved to be unnecessary. The offensive has ground to a halt, and the medical battalion that we were supposed to relieve was still in Kuban. For eight days we did nothing, living next to them. We got to know them well. They are a Guards* detachment and walked around proud as peacocks. Their leading surgeon was covered with decorations—a heroic figure.

Warm, early spring days. Black patches have appeared in the snow, and rooks make a terrific racket in the tall, leafless trees. Life. Kuban is a typical small Orel province village: tiny, neat houses, with thatched roofs. It was liberated on the 6th of March, undamaged. Usually the Germans, when retreating, leave special "fire commandos" behind to put everything to the torch. But that is where local partisans are invaluable. They often fall upon these arsonists and destroy them. That is what happened in Kuban.

Those partisans are our second front. The Communist Party leaves some of its members behind to organize this guerrilla warfare. In Byelorussia there are some large areas that the Germans could never penetrate. They are Soviet islands far behind the German lines. There are airfields there where our planes land to bring in supplies and evacuate the wounded. The guerrillas harass the Germans, blow up their trains, destroy their supply columns, and rid the towns and villages of their collaborators. The reprisals are savage, but that only works in our favor. Men and women run into the forests and join the partisans. Many German divisions are tied up fighting them, as well as German police regiments. It is savage warfare with no quarter asked or given, and they say that several thousands of these "people avenger" detachments are operating in the German rear at all times. Sometime, someone should write a book about those people.

The front line is close to Kuban. We can clearly hear machine gun bursts and shell and mine explosions.

---

*The units that distinguished themselves in action were designated as "Guard Units"—i.e., crack detachments. This distinction was highly valued.—Trans.

The streets are full of soldiers and supply carts. Our soldiers still wear felt boots despite the mud, but some carts are already on wheels. There are many officers of all ranks, including generals. This is a divisional rear area.

How the officers and soldiers have changed! The army does not look very elegant—soldiers are sloppily though very practically dressed, and shave irregularly. The officers look better in their well-fitting overcoats. But it is not the appearance that is striking; it is the general sense of confidence. In 1941 our soldiers were timid and frightened. They were forever scanning the sky for enemy aircraft, ready to run and hide. Now they pay no attention to the planes or gunfire. They smoke at night, and field kitchens are smoking in courtyards without any attempt at camouflage.

I spoke to some officers. According to them we now have air superiority, and our equipment, particularly T-34 tanks, are better than anything the Germans have. And our artillery has always been better; we were just outgunned before. Not any more. All the factories relocated in the Urals and Siberia are working full blast, and the railways are doing a tremendous job. Our *Katiusha* rocket launchers are particularly terrifying to the Germans. Strangely, they do not try to develop rocket artillery of their own. Why? No one seems to know. Much of the German equipment is slowly becoming obsolete.

In Kuban I first heard about the Kursk salient, a deep bulge into the German lines, carved during our winter offensive. One captain showed me his map. It looks dangerously exposed. To me it resembles a hernia.

"That's where they would probably strike," he told me. "Trying to pinch off the salient and stage their own Stalingrad. But I'm sure we're ready."

I hope we are. But I can't forget those first weeks of the war. We were all sure that we were ready then. And we were caught with our pants down. And what about last spring?

"Not again," the Captain said. Rear supply people are the best strategists.

MARCH 21, 1943

Last night, without any warning, the medical battalion moved out, turning their wounded over to us. We've inherited about 150 cases, which had come in during the last few days. Thirty of them are recovering from major surgery and are untransportable. The transfer was simple. They just carried the wounded from their tents into our huts. Head nurses counted sheets, blankets, and stretchers, and made us sign for them. The therapist told us very little about his charges—stomachs, chests, and skulls lying in two huts.

This time we were properly set up. All standards of organization and hygiene were adhered to, even though we are understaffed (part of our personnel and supplies are still in Ugolnaya). However, we've had ample time and ample manpower—our recovery battalion under Bessonoff's direction.

And we have organized "the Kuban University." A series of lectures for nurses about all the peculiarities of military surgery. Our new girls had come from three-month training schools, and knew very little. We run classes for three hours every day, much to the joy of our commissar, who is still watching their morals. Strange man.

He saw Lyda Denisenko and me walking together the other night and clumsily spoke to me about "our duty" to keep our girls "out of trouble." "Their mothers have entrusted them to us." I wanted to tell him that if he had to set out to fight human nature he had a losing battle on his hands, but I didn't. We have all learned not to contradict our political nannies; it's become second nature. But our commissar is an exceptionally fine man.

We've had very few new wounded. The fighting has slackened, and our front has become almost inactive. The troops must have outrun their supplies, what with the impassable roads and wrecked railways in all the liberated areas. The news from other fronts is not too good. Our troops left Kharkov and Belgorod. But our Western front has come to life and we have taken Rzhev, Gzhatsk, and Vyazma.

Some high-ranking officers visited us. First, our old friend with the Budenny moustache. Then the head of the Evacuation Area. He was satisfied with our organization. He sat for a while in our dressing station, getting acquainted with our nurses.

"Girls, why the trousers?" he said. "It's so pleasant to see a skirt once in a while."

He had been seeing plenty of skirts where he came from. But he had the right idea, so we all supported him. The girls agreed. Spring is approaching; everyone is perking up.

In the Red Army the term *commander* has been replaced by *officer*. And there are new uniforms with shoulder straps, much like those in the Czar's army. Perhaps it's a good idea—the continuation of tradition.

And we, the medical personnel, are going to receive the usual army ranks, too. Medical sergeants, lieutenants, captains, majors, colonels, and generals. I wonder what rank I will get. Rank means a great deal in the army.

MID-APRIL, 1943

The main problem is surgery. Our work is not much better than that of medical front-line units. Of course, our problems are different. Medical battalions do the primary wound treatment, and it is our job to see the wounded through.

Theoretically, the thorniest problem is stomach wounds. There are many abdominal wounds, and all of them should be attended to during the first six hours. Otherwise, there is no way of combating shock and peritonitis. In unsuccessful battles, soldiers with stomach wounds never reach the rear hospitals; they die in their division. Now we have a slack period, and yet . . . I saw one of the Guard surgeons perform a lightning-like laparotomy. Then he left, probably marking the operation as a success in his book. And now the man is dying.

Of the twelve laparotomy cases left to us, six have developed complications: limited peritonitis, intestinal abscesses, opening wounds, fecal fistulas. The reason for all this: poor surgery.

Bocharoff taught us the ABCs of abdominal surgery. One must operate fast, but thoroughly. I have tried his method on one young soldier. The boy has recovered very well.

The second problem is chest wounds. There are three main types. First, there are wounds that do not penetrate the pleural area. These are the simplest cases, and none of them die. Then, there are the deeper wounds without open pneumothorax. With small openings, the air does not escape from the pleural area, and lung injuries are slight. These cases also recover easily. The worst chest wounds are open wounds with open pneumothorax. The air comes in and out of the pleural area and the lungs are usually badly injured. There are many dangers: in the early stage, shock because of the disturbed breathing and blood circulation. Later, infection.

Open pneumothoraxes, along with abdominal wounds, are the main problem of front-line units. The usual procedure is to close the wound with ligatures without paying any attention to the lungs. They all do the same thing, and our medical battalion left us several such cases, assuring us that everything necessary had been done. But in practice it was not so at all.

For three days all went on normally. We were incising and draining blood, pleurorrhea—up to a liter a day. On the 5th and 6th days, all bandages started to grow soggy, and on the 10th to the 12th days, the air began to escape. Two days later the wounds fell apart, and there were open holes. There was no immediate catastrophe; the breathing was not badly disturbed, and no shock developed, but there was progressing sepsis, and it progressed much faster than in cases with extremity wounds.

Of course, we tried to sew up pneumothoraxes, whenever the wounds opened, but it was senseless. The longest the ligatures held was 3 to 4 days, and then everything was repeated. Within one month five of our twelve patients died. So even here we cannot correct the mistakes of front-line units. They must operate more radically. We have worked out the exact methods and verified them on corpses. During war, surgeons never lack "school supplies."

A medic from our hospital recovery battalion fooled around with a hand grenade. It exploded next to him and he received a number of wounds, two of them in the chest, with open pneumothorax. We operated on him in accordance with our new method: cut the wound wide open, resect the pieces of neighboring ribs, open the pleura, sew up the diaphragm to the ribs, tighten together the undamaged ribs, and then sew up everything at the different levels, including the skin. Each day we used punctures to remove blood and fluid. On the fifth day he was already walking, and on the twentieth he was discharged and went to work. Our commissar was particularly pleased that he could report this "extraordinary success" to the medical superiors and to the Special Section.*

But even our new method doesn't cover all cases. If there is a serious lung injury, the mere sewing up would not be effective. In such cases, the surgeon must operate on the lung as well. Unfortunately, all this speculation about complicated operations, minute surgical interference, lung surgery, and the like is fantasy. When the wounded are arriving in a steady stream, we have no time and no energy for any such complicated surgery. It is tragic that many of the wounded who die do not really have to die. It is sad to find this out only toward the end of the second year of the war. The most important elements are proper conditions, time, and facilities, and especially ample transport.

It's bad enough that many men die at once from enemy fire. But it's terrible that so many die needlessly as a result of surgical carelessness and lack of time and facilities. That is inexcusable. Don't they understand that proper medical facilities are just as important as tanks, planes, machine guns, and food supplies?

And meanwhile, the spring marches on over the broad Orel plains. It is the middle of April. The trees near our huts have

---

*The army counter-intelligence section charged with destruction of German spies and their collaborators, and with political work generally. Unofficially called "Smersh."—Trans.

become covered with green dawn—buds ready to burst. The sun is warm and bright. It is time to plant and sow, but no one is sowing around Kuban, even though the old *kolkhoze* farmers are coming back and looking around—planning to reorganize their shattered lives.

Mud. A sea of mud. All secondary roads are absolutely impassable. Only the Studebakers float slowly over the mud rivers—all other transport is at a standstill. Not much hope for our horses. One died from lack of fodder. Others are barely alive but will probably live long enough to graze on fresh grass. Soldiers, women, and small boys and girls are carrying mines and shells to the front lines on their backs—the only way to supply it. Wonderful people. Even small children clamor for work, although all they can carry is a few cartridge clips. The people's war.

Our Kuban University has finished its work. We conducted proper examinations. All our girls have passed them with flying colors. Now we shall have some efficient nurses.

Two more doctors have arrived, both men. One is "a cold urologist" from Moscow; the second has no particular specialty, probably a general practitioner. The urologist is over 40 and rather fat. He has been working in a regimental unit. There he became so frostbitten that now he will never remove his fur vest, even when he's sitting near the fire. But that's not why I call him "the cold urologist." I call him "cold" because he has never done any surgery; he's only treated men with lavations, probably gonorrhea cases.

Meanwhile, our girls are slowly developing romantic attachments. The major is trying to keep them in line, but it's difficult—they live in different huts. And no one will help him. We all feel his efforts are unnecessary and stupid. And what can the girls do? We've read all our books, and there is no way of getting new ones. The newspaper *The Red Army Man* reaches us sometimes, and we await each issue eagerly. We listen to the communiqués only occasionally: our major is too busy with supply problems and our girls' morals. All we have is about 40 wounded, and we are evacuating those who are transportable. We've reached a complete standstill on our front. Strange.

The major is no longer worrying about Lyda and me. Probably he has given us up as "incurables."

Finally I had my "showdown" with Lina. I had been dreading it ever since the appearance of Lyda Denisenko in our hospital. I hate reproaches, but there were no reproaches. It was very simple, very easy.

I was sitting outside our hospital tent reading an old newspaper. I didn't even notice when Lina sat down beside me on an upturned supply case. I only smelled the dry blood on her surgical gown.

"I must congratulate you, Doctor. She's a fine girl," she said. "What are you talking about?" I said, even though I knew very well what she was talking about. She has been calling me doctor ever since that stupid day in Kaluga when I tried to kill myself. She felt that I was tense and she smiled—a sad smile, I thought.

"Do you remember that old Chinese story about a thief who stole a little bell and hid it in his clothes? He was afraid to move lest the bell ring and he be found out. That's how you've been acting. Especially with me. But I heard your bell long ago, probably before anyone else."

Stories and song quotes. I had always disliked that aspect of Lina. "You heard nothing," I said flatly.

Lina put her arm around me in a way that indicates distance rather than proximity. "Relax, Doctor. I'm very happy for you. No hurt feelings. I'm absolutely honest about it, and I like Lyda. I think you two should get married. And I'll be the first to congratulate you. Do you remember that old Gypsy song, 'And now we're strangers . . . How strange!' Only we're not strangers. We're comrades."

Yes, we are comrades. Even more than comrades. I have learned to depend on Lina. She's been developing into a first-rate surgeon. Better than me? No. I have more depth, more imagination. But she's more careful, more thorough when it comes to routine surgery.

Women are strange. I'm sure Lina was sincere. And what about men? I should have been relieved. I was relieved. But also a little hurt. How easily she had discarded me. "Let's not talk about it," I said. "All right," she said. And then we talked about surgery. Particularly about hemorrhage cases. Lina does not like those and always leaves them to me.

I have performed several interesting hemorrhage operations. Once I even inserted a ligature under the abdominal aorta. Unfortunately, "interesting" operations usually end tragically. My patient died from fast-progressing sepsis. The autopsy showed a thrombosis of the inferior vena cava, all the way to the heart.

EARLY JUNE, 1943

Beginning April 20th, I spent an entire month attending lectures for leading surgeons in Eletz, at the front hospital base. It was not particularly interesting, but it was a fine diversion. Their hospitals and their surgery did not impress me at all. I flew home in a hospital plane, for the first time in my life. The plane was a crate for the wounded, but I liked flying. Too bad we don't have enough of these special planes.

I arrived in Vorovo, our new location, at midnight. It was dry and warm. There were many gardens but no houses. The village had been demolished during the winter offensive. With difficulty I located our hospital, a cluster of tents. My heart was beating very hard; it was homecoming for me.

I awakened the wound-dressing section. They were sleeping in a small army tent. The girls jumped out in night shirts and covered me with kisses. I never suspected I was so popular with them, except for Lyda Denisenko. But that is a special case. They insisted on showing me everything; after all, they had set up this operation by themselves, without me.

"The village doesn't exist . . . only some brick walls. It was quite a task putting up roofs, but now we have a first-class hospital, a marvel. But we, the wound-dressing section, are in tents."

Among some large apple trees there were three large tents,

joined together—first, a small reception ward, then a main dressing station, and then the operating theater. We developed this procedure in Kuban, and found it excellent. We call this arrangement "the sausage." The ward tents are placed nearby.

In general, everything had been done correctly. I complimented them and went to sleep in the doctors' house. The word *house* is a euphemism: the roof is made of loose tree branches, which provide no protection from rain. Therefore, inside they rigged up a regular army tent.

What can we say about our life in Vorovo? We have a health-resort existence. Even the food is good: American "Spam" has made its appearance. It's our favorite. The Studebakers and canned food are provided by our allies, whom we see at the front. We see the Studebakers only at a distance, and we are green with envy. However, our horses have put on some weight because there isn't much work for them. We have to set up 200 beds, according to all the rules. Our orders: keep the wounded here as short a time as possible and then send them to the rear. Could that mean another offensive? Ours or the Germans? For the present at least, there is no action.

I performed a good operation—an aneurism of the left subclavian artery. The wounded man was on the verge of death. Private Egorov, 19. Hemoglobin, 18%! The swelling under the left clavicle was as big as a child's head—pulsing and bubbling—horrible to look at. While I was away, the head front surgeon, Professor D. had been here. Lina showed him the patient, but he refused to touch him. "Evacuate by plane," he said. But how can one evacuate someone with an open, bleeding wound and a temperature of 39°C? I did everything properly. It was very difficult and very frightening, but I'm sure that Egorov will live. This time I have truly saved a life.

I also had a chance to experiment on my chest wound technique. Four pneumothorax cases and not a single fatality.

But what about hips and knees? This is a fine time to experiment and to show what can be done under war conditions by an experienced surgeon. But nothing conclusive can be proved because of the precise orders: "Do not clog up mobile field hospitals. Evacuate all transportable cases at once." At any moment we might be ordered to move. However, we did put eight high plaster casts on hips and knees with no complications—at least none while the men were with us.

In general, all has been confirmed. Even many of the most seriously wounded can be saved if one starts early and works without hurry. For this we need many field hospitals and sufficient transport, but that's so obvious there's no point in dwelling upon it. So far we're short of both.

JULY 12, 1943

All spring there have been rumors about the impending German offensive. How do these rumors originate? The political organs of the army are pretty tough on the "rumor-mongers", but front-line soldiers have an unerring instinct for those things. If I were a general I would conduct periodic studies of rumors among soldiers. They would produce valuable intelligence.

We all feel cocky after the Stalingrad victory, but we are also uneasy after the surprise the Germans gave us last summer. And then there is a general belief that summer months favor the Germans and winters favor us.

We discussed those things among ourselves, Lyda, Lina, and myself and sometimes Kansky. We also spoke to soldiers coming from the front lines. All of them felt sure that the summer battle will be fought near us—at the Kursk "hernia." To a surgeon, that makes sense. It is a tempting chance for the Germans to pinch it off.

"The Fritzes are building up," the soldiers say. "At night it's like thunder—their tanks and things coming into position. One can hardly sleep from all the noise. But in the morning all is quiet again."

The main highway runs two miles from Vorovo, and we, too, can hear tanks and trucks rumble by. Those are ours, of course, but the noise can be heard for miles around. Unless someone invents silent tanks and transport, any really surprising armored troop buildup is impossible. No, the Germans can't surprise us.

We also hear our reconnaissance planes. They fly over us all the time. And there are the partisans behind the German lines. Our high command must be well informed about every German move. Nevertheless, they did miscalculate last summer and at the beginning of the war.

By July, by some strange intuition, we became sure that the storm was about to break. Instinctively we all became tense, ready for whatever was to come.

It came during the night of the 5th of July.

None of us had ever heard anything like it. It was not the sound of guns firing; it was a steady roar, very much like a tremendous thunderstorm. At three o'clock in the morning we were all outside listening, shivering nervously.

"It's beginning."

But we didn't know *what* was beginning. None of us slept the rest of the night. In the morning the first wounded started to come. "The Fritzes are attacking!" they said. The main blow, it seemed, fell against our neighbor, the 13th Army. From our army only two divisions were involved so far.

We expected a stream of wounded, but all we got was about 80 men. They had been very well attended to in front-line units, and therefore there were no surgical problems.

And what wounded! We've never seen wounded men in such high spirits. One would think that we were attacking instead of trying to stop the enemy.

"This is where he's going to break off his teeth!"

"The ground is covered with dead Fascists. We're cutting them down like rye stalks."

"They throw tanks at us—we throw tanks at them—two for each one they have. Their tanks are burning like campfires!"

"And whole clouds of our planes!"

"And our artillery—it's mowing them down. Explosion after explosion."

"This time we've got the bastards."

For five days we worked, listening to the thunder of the battle—without a moment's letup, day and night. We kept asking the wounded for news, and all reports were good. Men were dead tired, dirty, sweaty, dusty, but not one was in a pessimistic mood. "We're cutting them down . . . We're killing the scum . . . We're tearing their guts out . . . " Even seriously injured men were smiling. Getting out of that hell alive at all was happiness.

On the fifth day the gunfire started to die down. And then came the reports. "The Germans went on the defensive along the whole front."

That meant one thing: they've failed.

On the 10th we got the news that some other field hospitals had received orders to move forward. We know that our turn will come soon. We were excited because we knew that this time it meant we were on the offensive.

This time we are ready. The first group—the dressing station and surgery ward, fifty folded beds with the minimum supplies and food—can be loaded onto our truck.

During this time there were operations, several amputations, and a few men died, but all that went on almost unnoticed. Everyone was talking about our offensive. Now that we had ground the Germans down to the Kursk hernia, our armies were ready to hit them before they could get their second breath.

On the morning of the 13th we again heard the rumble of gunfire. Now it was our turn!

By some wireless soldier telegraph we knew that our armies were attacking in the direction of Orel, breaking through the German defenses. We knew there was very hard fighting, but still we were on the sidelines, getting only a few wounded a day from our front section, which is still inactive.

We were growing impatient. Had they forgotten us again?

JULY 26, 1943

Finally, last night we got our orders: "Relocate immediately at Kamenka, and at 10 o'clock on the 26th, start receiving the wounded."

We looked at the map. It was nearly 50 miles to Kamenka—the village itself was located about eight miles from the main highway. So our troops had really broken through and were moving ahead!

Fortunately, we have only a few wounded. A medical plane arrives and picks up all the most serious cases. We turn the others over to the neighboring hospital. We load our truck, and by seven o'clock we are ready to leave. Fedya, our driver, walks around the truck shaking his head. "We're overloaded . . . we'll get stuck."

"Who cares? Let's go."

Our chief gets into the cabin. The girls, Kansky, and I climb on top of the overloaded truck, holding onto each other to stay on. Our horses will not be there for two days at least, but we have everything we need to handle the first cases. Later our truck can go back and forth and bring in reinforcements as we need them.

The weather is cloudy. We scan the sky, not for enemy planes but for rain. If it should rain we will get stuck. Our poor truck is groaning under its load.

But we're in high spirits, even though we didn't sleep last night, and we sing. Along the highway we see wrecked tanks and trucks, both ours and the Germans'. We pass a marching detachment and the men wave at us, shouting, "Where the hell did you get all those girls? Leave some for us!"

We pass some German prisoners being marched back, dirty, dishevelled, gloomy. It's surprising how quickly well-dressed soldiers become tramps when captured. We call to them, "Hitler kaput! Hitler kaput!" They look at us; several of them grin, but most pay no attention. They look tired and dazed. Some are young, no more than sixteen. Will they ever understand how a single maniac got them where they are?

We arrive in Kamenka at noon. A terrible sight. A high slope with some torn, shell-broken trees on top, two small huts, a hospital tent. Beyond, there is a deep ravine, and on the other side, about twenty small peasant huts.

The entire slope is covered with the wounded. They are lying on bare ground, some flat on their backs, some sitting up. A few are crawling about. How many? Two hundred or more?

We drive up to the tent. Here the picture is even more depressing. What can we do with our fifty beds? Again this looks like Ugolnaya, or like Kaluga.

The chief and I walk toward the tent. A soldier carries out a zinc basin with a severed leg. A familiar scene. Then a doctor walks out, surgical mask around his neck. We introduce ourselves and inquire about the conditions.

"Yes, probably about two hundred cases. The walking have all gone off on foot. Our medical battalion has gone ahead and left us here, two doctors, three nurses, a bit of food."

"How many men have been attended to?"

"Are you joking? What could we do under these circumstances? Perhaps around twenty have had their wounds redressed. Others came from their regiments today and last night. Thank God, there is no rain."

Food is being passed around. Noise, swearing. Everyone's hungry. No order at all. And now two more trucks drive in, loaded with wounded men.

"Where do we put them?"

"Well, under the apple trees there . . . there's a bit of room. Ivan, help them."

Moaning, curses.

We begin our negotiations. "We'll set up our dressing station at once, but we can't feed all this mob. Please leave your kitchens here until our truck makes another trip . . . until tonight, all right?"

The doctor agrees.

We're looking for a place for our three connecting tents, our dressing room sausage. We must move the wounded out of the way to make room. It's very hot in the sun, the men don't want to leave the shade.

"Oh God . . . What are you trying to do, bake us alive? Let us die in peace, at least . . . "

"Bastards . . . torturers . . . " (This in whispers. We are used to it.)

"Unload! Set up the tents! Kansky, get going! Lyda, don't lose time. One, two, three."

The doctor and I go into the two hospital "wards"—the small huts next to the tent. After the sunlight outside, it is dark. Miniature windows, masked with rags. Ugolnaya comes to my mind. This is almost an exact repetition. It is warm, and there are swarms of flies. They attack us, trying to get at the eyes and mouth. I don't think I have ever seen so many flies before.

On the floor, on the thin straw, lie the wounded—perhaps about thirty. Some are covered by overcoats; others are almost naked, covered with flies. In the middle there is a skull case. He's delirious. I try to find his pulse. No pulse. A living corpse. Next to him is a stomach case. "Wa-ter . . . wa-ter . . . " As my eyes become accustomed to the semidarkness, I see chest cases, sitting up, gasping for breath. One soldier has an amputated leg and a bandaged head. A big soldier with a bandaged arm walks among them with a large pail of water, giving it to everyone, including the stomach cases.

"We've no medics," the doctor says. "This one came last night. We drafted him to help."

Some help.

And the flies! The bandages are black and crawling with them.

"Yes, not a cheerful picture," I say.

To put the wounded through an official reception procedure would be senseless. I let the doctor go—he has a man on the table. I send Lyda to help him and we start checking the cards. Many men don't have them. I issue an order: no water to stomach cases. The men grumble and curse me.

Two hospital carts come in, bringing Bronya, three nurses, and equipment for forty more beds. Now we can put postoperative cases into beds.

By three o'clock our dressing operating station is ready—three connected tents. Lyda and the girls are putting on the last touches. We must start working. The people from the medical battalion are ready to leave, loading their horse cart. The doctor, already minus his white gown, tired but smiling, is climbing on.

"Now, back to the front . . . It's better than this. Thanks, I thought I'd perish here. Good luck."

We'll need luck. By this time we've set up the hospital tent with stretchers instead of beds, but with sheets and pillows. We can start transferring surgery cases there.

But the damned elements are against us! The sky is covered with dark clouds. Rain might come down at any moment. There's no time for wound dressing—we must save the wounded from the rain. The last thing they need is to get drenched now.

"Don't move them from the huts yet! Set up the third tent! Remove all stretchers, let them lie on the ground. There will be more room! All those who can move, move to the village beyond the ravine! Cover them with tarpaulins!"

Everyone is dashing about, and the first rain drops are already falling.

"Quick, quick! Boys, crawl under the tarpaulin, into the tents! Medics, carry those who can't move! Faster, faster!"

A real downpour starts by six o'clock, but by then we have everyone under cover. Tents and huts are bursting with moaning, groaning men pressed together like sardines.

By seven o'clock I start surgery. The first case is on the table, a chest case. When we remove the blood-soaked bandage on the right side, we see a tremendous wound, 10 centimeters by 12. Steam rises from it to the rhythm of breathing. Three broken ribs—we see the diaphragm, badly injured, and a bleeding liver. Here it is, the chance to put our chest surgery methods into practice.

We do everything as we planned: a large resection of the ribs and an economical one of the diaphragm wound. Ligatures on the liver. I open up the stomach for drainage. Blood transfusion by drops. The blood pressure after the operation is 80. We spend almost three hours.

"Where do we put him?"

The rain is drumming on the canvas roof. All our plans for organized work have collapsed. In addition, the damned generator won't start—no matter what we do—and we must work with oil lamps. Kansky is working with the generators. I swear at him between operations.

A simple amputation. Several large wound debridements. Lina and Bykova walk among the wounded, oil lamps in their hands, selecting men for immediate surgery. They have to step over the bodies as they go.

Toward midnight we get our electricity. Kansky is a miracle worker.

We are trying to preserve strict asepsis, all the wounded are undressed before surgery. But now the flies have invaded our tents, taking cover from the rain.

At one in the morning I call a halt. We all collapse on the floor in the wound dressing tent. How many will die during the night in their huts and tents? But we are at the very end of our endurance. To try further is senseless. We can't move, can't talk. Lyda and I sleep side by side, but we could be two logs, for all our feelings.

Outside, the rain continues, and I can't stop my thoughts. They keep crowding into my brain.

So the Germans have suffered another disastrous defeat. Surely, nothing can save their rotten "empire" any longer. But how many more men must die just to permit those dull, traditionally stupid German generals to draw their pay? Medically, one can understand Hitler and his cronies as sick people, madmen; but what about these generals? Cold, calculating murderers, sacrificing thousands of men's lives—their own men's lives—just for the privilege of strutting in their glittering uniforms for a few more months.

History might forgive Hitler. He's a miserable, psychopathic moron. But not those heel-clicking idiots. They should be brought to justice after the war and hanged.

Strange. The more tired I am, the more lucid my brain is. Or perhaps it just seems so to me. There is a fatigue limit beyond which man's body dies but the brain continues to function. It is the most durable organ, the most tireless.

I don't think I have slept one minute during this rainy night. If I did, I didn't notice it.

JULY 27, 1943

The next morning started with a monumental dressing down

delivered to us by a colonel from our Army Medical Service. Our chief stood at attention while the colonel yelled at him. "Where is the sorting station? Where is the shock ward?" And so on. It is good to be an officer in the army; one need not think, just have a sonorous voice and aplomb. All that the colonel said was true, but what about the rain and the lack of facilities?

It rained the whole day, intermittently, and the whole day we were trying to get organized. Unsuccessfully, because of the new wounded coming in. Toward noon we succeeded in setting up a post-operative tent. All the wounded who could walk were sent across the ravine into the village. It is deserted. We set up a small wound dressing station there as well, in one of the abandoned huts.

Even though we had no sorting station we did not drown in the stream of injured men. All men went through Bykova. They were registered, superficially examined, and sent to the barn, the pig-sty, the granary—our "departments."

All tents became soaked through. Murderous mud. Swarms of flies. Some asepsis! The germs must be having a field day.

We received 530 wounded. No evacuation: all roads are streams of sticky mud.

We worked from six in the morning until midnight. 120 men had their wounds redressed. We performed 42 operations, and about 80 men went through our small dressing room behind the ravine. This is little compared with the need, but reasonable considering our means.

The rain let up toward night. But the night was cold, and the wounded lying in barns and pig-pens were miserable. Most of them had nothing on but shirts, and we had just a few blankets.

AUGUST 3, 1943

Many cases of gaseous gangrene have begun to appear. Many. More than ever before. Small wonder: all wounds have been cleaned up late and carelessly, and many men have had no bandage change since their injuries. Every night Lyda, Kansky, and I have been handling gangrene. Most are amputations; we've no time and no facilities for proper treatment. If anyone were to line up all those severed limbs, the line would probably stretch from here to Siberia.

We've had many fatalities. Out of the thirty men left to us by the medical battalion, more than half have perished. All our chest methods have gone to hell. How could we do any proper drainage and suction while the wounded were lying on the ground on wet straw? All pneumothorax wounds sewed up by the medical battalion surgeons have come apart. Out of my five chest cases, however, only one died. Even the man with that terrible open chest wound, that open hole, was still alive and giving us some hope.

Flies continue to plague us. Every day we interrupt our work twice and spray anti-fly powder. In a few minutes the floor is covered with a thick cushion of dead insects. We sweep them out and burn them, but an hour later, they appear again. From nowhere. The damned bastards crawl over infected wounds and then over the clean . . . a nightmare.

On the fourth day after our arrival, maggots made their appearance. We would remove a bandage and see fat, wriggling larvae. The wounded would become panicky. "Infection!" Of course we know that the larvae are harmless. On the contrary, they devour dead material in the wound, cleaning it. In fact, maggoty wounds heal quicker than those without those ugly things.

We organized our morgue near the river in a half-wrecked bathhouse. The dead are taken there by some men from our recovery battalion. "Take him to the river!" has become a familiar command.

There were two *Kazakhs** who could not understand the

---

*Not to be confused with the Cossacks. The Kazhakhs are a nationality in Soviet Central Asia.—Trans.

Russians very well, and we had a scandal because of them.

Toward the evening of the fourth day, some lieutenant-colonel came to our chief, trembling with indignation:

"Are you the chief here?"

"Yes. What do you want?"

"How dare you outrage the feelings of the defenders of our Motherland? I'll report you for this! There are common norms of human decency . . . " and so on—quite an angry lecture.

He had been driving past the river and wanted to wash his feet. He had come down to the water and saw corpses dumped on the ground with their bare feet in the water.

We went to see. Yes, it was true. There were the naked, rotting bodies.

We have absolutely no room for any new wounded. Even though the original stream has slackened, we have on hand about 700 cases, all requiring evacuation. Those who could walk have been sent on foot to the highway. About 100 cases are absolutely untransportable. And no evacuation cars from the Army Medical Service.

On July 31st we set up three posts on the highway to intercept empty vehicles going to the rear. They did not work as effectively as during the winter, but still we netted about twenty vehicles every day. We brought up enough straw to put in every car. So the evacuation was at last organized.

AUGUST 5, 1943

Glorious news. Our troops liberated Orel and Belgorod! So those boys near the river did not give their lives in vain. Our first great summer offensive! This must be the turning point of the war.

No more wounded coming our way. The front moved forward, and other hospitals followed them. We are doing the cleanup work.

Untransportable cases are those that cannot be moved even for a short distance. They might perish on the way, even in ambulance cars. The doctrine is strict! Do not move any critical cases. Is this correct? Yes. This evacuation rush is a terribly contagious disease. Everyone is trying to pass the wounded to the rear. To doctors the wounded become impersonal, even in peacetime. And especially during the war. "Charge it all to the war." The value of human life has depreciated shockingly. And then there is the usual alibi: "They can take care of them better in the rear." Therefore, the chiefs of field hospitals pressure us surgeons to evacuate. But surgeons must resist this pressure. They represent medical humanism.

And yet, God help anyone who becomes untransportable while the front is in motion. It is best to get sent back, even at the risk of one's life.

The practice of the army medical service is as follows. The troops move forward, and hospitals must follow them. Therefore, all the wounded who can be sent back are sent back, and those who can't be moved are left behind. Generally, hospitals assemble them in a single peasant hut, assign the worst doctor and least experienced nurses to them, leave the minimum of supplies and food, and an ambiguous instruction to evacuate the wounded "eventually." But in fact this means to bury them for few of them survive. And everyone knows this very well, including the wounded. There are heartbreaking scenes every time we leave those men behind: "Send us back! Don't leave us here to die like dogs!" But we must follow our orders.

Had I the power, I would have changed the rules. To evacuate untransportable cases when the front is stable and there are time and facilities for treating them *is* a crime. And it should be forbidden. But when the armies are in motion, *everyone* should be evacuated. Only completely hopeless cases should be left behind to die. Of course, some untransportable cases would die on the way, but many would have a chance to recover. But leaving them behind, as we are doing, dooms at least half of those who could have been saved otherwise. It is a matter of cruel mathematics.

That is why we are trying our damnedest to evacuate as many cases as we can, even taking chances now and then.

Special hospital planes are our guardian angels. By air we can evacuate even otherwise untransportable cases. There are few such planes, and not all of them can land on rough ground. But some of them do, and every time it happens there is an outburst of excitement.

"Nikolai Mikhailovich! A hospital plane! It landed in the field across the ravine!"

"Who is the pilot—a man?"

"Yes."

"Run there at once! Take him directly to Chapliuk. Get some alcohol from Lyda! Quickly!"

Women pilots are easier to handle. They have compassion. But men often act like primadonnas. We must butter them up. Otherwise its "Sorry, I can't take off with a full load from the ground like this." And that's all. We can't argue with them or give them orders. They must protect their machines; to them they are more important than men.

AUGUST 7, 1943

We have been lucky. We've been able to evacuate all our untransportable cases by air to Eletz. Only one has been left behind, a young soldier dying of tetanus.

Our stay at Kamenka is drawing to a close. We can total up our figures. Our surgical diaries have been strictly kept, and individual surgeons have their own notes to go by.

And so, we have handled 1,700 cases, most of them bed cases. About 110 men with gaseous gangrene. One third of all gangrene cases died, 37 men altogether. That's not too bad, but also not very good. True, we had no "negligence cases." Those are the cases not diagnosed in time, those untreated for shock, and those abdominal wounds not operated on quickly enough to save men. Our nurses have become better, more attentive, more professional. Our Kuban University has paid off. When the hospital is bursting with 700 or more wounded, only ward nurses can pick out those needing immediate attention. And we have only four doctors. No, now five. The last one has just arrived—Anna Malakhova. She came to us in her own summer dress and fashionable white slippers. A very modest girl with long dark hair. Very taciturn. We still don't know where she came from or anything about her. But she works hard and conscientiously.

She and Lina took to each other immediately. Pleasant. I can't help feeling that Lina is very lonely. Especially after our famous showdown. Or is it my masculine vanity? Those who came with us from Cherepovets knew about our previous relationship. And now they know about my infatuation with Lyda. We are a small collective, and we live and work too close together. No secrets. The major spoke to me again, very tactfully, not even mentioning Lyda. Just about man-woman relationships during the war. "If it is serious, it's one thing. But if this is just a diversion, it must be discouraged."

Poor man. His own family had fallen apart before the war. His wife went to another man, I think. She was evacuated to Siberia and she took their children with her. I don't know how people find out those things—I am sure the major has never discussed this with anyone. But we seem to know everything about one another. It is really amazing. And I agreed with him in principle. During the war men should not "practice love like sport." That is from Mayakovsky. Millions of men are separated from their women; women are lonely, and they fall easy prey to adventurous Romeos.

AUGUST 11, 1943

We are advancing! A beautiful feeling, if one did not have to see the medical side of the victories. If we could only go this way all the way to Berlin! Why don't the Germans give up? Their war is already lost, irretrievably. They can never recover after our "Kursk hernia" operation.

Their losses must be enormous. At least four million young Germans grow old enough to become soldiers every year, and yet they are drafting workers from all over Europe to replace old men sent to the front—scraping the bottom of their stinking barrel.

But Hitler is a fanatic, and the Germans still obey him. Their resistance is as desperate as ever.

Our own army seems to be left on the sidelines. At first we belonged to the Briansk front, then to the Central, and now they are moving us south.* For a PPG, however, it is immaterial what front it belongs to. The medical branch of our particular army is not very good. We have insufficient transport and no supervision. We are working according to our instructions, with no new methods or ideas. And there must be new methods—what with millions of wounded men!

Generally, I like our military medical service. We have our own doctrine, and everything is planned well and organized economically. Our main leaders, Smirnov and Burdenko, have worked out everything in detail. But our poverty is depressing. Not enough personnel, transport, facilities. Few people understand that medical service is just as important as front-line troops, that it is saving lives, preventing men from becoming cripples, and returning men back to the fighting ranks.

Well, enough of criticism. No one listens to us or asks our advice.

We are advancing! That is the thing that's important.

AUGUST 13, 1943
Finally we got our new orders. We are to move to the

In the Soviet military parlance groups of armies were known as "fronts."—Trans.

Dmitrovo-Lgovo area, 120 miles to the west, using our single truck and a few horse carts. (But we noticed that the Germans are using many horses as well. Either they are short of motor transport or have found horses more practical for our roads.)

Once again we loaded our dressing and sorting equipment on our Zis truck. Again Fedya swore under his breath, walking around and kicking the tires. "They won't stand up. This is the end." Again we climb on top of bundles with linens and supplies. A good place as long as there is no rain. Soldiers and officers wave to us as we go by. "Look at all those girls! Where the hell did they get them?" War seems to sharpen the sex instinct in men.

And what about the women? There are many stories about the Germans raping our girls in occupied territories. And many become pregnant and give birth to children. But I don't think that rape is easy—if the woman resists. Many of them probably did not resist. They were just lonely, lost and scared.

People in the areas liberated by us shun those poor women and the children born of those unions. This is very cruel. Some women cooperated to protect their families or to avoid being sent to Germany. And they say that the Germans operated regular field bordellos for soldiers, forcing young girls into them. If this is true, it is the lowest form of barbarism. No wonder some girls took up with Germans to avoid this fate. And now they have to pay the price.

I tried to speak to our major about it. He was lost. No, he did not defend those poor girls. He felt that many of them were "criminally weak," as he put it. But he was sorry for the children. They were not to blame for what their mothers did. "The best thing is to take them away from their mothers and bring them up as good Soviet citizens." That is easy to say. To me that was no solution. It was much too mechanical. And I did not feel that the major was too sure about it. He is very humane. "Well, the main thing is to win the war," he said. "We can sort those things out later on."

From what I have seen, morals seem to be high among our men. Our laws are severe—any real rape case would lead to a firing squad. But once I overheard two of our medics speaking about women. "Just wait till we get to Germany. We will show a thing or two to those bitches." That is ugly, but understandable.

Our poor Zis is holding up even though Fedya is almost crying behind his wheel. "We're overloaded. We are murdering this machine. She's good only for a few more kilometers." But it is rolling on and on despite Fedya's pessimism.

And somewhere, far behind, is our horse-drawn train. For as long as we are without it, we are crippled. We are short of this and short of that. It is impossible to calculate all contingencies.

The country is barbarically devastated. The German occupation was savage. What were they trying to do—exterminate the entire population and wreck everything? Even old village churches are burned down or blown up. On our way we mentally appraise the things we pass. A large barn—a sorting ward. Another for walking wounded. Standing buildings for hospital wards. And if we see a large brick building, even burned out, we lick our chops—a dream! Troop commanders appraise the land this way: a good defensive position, a good staging area. But we are thinking about the wounded.

Some villages have remained untouched—those the Germans had no time to destroy. They are no longer retreating, but often simply running, abandoning weapons and transport, even completely undamaged tanks and guns.

We set up our hospital in the village of Lubashovo, without any rush. The wounded started to arrive in two days—about 250 men. But even before we could start working properly, we got another order: "Evacuate all cases, and move forward."

LATE AUGUST, 1943

This time we have jumped forward 70 miles. This is lush country. The Germans ran so fast that they had no time to burn down villages all the way to the Desna river. The local peasants have been living well, raising beets and making home-grown vodka. All our medics and recovering soldiers are walking about slightly drunk, or even really drunk. They're all so cheerful and polite. Alcohol may be evil, but it has its points, used in moderation. Unfortunately, we Russians are not good at moderation. Still, sometimes I am sorry I have never learned to drink.

Speaking of drinking, we got news of Khaminoff. He was assigned to a regimental hospital during the worst days of last summer's retreat. He distinguished himself by evacuating the wounded. He was fully rehabilitated, and then was killed in Stalingrad. There surgeons had to work in front-line trenches and blockhouses. He was a good man. I am very sorry for him.

The village of Oleshok, our new destination, is large and rich, and is completely undamaged. They say that the local *starosta* appointed by the Germans worked with the local partisans and led them when the Germans were ready to leave. They fell upon the Germans before their "fire-commandos" could do their work and killed all those would-be arsonists. But the *starosta* was killed as well. This, they say, is not an extraordinary case. Many so-called collaborators secretly work with the partisans and send intelligence reports to our troops.

We had two full days to get ready, and from then on we could easily process up to 200 wounded each day and evacuate them on military vehicles going back.

Bykova has organized her department perfectly: reception, sorting, primary examination. I am less happy with the head ward nurse, Bronya. She came to us along with the commissar. His former love? She is not a bad worker, but she lies and intrigues and uses her pull with him. And, after all, one must consider the commissar. He represents the Party with us. And we all respect the Party for its enormous organizational work during this war. It held us together during the worst days.

But Bronya is out of luck. The poor major has fallen hopelessly in love with one of our nurses, Tacia. He is like a schoolboy. Everyone notices this and makes fun of him behind his back. As soon as Tacia looks favorably at some officer, or if someone looks at her, we have a bad period: strict discipline, night checks, stern lectures. The girls hate those periods, since the major has appointed himself the guardian of their morals. But as soon as Tacia smiles at him, the major becomes an angel in uniform.

The girls beg her, "Come on, Tacia, soften up a bit . . . just a little . . . for a week or so . . . then, when the wounded start coming, you can tell him off."

But Tacia does not like our major. Even though she is a natural flirt and is flattered by the major's attention, she is romantic as well, waiting for her great love. Perhaps she would give him a few smiles, but only for "the good of the collective." A very strict girl.

Bronya gets more and more upset. She is quarrelling with Bykova, since Tacia works for her. And Bykova complains to me. To hell with women. But our women have kept up our morale during the darkest days.

> You are waiting for me, this I know,
> My beloved, my darling, my love,
> And because of your love, this I know,
> Nothing will happen to me . . .

A young instructor from the political section used to sing this. He used to come and visit us in the spring. He was killed near Orel. The girls cried when they heard about it. He was their favorite.

In Ugolnaya and in Kuban we had no time to think about love. All potential Romeos were too busy. But in Vorovo, while the front was quiet, the apple trees were in full bloom, and nightingales filled the nights with their trills, things changed. Young officers and sergeants from our regiments kept driving in; there were rendezvous and long night walks after evening lights-out. And the major with the mighty Party behind him could do nothing about it. Finally he had to give up. He just sighed, watching Tacia. We are young, and even war cannot conquer nature.

I must confess, too. I am falling in love with Lyda Denisenko. Not without reciprocity, I think.

Today I have the rank of major of medical services. Lina is a captain. Lyda a junior lieutenant. Finally our orders have come through. We got our shoulder straps with stars—very imposing. But it's only fair; our work is just as important as that of those who drive tanks and fire guns.

SEPTEMBER, 1943

From the drunken Oleshok we moved to the village of Vovno and sat there waiting until our troops would force the Desna and liberate Novgorod-Volynsky. Vovno is a large, comfortable village, left completely undamaged, and we have nothing to do.

Then our troops jumped across the Desna, and we got orders to move to the village of Semenovka, a regional center of Sumsk Province. The Ukraine!

We arrived at night and immediately appraised the place. The old village hospital is completely intact—several hospital buildings, bathhouse, kitchen, laundry. The Germans also had their hospital here. All the walls are covered with German graffiti. There are double-decker beds. We also found mattresses and sheets and pillowcases made out of some synthetic material, thin and cheap. Our first battle trophies. We even found a portrait of Hitler in the basement, riddled with bullets. But everything else of any value has already been picked up by our predecessors. Many soldiers now wear German wristwatches, but all claim that German equipment is of poor quality, including their uniforms. This is strange, with all of Europe working for them.

In Semenovka we were immediately hit with a transport of 300 wounded, and then more and more. But we were able to cope with no confusion.

Surgical problems are still with us. Many early urinal and fecal fistulas. Open pneumothoraxes with old ligatures in shreds. We need an X-ray cabinet. It is simply impossible to treat chest cases without X-ray. We have only one for the whole army, and it is almost always out of order. Even skull cases are often operated on without X-ray plates.

I must once again do some skull and even eye surgery. The special neurosurgical hospital has fallen behind, and we accept all comers. I have performed four trephinations. One man died; three are still alive. It's good that I had some experience in Kaluga. I also performed four enucleations—removal of eyeballs. When there are serious eye injuries enucleations must sometimes be done to save the second eye.

What beautiful birches are growing near our hospital! A whole grove of those delicate beauties. Some leaves are turning yellow, but that makes the trees look even more beautiful. We go for walks there at night. It is impossible to resist romance. Our men and girls are emotionally starved. But the flighty affairs of some young officers irritate me. Here I find myself allied with our major. It is dishonest to take advantage of our girls' loneliness unless there are serious intentions.

Once again we cannot evacuate all our wounded. We have no special transport, and the nearest supply base is almost 200 kilometers away. But there is a new practice: empty vehicles come here to take away the wounded. We no longer have to catch them on the roads as before. But actually we need ambulances, not trucks.

There was an unpleasant occurrence. One of our wounded whom we had sent back died on the way. We learned about it from the driver of a truck who stopped on his way back to the front.

"We had driven about fifteen kilometers from Semonovka when I hear someone knocking on the back window of my cabin. I think somebody has to take a crap. I don't want to fall behind the column, so I signal them to wait a while. But they keep knocking, more and more. So I stop. 'What the hell, couldn't you wait a little?' I say, and I add a few salty words, too. But they are terror-stricken. A man has died! I get inside. It's true. A young man, bandaged head, but no blood. What to do? Well, boys, I say, you'll have to keep him company. So they just unloaded him when we came to the hospital. Didn't ask me anything. The place is absolutely packed with the wounded—thousands."

The chief and the major looked at me with reproach. And what could I say? Was it my fault? Am I responsible? We check all the wounded before evacuation. We must redouble our attention. but it's impossible to examine everyone thoroughly when we are sending a hundred or two hundred men all at once. They often deliver corpses to us along with the wounded, and we never question anyone. War.

OCTOBER 7, 1943

Another order to relocate. The wounded have not been coming for a few days, and we have safely evacuated most of ours. We had only 54 very serious cases. We sent them away in empty vehicles, but this time we sent our own medics along with them.

They were all delivered safely. Such a load off our minds.

Farewell, Semenovka! We have worked well there. Almost 2,-000 have gone through our hospital. We'll forever remember those white birches, small streets with neat little houses, warm nights, aromatic apples, fresh rye bread. And what wonderful borscht Chapliuk used to cook there!

Of course we had our quota of terror tales about German atrocities. Not a single Jew was left. They were all killed behind the hospital building. Old men, women, little children. But generally Semenovka was spared real devastation because it was a German military staging point, run by the Wehrmacht rather than the SS or the Gestapo.

We are moving west, so far without any final destination and without undue hurry. We drive for a while, then stop and wait for our horse train to catch up with us.

Byelorussia . . . dry, warm autumn . . . fields and forests. Some signs of fighting: shell craters, trenches. But not many—the Germans ran like rabbits here. This was guerrilla country; the Germans held only the main highways. Every second village is burned to the ground. Reprisals. Why this senseless barbarity? One cannot stop advancing troops by burning villages in the summer. They don't need shelter.

Generally, this is poor country with many marshes and bogs. The people who have remained subsist on potatoes and turnips. They are in for a hungry winter. Here and there they are working in the fields. Autumn sowing. The plows are pulled by miserable cows and thin horses, and in some instances by old women. People are trying to avert famine.

We stop in several villages. "Where are the people?" we ask.

"What people? Some were taken by the Germans . . . Almost all the girls were sent away. The men are in the army . . . Others went into the forests, then joined up when the Red Army came back. Many died, particularly the children. Others got killed by the Germans. So we are the only ones left. It's just as well—we haven't got enough food for even those who are here. And where would they live in the winter?"

Where indeed? The further we move into Byelorussia, the more devastation we encounter. The Germans did not even try to occupy these places; they just destroyed them, often with their entire population. Here they could not move without army escort and only in the daytime. We saw several German trains burned out, lying near the railway: they had been ambushed and destroyed by our partisans. The Byelorussians are the nearest Slav people to the Russians, and their country was a traditional route for invaders. Napoleon lost half of his army retreating through Byelorussia. Peasants attacked his column with axes and pitchforks.

When one sees these bedraggled women and children digging in what is left of their burned homes or watching us eat with hungry eyes, one feels a rising hatred against the Germans.

One is terrified at watching human nature deteriorate during war. If a small group of murderous fanatics could do this with a great, strong, cultured nation, then where is the limit? It means that deep inside human nature there is cruelty and avarice, thinly covered with a veneer of civilization.

There is cruelty on both sides, of course. True, on our side it is not so senseless as it is with the Germans, but still . . . I am amazed and frightened at the indifference and lack of compassion shown for our wounded soldiers. It is so difficult to plead for any help. Nonetheless, on the whole our people are kind. The Russians have never had any hatred toward other peoples, maybe because our nation is composed of so many different ethnic groups.

Not long ago they brought us a group of wounded Germans. Light injuries, all of them walking. They unloaded them along with our men. It was warm. The sorting tent was filled and the men sat outside on the ground. The Germans looked miserable. They sat together, spoke to each other in whispers, and kept turning their heads around as though expecting a sudden assault.

Our soldiers were cheerful. The offensive was going well. Their injuries did not endanger their lives but were sufficient for a long rest in the rear. They talked, laughed, and shared tobacco, watching the Germans.

"Look at the Fritzes . . . so quiet all of a sudden . . . And why do they take them? They should have shot the bastards on the spot."

"Yes. Did you see those villages? They have been exterminating our people. And if you asked them, they would say, 'That's not us. That's the SS . . . the Gestapo . . . Hitler kaput.' "

The Germans heard the familiar words and started nodding and mumbling, "Ja . . . Ja . . . Hitler kaput."

"We know he's kaput. But why do you burn down our villages?"

"No understand . . . no understand . . . Hitler kaput . . . Deutschland kaput."

For a while this is the extent of the conversation.

Then the Germans seemed to understand that no one would murder them here. They twitched their noses, smelling the tobacco smoke drifting their way. And our men silently watched them.

"Look at those bastards, twitching their noses."

"Sure, they want to smoke. They don't have tobacco. Officers yes, but all the soldiers get is straw treated with tobacco juice."

It was obvious that our men wanted to offer their tobacco to the Germans. But they were embarrassed to show compassion for the enemy.

Then a sergeant could not restrain himself. He got up and untied his tobacco pouch.

"Okay, bastards. Taste some real tobacco for a change. You won't have any till we get to Berlin."

The Germans started to smile and nod. Some got up and came nearer. Our men approved of their comrade's kindness.

"Let them smoke. To hell with the scum. They are human beings too."

This opened up a conversation session. Curiosity and the lack of any chauvinistic feeling among our men was evident. One of the soldiers could speak a little German, just a few words. That was enough. Our soldiers respect the Germans for their bravery, their tenacity, but they do not compare with our men. "No, a German can't stand up against a Russian. His gut is too thin for that." This is peculiar Soviet pride. We all feel it. After all, the Germans were rolling over everyone in Europe, but we not only stopped them, we are driving them back. And we all know that we will drive them back all the way to Berlin. They know it, too.

It is strange to hear the captured Germans speak of Hitler with hatred. They swear and spit when they hear his name. And it seems to be genuine. Dumb as they look, they must realize that this one miserable maniac has brought Germany to the brink of a national catastrophe. But still they fight for every inch of ground for as long as their officers tell them to fight. Peculiar people.

LATE OCTOBER, 1943

We are moving toward Gomel. We have been told that we will be working there when Gomel is liberated. Everyone is happy. We are tired of tents and peasant huts. Gomel is a real city.

We listen to Stalin's orders of the day every evening. He mentions divisions and regiments that have distinguished themselves in each operation. That's strange; usually troop disposition is a military secret. Maybe our comander-in-chief feels that we do not have to keep secrets any longer, because the communiqués also mention not only liberated towns but the units that liberated them. It is difficult to trace our advance. We have no map of the Soviet Union, only military topographical maps, each covering a small sector. Before we can get new ones, our troops outrun the maps we have. Wonderful.

We stopped near Gomel in the village called Lavrischevo. The front seems to have temporarily stabilized. All we hear is artillery fire and mine explosions. There are many planes in the air, all of them ours. We haven't seen a German plane for quite a while except those burned on the ground where they crashed.

We are crammed into a few huts. Not much work. Bronya finally has left us. She was transferred to the rear hospital area. And Tacia has been promoted. She is now a head hospital ward nurse. Some think that the commissar had a hand in all this, but that isn't true. Tacia is a good worker, and she has acquired a boy friend—a young tank commander. He comes to visit her now and then, and they plan to get married after the war. The major seems to have reconciled himself to the situation. He is a good man, after all.

We have only a few cases coming in, none of them serious. This is our rest period. The boys go to the Iput river to fish, using dynamite sticks to stun the fish. The girls cook delicious fish dinners. I am a frequent visitor in their quarters. Probably too frequent. My infatuation with Lyda is no longer a secret. We take long walks together, talking about small, insignificant things as people in love usually do. No, we have not as yet discussed our future, but I think we both know that we will share it. The country is very pretty. The forests are aflame with autumn leaves—yellow, red, orange.

Some people from Gomel filter through the front to our side. They all speak of German atrocities. Before the war Gomel was a flourishing Jewish center. It had a large community of Orthodox Jews. Now not a single Jew is left in the city. Some were killed on the spot; others were deported to extermination camps and killed there.

Why didn't they try to escape when the Germans were approaching? They brought into our hospital a young boy who had been fighting with the Gomel partisans since the earliest days of the war. He hated the Germans, who had killed all his family, but he was particularly bitter about some leaders of the Jewish community.

"Before the revolution my father was a Rabbi," he told us. "Then he worked as a cobbler in a shoe factory, but still he would go to pray in the synagogue every Friday night. He was very religious, and he dominated my mother and my sister—she was four years older than I. When he learned that I had joined the Young Communist League, he cursed me and drove me out of the house. I lived in the school dormitory. When the war started, I came home and pleaded with my mother and sister to flee, but then father came in and started screaming at me. He said that all the rumors about the Germans persecuting the Jews were Soviet propaganda, and that Hitler at least was not against God like the Bolsheviks. You see, the Germans had been in Gomel in 1918, and that time they didn't touch the Jews. On the contrary, the Germans were friendly with them because they spoke Yiddish and the Germans could understand them. Father said that there had been a meeting at the synagogue and they had decided to stay. And he forbade my mother and sister to leave. I am sure that many Jews stayed in Gomel because of him and people like him. I was too young to join the Red Army, but I ran away and joined some partisans. We knew what was happening in the city. The Germans assembled Jews in their synagogues, set the buildings on fire, and shot all those who tried to escape. It was the same all over the Ukraine. In Kiev they killed off all the Jews in two days, and all because of some bigoted men like my father."

The boy had been wounded three times, and when he was brought to us he had a bad untreated abdominal wound. We did all we could, but it was too late to save him. Peritonitis. We listened to his story with tears in our eyes.

We have had many Jewish wounded with us, but this boy's story was particularly tragic. It was hard to believe that people were exterminated only because they belonged to a certain race, but it was true. And not only the Jews. The Gypsies were all killed off by the Germans, for no reason at all.

We all knew that many religious Jews were antagonistic to the Soviet regime. Religion was the most important part of their life, and they influenced other Jews, many of whom stayed behind when the Germans came. Because Soviet authorities did not recognize their religious customs, the Jews thought they were anti-Semitic. That is one of the great tragedies of this war. And if it were not for the millions of Russian soldiers who died, there would not be a single Jew left in Europe today. It is true that religious Jews were forced to work on Saturdays and during their religious holidays, but that applied to all Soviet citizens. And there was not a single Jewish pogrom under Soviet rule—even in regions where, under the Czars, pogroms were quite common.

Although religions differ, historically they have all been responsible for more hatred and bloodshed than other philosophies. And that is strange, because all of them teach love and compassion.

NOVEMBER 4, 1943

We have been assigned to a new place and have arrived to-day at our new destination. We are now a part of the Hospital Army Base. This sounds important, but in fact the base consists of one rather small evacuation center and our hospital. We will have to work really hard here.

We arrived in our Zis truck toward evening at the large

village of Khorobichi. Almost 450 houses, and almost all of them intact. There is a railway station nearby. It is the feeder channel for our army, which is advancing south of Gomel.

Our orders are to intercept all vehicles bringing the wounded, sort them on the spot, remove all serious cases, and send light and walking cases to the Evacuation Center five miles away. We can imagine all the difficulties. Drivers will resist: "No time, no fuel, and our motor's all shot. Take them off here." And there is mud, rain, snow, early winter darkness, frozen wounded men. Yes, this will be a new trial.

But at the moment we are not thinking about the future. We have no place to set up our hospital! Every building is occupied by an Aviation Division. Their general refused even to discuss it with us. "No room. Do whatever you want," he said.

We have tried the neighboring villages. Not an empty hut. We'll have to set up our tents in the mud. Some arrangements! The worst yet.

NOVEMBER 6, 1943

There is divine justice. This morning the Aviation Division got orders to move on. Their general was big-hearted enough to turn over his staff buildings to us before someone else could grab them. And some glorious news—Kiev has been liberated! The largest Soviet city ever occupied by the Germans, the capital of the Ukraine, "the mother of all Russian cities."

We saw Ukrainian soldiers crying and hugging one another, but it is truly a holiday for all of us.

Our new housing facilities are fine—a school, a club, and about twenty houses for our personnel. We couldn't dream of anything better.

NOVEMBER 10, 1943

During the November holidays we got set up. We have thought of everything, and we're ready for some intensive work. The approaching problems: winter and lice. But we shall not repeat Ugolnaya. Under no circumstances.

This is our setup:

The reception-sorting section is in three large tents. From there the wounded go to the bathhouse, naked and wrapped in blankets and bathrobes, and then to a special tent—we call it "the buffer"—where they will await wound dressing. This is an important innovation. Here they get fresh linen, and only then are they passed into the hospital wards. But not all are passed along. Those with light injuries go back to the buffer, then they get dressed in their deloused clothes and are sent to the Evacuation Center. An impassable barrier for lice!

We have placed the hospital wards in the school building: 200 beds. There are 220 more beds in the evacuation wards, in the club house, and in the building belonging to the village Soviet. In a crunch we can take 600 cases. And there is reserve space for 400 more in several small houses.

The dressing station and operating theater have been set up in the house formerly occupied by school teachers. We broke down a wall and put in six tables for wound dressing. Then a separate operating room.

Never before have we been so well prepared for what was to come.

So we thought. Until today we have been filled with self-admiration.

And then the roof collapsed upon us.

LATE NOVEMBER, 1943

It all started when they suddenly dumped on us all the untransportable cases from the front-line medical units and from a hospital specializing in head wounds. These men immediately occupied almost all our beds in the club and school building. There were men with sewed-up pneumothoraxes that had split open, with developing fecal fistulas, with jaw wounds. There was no sign of any coming evacuation. Our army's hospital trains had got stuck somewhere in a distant station because of the changes in the general evacuation plans.

Then our 48th Army started a drive toward Rechitsa, south of Gomel, on November 13th. But for three days we knew nothing about it, since the communiqués never mention operations that are still indecisive.

November the 16th was cold and wet. Intermittent snow and rain had turned Khorobichi into a sea of mud. We spent the whole day doing routine surgical work. We had plenty of that, with about 185 serious bed cases and no prospective evacuation. Meanwhile two chest cases died. One of them was a German prisoner. He came to us along with our wounded. I postponed an operation on him to operate on a Russian soldier in similar condition. Generally we treat the German wounded on equal terms with our own, but this man was silent and did not complain. He was terribly scared. He believed, like most German soldiers, that we tortured and killed all German prisoners. This propaganda of Goebbels is truly diabolical because it affects the treatment of our prisoners by the Germans, and that, in turn, angers our soldiers. A chain reaction of hatred. As our troops advance, they find mass graves of Soviet prisoners killed after their capture. It is hardly surprising that some Germans are shot rather than taken prisoner. There are strict orders against this, but it is hard to enforce them in the heat of battle. German wounded reaching our hospital, however, have always been treated as well as we could treat them without neglecting our men.

No, my conscience is clear. I gave priority to our soldier, but that was only normal. I could not have done otherwise.

We were busy in surgery, but our reception-sorting department, run by Liubov Vladimirovna Bykova, was still living in a fool's paradise. Everything there was in perfect order. Even the labels for soldiers' clothing were all neatly prepared. They thought that they were ready for whatever was coming their way.

I finished my work by about eight o'clock and had my supper. It was an average day, with six operations and only two amputations. I went to my quarters. They had assigned a good room to me in a small wooden house next to the school. It belonged to some lonely old woman, a daughter of some famous Czarist general. In my room stood an ancient piano without strings and a large gut-sprung divan infested with bedbugs. I was tired and I went to sleep at once.

At about midnight Bessonoff burst into my room and shook me. "Nikolai Mikhailovich! Wake up! They have brought them in! It's terrible!"

I could hear a steady rumble of many motors, rather like the sound of a large flight of planes. In the windows, the dancing glow of many headlights.

I dressed quickly, and ran out.

The entire square in front of the school was filled with moving, grumbling Studebakers. Here and there headlights were being switched on and off, like projectors. A deafening chorus of agonized screaming. The mud, whipped up by automobile tires, was almost knee-deep. It looked like some fantastic Martian invasion.

Near the reception tent we heard shouting and swearing. A crowd of drivers had surrounded Liubov Vladimirovna, shouting obscenities and threats.

"Take them in, you old bag!"

"Can't you hear them screaming? They are frozen stiff!"

Yes, there was screaming—a discordant chorus of moans, groans, cries, curses. Pandemonium.

"We're going to throw them out in the mud, you old slut!"

"Come on, move your ass!"

It was a critical moment. I should have used my own arsenal of obscenities, the way I used it as a shift boss at the electric station. But I couldn't do it in the presence of Liubochka. Unthinkable. She's a lady.

"Shut up, all of you!" I said. "Where's your commanding officer, you bastards?"

He was a middle-aged, weary captain. He knew his orders. But the prospect of driving farther to Gorodnya through the sea of mud was frightening. They were all dead tired.

"I'm Major Amosoff. How many cars?"

"Forty-three."

"How many wounded?"

"Who knows? We didn't count them. Five, six hundred."

"Don't you dare unload them! We are taking only bed cases. The rest are going to Gorodnya. Do you know your orders?"

"I know, I know . . . but do it quickly . . . They are completely frozen, all of them."

By then I was in command of the situation.

"We'll sort them in the cars. Medics! Get the stretchers! Take only men with proper cards. If anyone gets out of any car on his own, make him go back! Come on, Liubov Vladimirovna! Anna!"

We started working. In the cars, the wounded were lying on the frozen straw or even on the iron floors, without blankets or sleeping bags, only their overcoats. Among them were crouching figures with bandaged heads, arms and legs in splints, cut-away sleeves and trouser legs. All wet, powdered with snow. How could we send people like that away? But no. If we had taken them all, we would have filled all our buildings. And what would we have done the next day? And the day after? Soldiers must be prepared to suffer. That is their duty. But there were those hundreds of screaming, weeping, cursing men.

Bykova and I went from car to car, followed by medics with stretchers and pursued by the cries of the wounded.

"Take us in! What are you looking for?"

"What cards? We are all wounded!"

"Who do you think we are—Fritzes? Take us off this train, you sons-of-bitches!"

"Murderers! Butchers!"

We had no time to explain or argue, and it was no time to lose one's temper. We had to be calm and firm.

"Where is your wound?"

"Here in the arm—"

"You're going on. And you?"

"I was hit in the chest."

"Did you spit blood? No? You're going on!"

"Where?!"

"To the Evacuation Center, five kilometers farther."

The word *evacuation* has some effect. Everyone wants to go as far to the rear as possible. Meanwhile, medics were taking off stretcher cases. All walking and sitting cases were left in the cars.

Bykova, Lina, and Anna checked other cars. We worked quickly. The sorting tent began to fill up. We put them down on the floor, row after row. Inside, the men instantly fell silent. The barrel stove was ablaze, the wood was dry. We had plenty of time to bring it in.

I noticed that in some cars the drivers were pushing the wounded men off.

"Get the hell off! They won't force you back!"

But we were merciless. Medics drove all those who could move out of the sorting tent. Of course there were some men who tried to fool us, acting as if they were dying. We knew we'd need some of them for our recovery battalion, so we passed a few obvious fakes. They'll pay for their trickery with hard work.

Meanwhile, I was glad to see that the chief and the commissar were arguing with the captain and the drivers. I am too short-tempered. When I saw those bastards push the wounded out of the car, I was sorry I had no revolver.

Gradually, some cars began to move. The headlights were switched on, and the machines began to leave the square one by one, floating through the sea of mud. Eventually the command car with the captain left. The whole operation had taken us a mere half hour. I was bathed in sweat despite the fact that I was wearing only my shirt.

The reception-sorting tents were boiling with activity. First of all, all the men had to be warmed and given hot tea. The stove was roaring. Large tea kettles were hissing. The spirits of the wounded began to rise and we heard no more screaming or complaints. Here and there there were even words of gratitude.

"Thank you, sister. I thought I'd freeze to death."

"Will you feed us?"

"What about taking a crap? Pass me that pan, brother."

"Give me some tea. Make it hot!"

Only then did they talk about their wounds.

Altogether we took 125 wounded and one dead. All three tents were filled to capacity. There was no room for all of them to lie down, and some had to sit up. Medics placed them in tiers, on straw covered with tarpaulin. We couldn't leave them on stretchers; they would have taken up too much room.

We checked everyone, selecting those that required immediate attention, but we left most of them until morning. The chief and I decided to risk losing some that might not survive the night. If we work day and night, we won't last long, and it looked as if we had enough work to last for months.

DATE UNKNOWN

From that night on we have been living in a perpetual nightmare. Every night they bring us several hundred badly injured men. For a few days we succeeded in keeping the sorting procedure going, washing and redressing all the wounds that needed redressing. We set aside all the evacuable cases, putting them in tents and small houses. The club, the Soviet building, and the school are filled with critical cases. In three days every inch of space was taken, and we started spreading into the neighboring peasant houses.

By the fifth day, when the number of wounded went over 1,000, we began to flounder. The sorting tent was crammed. We had no room and no time even to check the wounds and see that they were properly dressed.

And the wounded keep coming and coming. We take off only absolutely critical cases, but there is no room even for those.

We've started to requisition peasant houses, street by street. All are occupied, of course, but we have no choice. Our commissar has proved invaluable at this task. The cart with the wounded comes to a peasant hut, and the commissar knocks on the door with the butt of his revolver. For emphasis.

"Come on, *khazyaika!** Open up! The wounded!" he says.

Usually some officer comes out and starts screaming that there is no room, that the place has been assigned to him. But the commissar doesn't listen to him. Meanwhile, the medics carry the wounded inside, putting them on beds, benches, or even the floors. The commissar tells the military tenant that he can stay and share the place with the wounded. And the peasant women who own the huts usually take our side and help the wounded all they can.

DATE UNKNOWN

Two more days have passed and the number of cases is beginning to approach 1,500.

Our most pressing problem is feeding everyone and providing the most rudimentary medical help. We quickly form a recovery battalion—at first about 100 men, and then even more, all under Bessonoff's direction. Bessonoff is truly a dedicated man. Officially, he has been demobilized and could go home, but he has stayed with us as a voluntary worker, without rank or pay, purely out of compassion for his suffering comrades. A former skull case, he is odd at times, but he projects an image of absolute authority without ever raising his voice.

But of course, the men in the recovery battalion, injured themselves, cannot take care of all the wounded. Over 90% of our

---

Literally, "householder," but in peasant parlance there is a warmer connotation, rather like "house mother."—Trans.

patients are immobilized bed cases, and only a few are able to move without help. They all must be fed and given water, bed-pans, urine bottles.

We've tried to bring some order into this impossible situation. For each street or two, we've assigned a nurse and a senior medic. Each street is assigned a doctor who, of course, must also take care of the critical cases in our hospital wards. And we have only five doctors! But the peasant women in their huts are taking good care of their helpless tenants. They come to the kitchen to get food for them, in accordance with special cards we issue to them. Some of them take food and cook it themselves. They say that their home-cooked food is better than the stuff Chapliuk can conjure up with his small staff. The women who own some of the better houses are especially compassionate, and the wounded in those houses are lying on mattresses and homemade pallets, but bare straw has to do in most cases.

For transport we have mobilized local *kolkhoz* peasants with their horse carts. Our own carts can handle only the supplies and cannot be used as ambulances. There are days when we must provide up to 2,000 kilograms of bread alone! We have no bakery, so we have had to improvise one. Several local women, all good bread-makers, have been enlisted for this work. All the women work with devotion, and we are enormously grateful to them. The men do not measure up to them. Now and then a horse cart disappears just as we are ready to move some critical cases to surgery. May God forgive me, but I have blown up several times, using the roughest language in the presence of our girls. I even gave one of those old bastards a pretty good shake.

Our supply people are performing miracles. Everyone is fed amply if not luxuriously.

The medical supply problems are more serious. We have to wash and reuse our bandages. We operate only in emergency cases. I have learned to perform amputations within five minutes. I don't know whether I should be proud of this efficiency, but it is saving lives—some lives at least. Fortunately, almost all cases have been well taken care of in front-line medical battalions because the front has been moving slowly, and because doctors, nurses, and medics have become more experienced as the war drags on.

We have increased the efficiency of our main wound-dressing station to 240 cases a day. In addition, nurses are doing some wound dressing in the houses, so in all we can process up to 400 cases a day. Every 4 or 5 days all the wounded are checked for complications and have their wounds re-dressed when necessary. Still, many wounds become suppurated, and bandages become soggy and slip off.

We are working from six o'clock in the morning until midnight, eating while we work.

Of course, it isn't physically possible for doctors to look at all their cases, but nurses inspect their streets at least twice a day, even taking temperatures now and then. How these frail girls can stand the stress I do not know. But they stand up even when husky male medics are about to collapse.

NOVEMBER 23, 1943

This morning we have 2,350 cases on our rolls! This is absolute madness. Only 150 of these cases are in our recovery battalion, and those are the *only* walking cases in our hospital. And some of them shouldn't really be walking.

We had to place about 700 bed cases in distant houses, nearly two miles from our reception tent. They did not have any proper wound debridement, but most of them had their wounds re-dressed by nurses and medics wherever they lay. All others have been washed. Surprisingly, lice have not made their appearance. This is important because cases of typhus have been reported from the neighboring villages.

No, we did not "sink" in our surgical department, but only because of experienced, dedicated nurses and proper sorting procedures. At least eight peasant carts are working each day from dawn to dusk moving the wounded from place to place. I think we have succeeded in spotting all the most critically wounded and moving them closer to surgery. Only two men were found dead today, and one had had no pulse when he was brought into surgery. An overlooked case of gaseous gangrene. It was senseless to even try to save him.

All this is "within tolerable limits," but obviously we cannot go on like this. If this continues we will have to let men die where they lie—unless they send us some help. The chief and the commissar have been sending S.O.S. messages to everyone they could think of, but so far there are no responses.

To add to all our problems, there are hemorrhages. Many men have been lying here for two or three weeks and are developing infections. That is the danger point—artery walls become destroyed by suppuration, and then the so-called secondary hemorrhages occur. How can we spot such a case in time, nearly two miles away, often at night? And help must be immediate. First, pressure must be applied to the hemorrhaging area by hand; then—whenever possible—a tourniquet must be applied. And then, an operation.

Applying direct pressure to the wound is most important. The hemorrhage must be caught in time. We are teaching peasant women how to do it. While they are lining up for food rations, nurses and medics explain to them how to apply pressure to the hemorrhaging wound the moment they spot fresh red blood. The wounded themselves are also instructed how to do it, but there is that moment of blind panic which might prove fatal. And only experienced medics can apply a tourniquet properly. We have one on duty 24 hours a day and a horse cart waiting. Bessonoff, who sleeps in the wound-dressing tent, also knows how to act in an emergency.

Often a trembling, white-faced little boy runs in at night, calling for help. "Come, quickly! Blood! Mother is holding it, but he is dying!"

Bessonoff, who always sleeps fully dressed, jumps up, puts a medic and the boy in the cart and drives full speed to the scene of the emergency, standing up in the cart and snapping his whip like a Roman charioteer. In the house there is excitement. In the light of a smoking kerosene lamp, a frightened woman tries to press down the wound while all the other wounded watch in terror. The poor man is pale and barely alive. As often as not he has already lost a great deal of blood before the bleeding was noticed. The tourniquet is applied whenever possible, or Bessonoff takes over and applies pressure while the man is taken out, put into the cart, and driven full speed to surgery. By this time Lyda or Masha Poletova are already waiting, in surgical gowns and gloves. The wounded man is quickly undressed and put on a table. Kansky cuts away the blood-soaked bandage, and slowly loosens the tourniquet. These secondary hemorrhages are tricky. Sometimes they stop under the tourniquet, only to reappear again in two or three days, or even in a few hours. In other instances the blood spurts up the moment the tourniquet is loosened. Then I have to operate at once, assisted by Lyda, who has become my best assistant, while Kansky transfuses blood and glucose. But whenever possible we postpone the operation until morning, and the patient sleeps in the tent next to the medics, who watch him all the time. They would never let him bleed to death. It is really quite an achievement that we have not lost a single hemorrhage case.

I've become good at blood vessel operations. Neither Lina nor our new doctor, Anna (quite a good surgeon), has ever touched a hemorrhage case. But finding and tying up an artery is a time-consuming thing. Some arteries are easy, such as the carotid and the femoral, but others are tricky, particularly the gluteal and the subclavian.

Our women doctors have had special problems ever since we began working in recently liberated territories. Young girls beg them for abortions. All of them claim they were raped by Germans, and some threaten suicide. But abortions have been forbidden, and the commissar is watching this with an eagle's eye.

Of course, during rush periods like this one we are too exhausted even to eat and sleep, much less to treat any civilian patients.

NOVEMBER 25, 1943

This morning the first hospital train came to the station. They assigned 15 boxcars to us, but we took a few extra ones by storm. What a day! We loaded almost 700 bed cases. Even though the distance is short, only about three miles, it is quite a task. Each man had to be checked and his wound redressed if necessary. Then he had to be dressed, put on a horse cart, and taken to the station. All usual work was stopped (fortunately we had no new cases brought in the night before) and we mobilized all our transport facilities. Everyone worked until dark, and finally we accomplished what seemed an impossible task. It is surprising what people can do under pressure.

NOVEMBER 26, 1943

Today we must clear out the sorting department and put through as many previously unattended wounded as possible. With luck, we can process up to 400 men. The clubhouse is almost empty. We've evacuated over 80 cases from it, in Dietrich splints. Poor boys. Some of them had been lying there in splints for two weeks, without traction, without casts. How many of them will pay for it with their legs? Or with their lives?

Just as we start working the chief and the major arrive. They announce that I have been awarded The Order of The Red Star! I am flattered. This is the first decoration in our hospital. I know it's childish, but I'm pleased. It's as if the Motherland itself recognized my work. The commissar is particularly warm. "Congratulations, Nikolai," he says. "You have certainly earned this."

"Thank you, thank you."

I wanted to say "I serve the Soviet Union," but somehow it again slips my mind.

They leave, and all our people congratulate me—Kansky, our doctors . . . even Lina. I think our people actually like me—particularly the girls—despite the fact that I am often very curt and even unpleasant during operations. I don't forgive sloppiness. It has no place in our work when men's lives depend on our skill.

Lina says, "You certainly deserve this, Doctor." After our talk about Lyda and me there has been some invisible barrier growing between us. No, the past cannot be erased that simply. I have been watching Lina carefully. I don't think that she has formed any particular friendship with any man. And she has never mentioned her husband once. She left him in Leningrad and she has had no news of him. Strange girl. She seems unemotional and cold, but I know how warm and affectionate she can be. Too affectionate, in fact. Is she still interested in me—secretly? I don't think so; at least she never shows it. And anyway that thing between us in Cherepovets was obviously a mistake. I think we both knew it even while it was going on. And her strange marriage—the whole thing was very strange, and now as I look back, it seems unreal to me.

It is very different with Lyda. First of all, I am older. Not so much in years as in my outlook on life. Sometimes I feel fifty years old. And Lyda is a very serious girl, very dedicated to her work, very levelheaded. She is also older than her age. She went through hell, which could have destroyed many women. No, this is different. And real.

Finally the congratulations are over.

"Very well, comrades, let's go to work. Sorry, no banquet."

I sit down to record the operations I performed during the night, and then a lieutenant-colonel comes in, in his overcoat. A stranger. Lyda tries to stop him. "Comrade Colonel, please take off your overcoat," she says. But he just brushes past her and walks straight to me.

"Dr. Amosoff? I'm from the hospital train. It didn't leave last night. Go to the station at once. Several of your wounded have died, and others are dying. And it is only the first night! We have to go for four days! What will we bring—a train of corpses? Is that the way you're working here?!"

I feel that my heart is ready to stop. To hell with all those decorations and congratulations.

"This can't be true!"

"Go and see."

No more arguments. I must go, and I must see.

"Kansky! Tell the chief to go to the station . . . You, too. Take a couple of medics. No, four. Two carts. No, three. Get moving."

Some banquet!

I run out. There stands a horse—brought in to relieve the one that worked last night. As a young boy I could ride bareback. I jump on the cart and then on the horse—in my surgical gown.

"Come on!"

I hit the horse's flanks with my boots. The mud's flying from under the hooves. Surprisingly, I have not lost my sense of balance.

In ten minutes I am at the train. It's easy to find the hospital train. There are groups of walking wounded. I have not seen these trains since Sukhinichi, but this one is different. About thirty boxcars and only one passenger car, probably a kitchen. Most doors are partly open. Stove pipes, some of them smoking.

I jump down like a true cavalryman. Must look stupid in my surgical cap and white gown.

I see a man with narrow shoulder straps.

"Are you the train commandant, Colonel?"

"Yes, what do you want?"

"I'm the leading surgeon. Where are the corpses?"

"Right there, on a stretcher, covered with a sheet."

Yes, I see it.

"Just one?"

"And how many would you like—ten? There will be others, don't worry! Follow me!"

We go along the train, silently. The colonel stops in front of one of the boxcars.

"Take a look inside."

We get in. Double tiers on two sides. A small burning stove in the middle, tended by a young soldier.

A chorus of voices. "Comrade Doctor . . . Nikolai Mikhailovich! Order them to feed us. They want to leave us behind—all fistula cases! We are ready to lie here like this—wet. Tell them not to touch us."

A warm feeling. Those are "my" boys, from the main hospital ward. None of them is critical. I turn to the colonel.

"Who's dying here?"

"No one so far, but with fecal fistulas, with tubes, they are untransportable."

"Don't listen to him! We're transportable!"

"Keep quiet, boys!" I say. "I'm not the boss here."

I begin to check them. This whole boxcar is filled with my cases. They aren't in danger, but the stench, the bandages soaked through with feces . . . They loaded them carelessly, urinary cases on the upper tiers. Urine is dropping down. They are all wet, with dirty beards, looking miserable. But no one is dying.

The colonel realizes that they have exaggerated the situation and speaks defensively, "You understand, Doctor. We have orders: no urinary or fecal cases. Those must be evacuated by air."

"Planes don't come to us."

"That's not my fault. See for yourself. Is it possible to drag them along like that for several days?"

Yes, that would be bad. No, impossible.

"Listen, boys, we must take you back," I say. "Maybe they will send planes to take you out."

"We don't want to go! Leave us here!"

"I can't. There are orders."

"Then why did you drag us here? Just for exercise?"

They're right. This is my fault. I simply did not know that such cases were classed as untransportable. From Kaluga we evacuated everybody, but maybe those were different trains. Just then the chief arrived, and Kansky with the carts. Medics brought stretchers.

"Unload them, boys . . . this one . . . and this . . . and this."

We walk through the train. Not a single dying man, but the colonels complained with a good reason. Many bandages have become wet; others have slipped. Of course every hospital train carries a wound-dressing team, but obviously we did not do everything properly.

"Yes, our fault, but just think—almost two thousand and a half bed cases for five doctors—three of them women!"

"We understand, but there must be some order. We'll have to send a report to the Medical Department."

"All right, send it, damn it!"

The chief becomes worried and tries to talk them out of it. Meanwhile I go to see the dead man.

In the shirt pocket I find a card. Wounded 13 days ago. Attended to by a Medical Battalion. Sent to us only yesterday. And there is no exit card at all.

I pull off the sheet. Lean, septic-looking corpse. The bandage is very wet. I smell it.

"Urine! A bladder wound—urosepsis! We could not possibly have sent him here. Where did he come from?"

A quick investigation shows that we did not send this man at all. It appears that some soft-hearted peasants brought their "tenants" here on their own, and they were loaded in without our authority. And this boy belonged to such "private patients." He has never even been examined by us.

The colonels become apologetic. "That's your internal affair. It means you didn't organize the evacuation properly, but we have our orders."

That ends it. All we have to take back is about a dozen fistula cases.

I ride back on my horse. One of the medics has brought me an overcoat. I am satisfied. Yes, a man died, but our system was not to blame for it. I'm sorry for those fistula cases, but we simply did not know the rules. What are we to do with them? We already have about thirty of them back "home."

But we must prepare evacuations more thoroughly. We did make many mistakes, fortunately none of them fatal.

We go back to work. At night they bring us another hundred or so wounded. Again our sorting tent overflows, but finally we process them all. Not a single one goes to the village.

Bad luck always seems to follow gifts and decorations. I wish they would forget about me.

NOVEMBER 30, 1943

Four days ago our troops finally liberated Rechitsa. We learned about it two days later from the wounded. We have been so overworked since we came to Khorobichi that we hardly listen to communiqués.

The stream of wounded has slackened. The front has moved forward. It's almost 120 miles to Rechitsa, and meanwhile winter has set in. The few wounded that arrive come in half-frozen. There aren't enough blankets or sleeping bags to supply them all. And what happened to all those wonderful fur bags we had at the beginning of the war?

After the departure of the second hospital train, we had only about 1,500 cases left, so we were able to bring some order into our work. We brought in all the wounded from distant streets closer to our base. And we have processed all the men who had been unattended during those nightmarish days when we were drowning in moaning, groaning, screaming, dying men.

Yes, we have had our dead. Every day. We will leave quite a cemetery in Khorobichi.

On the 29th the Evacuation Center moved forward. Now we are receiving all the wounded. Light cases give us no trouble. We feed them, dress their wounds, and send them on foot to the station. Hospital trains are now passing by almost every day, and slowly but surely we are unloading our wards.

Only now can we live like human beings, have our meals together, and exchange experiences of the past weeks. The chief told us that during one of our worst days, the chief surgeon of our front, Professor Popov, passed Khorobichi. He summoned the chief to his railway car.

"What hospital are you?"

"PPG-2266, Comrade General. Attached to the hospital base of the 48th Army."

"What's your maximum capacity?"

"About 800 cases."

"And how many on hand?"

"2,300, Comrade General. Not counting walking cases."

"Then I needn't look in."

And he left. Probably he has seen such things before and knew that no one but God could help us.

I think that my romance with Lyda has been accepted by everyone. Even Lina. No one speaks about it, of course, but it is taken for granted. Even our moral-bound major no longer speaks to me about the necessity of "protecting our girls." Our girls need no protection. Most of them have strict morals, but some permanent liaisons are formed now and then. This is natural. In the old army there were practically no women. But in our army there are many of them—in signals, in traffic control, in aviation, even in the ranks. And medical services are largely sustained by women.

EARLY DECEMBER, 1943

On December 6th I had my 30th birthday. My youth is gone. I don't know whether I'm sorry or not. It seems to me that I have aged twenty years since the beginning of the war. My pre-war life seems distant and unreal to me, rather like a dream.

During the last week we have been having an easy time—just 5 to 10 new wounded a day. Our long-suffering reception-sorting department is resting. They have had the toughest part of it all. When I remember that first night with the square filled with rumbling Studebakers, I feel shivers running up and down my spine. That chorus of agonizing screams. I don't know how Liubov Vladimirovna, our Liubochka, could stand it all. She's a cultured, refined woman, over 50 years old. I can see her crawling among the cars, arguing and fighting with the swearing drivers, and trying to solve absolutely unsolvable problems. Our women are extraordinary, all of them, from the doctors to those old women in the peasant huts.

I celebrated my birthday at the pharmacy tent with our pharmacist, Zina. I had a headache and I came in to ask for aspirin. It was about nine o'clock at night, and the accumulation of fatigue was beginning to get me. I told her about my depression, and about my birthday.

"Come on, Nikolai Mikhailovich, have a drink."

She poured me a glass of captured port wine. I drank it all at once, and indeed I felt better. Zina is a good friend. She tried to ask me about Lyda and myself, but I did not succumb to the temptation to unburden my heart. I even refused another glass. It's disturbing that our relationship is being discussed so widely. But one thing I have decided: I will never put Lyda in a position where she could be referred to as a PPZH.* We must be more careful.

That night I could not sleep, and as always I tried to think about our work. Surgical problems. Khorobichi has been marked by hemorr ages. I have never seen so many of them. From the middle of November there has hardly been a night when Lyda and I did not operate. And sometimes two or three cases per night. At first I got panicky, but gradually I developed my own methods. First of all, one should not get nervous. No one dies immediately. As soon as the flow is stopped, either by tourniquet or pressure, give a blood transfusion. When the blood pressure is stabilized, operate. First of all, locate the source of the hemorrhage. Once the source is found, insert a ligature under the vessel and tie it up. This, however, is not enough. In two or three days the vessel wall under the ligature disintegrates, and everything starts all over

---

*The Russian initials for "mobile field wife." Soldiers' slang for wartime girlfriends.—Trans.

again. Therefore, one must tie up the artery outside the wound through special incisions. But even that is not always sufficient. I had a case in Khorobichi. We called him simply "Nose." A man of 46, a blacksmith in civilian life. A small shell fragment wound on the right side of the nose, under the eye. We immediately took him into our recovery battalion—we needed blacksmiths. All went well for several days. Then one night he burst into our tent, his overcoat covered with fresh red blood. We undressed him and put him on the table. This was no ordinary nosebleed. I tamponed his nostril, but the blood started to flow into his mouth, choking him. For the first time in my life I tamponed a nose from inside the mouth, and the bleeding stopped. However, in a few hours the bleeding started again. More tamponing. The next night Bessonoff came in again. "Nose!" I was barely standing on my feet. "Hell! Again? Lyda—surgery!" I tied up his external carotid artery. The bleeding stopped. But in three days he had another hemorrhage, and this time there was a danger he might die. What to do? To the front base hospital, 130 miles? I figured out that the blood flowed from the brain region through anastomoses. I performed a second operation and tied up the internal right carotid artery. This was dangerous for the brain, but fortunately there was no paralysis. The bleeding stopped. In five days "Nose" was walking, and suddenly—another hemorrhage, stronger than ever! I was desperate. This time I tied the left external carotid. There was absolutely nothing further I could do; there was nothing else to tie up.

And nature surrendered. The man got well and started working. He is still with us. But now and then he still complains. "When I drink home-brew vodka, Nikolai Mikhailovich," he says, "my snot turns pink."

"Don't drink!"

"Impossible for a blacksmith, Nikolai Mikhailovich. It's a part of my trade."

The next worst problem was urinary cases. In front-line medical units and the PPG's we knew only a single operation—urethrotomy, which was not always effective. It is here that our "cold urologist" was invaluable. He walks around in a hot tent wearing his fur vest carrying a revolver in a holster, reeking of sweat and urine. But he has saved many men who would otherwise have been doomed, without his professional care.

Our old problems—chests, hips, and joints—remain unsolved. We could not treat them without X-ray, retention table, plaster casts, and most of all, time. We could only try to keep them from dying until evacuation. And they were growing progressively more and more critical. How many of them would survive? As a last resort we did amputations. Four minutes for a leg, seven for an arm. Terrible.

Altogether some 8,000 cases have gone through our PPG here in Khorobichi. Deaths, about 250. That's here. But how many of them died later in evacuation and base hospitals? I am terrified to think.

And who is to blame?

First of all, the war. Ammunition trains are more important than the hospital. That's axiomatic during defensive battles such as Moscow, Leningrad, Stalingrad, the Caucasus. But now? I don't believe it is impossible to spare proper transport for the wounded. Two, three dozen good automobiles for each army would have helped enormously. But there are no such cars. At best, some broken-down trucks.

But there is a cruel and stupid doctrine: "everything for those who can still fight." And no one protests. And what can a mere surgeon like myself do? Just suffer with the men who are suffering. But they die, while I stay alive, accumulating "experience."

DECEMBER 16, 1943

This morning we received new orders; we are to relocate. And we have 87 absolutely untransportable cases. We'll follow the usual procedure: leave them behind with sufficient personnel and supplies.

We are leaving our cold urologist, a few ward nurses, one cook, and a recovery battalion of 20 men. We are leaving enough supplies, but what about knowledge and experience? Most of these men are doomed. Legally, everything is correct, all according to orders. But on a human level?

The wounded seem to know what awaits them. "You're leaving us to die," they say. I try to encourage them, but I don't sound very convincing. They are right, and I am lying.

We are wrapping up this operation.

DECEMBER 19, 1943

We loaded our hospital into a boxcar train. Our new destination is Buda Koshelevskaya, to the northwest of Gomel. The chief and I are going in our old Zis truck. We left 85 critical cases behind. (Two died during the last three days.)

Once again I am sitting on top of the bags and boxes, wrapped up in everything I could put on. I am both sad and happy—sad because I had to leave my poor wounded, happy because I do not have to think, because momentarily I have no responsibilities, because everything is being decided for me somewhere. I have only to follow the current.

Fresh snow has covered the tortured earth and the burned-out villages. People live like moles, deep under the ground in snowdrifts with stovepipes sticking out of them. The snow in the road has been packed down by military cars. We are going fairly fast—the river Sozh, a temporary bridge, Gomel. What is left of it. The long street we drive down is flanked by burned-out skeletons of brick buildings. There is hardly a building left undamaged. But already some windows are boarded up, and black stovepipes are smoking. This was one of the prettiest towns in Byelorussia. How many towns and cities have been so barbarically murdered? And how many will be leveled before this damned war is over? And how many thousands—millions—of poor Russian soldiers will be dead and crippled before the terrible Nazi dream is finally submerged in our people's blood? Do people in Europe and America realize the price we are paying to free the world from this plague?

I don't think so. For them there are moving fronts—just names in communiqués—advances, retreats, battles, an impersonal chess game, played by staff generals on maps. Victories, defeats, tactical and strategic mistakes. If only future historians could spend some time in our hospitals with the mangled, screaming men.

If I live through this war, I might try to write about it. But, of course, no one will publish what I write or read it. Everyone will try to forget. It's human nature: Let's forget and get ready for the next war. Hitler wrote "War is a natural state for any healthy man." Maybe he knew human nature better than we do.

I don't want to believe it. It is best not to think during war. Just cut off men's legs and arms, and let it go at that.

What awaits us at our new destination?

LATE DECEMBER, 1943

We arrived in Buda Koshelevskaya late at night. Our train with the hospital was not there yet. We stopped in front of the blown-up railway station. Our chief went to look for the station commandant. It was dark, cold, and miserable. Fedya went out to reconnoiter on his own, to speak to the drivers. He returned in low spirits. This station supplies two armies. Everything is crowded with rear-echelon organizations and staffs.

Then the chief came back, looking even bulkier in his fur coat. He, too, was pessimistic. "Nothing at all, not a centimeter of space." We spent the night in a peasant hut requisitioned for the Evacuation Center. We slept on the wooden plank beds prepared for the wounded. It was warm inside. The owner of the hut, an old peasant, kept the stove going the whole night, brewing some homemade vodka.

The next day we drove around for miles. Hopeless. Rear-echelon offices, stores, dumps, everything except a place for the wounded.

In the evening, coming back, we saw a large two-story schoolhouse without doors or windowpanes. The car came to a stop. The chief got off.

"Let's go and look in," he said. "We have nothing to do in any event."

We inspected the building. All the doors and windows were gone, even some of the door frames; all hinges and bolts had been stolen. But floors and ceilings were intact, and so was the roof.

"This could be a good hospital, don't you think?"

"Excellent. But how will we put this in order?"

They told us that in 1941 the Germans brought all the Jews of the town into this school and kept them here before killing them off.

Later in the night our hospital train arrived. We unloaded because the cars were needed elsewhere; they gave us half an hour to vacate them. We set up our tents near the railway track and went to look at our empty school.

There was no way out. We had to do what we could. In the morning we started working. We had about a hundred men in our recovery battalion, some construction workers among them. But we had no materials. We started a house-to-house search. We found a few stolen doors and some hinges. Local people had done pretty well for themselves. But we didn't stand on ceremony. There was no arguing with us; we took what we needed.

Our real bottleneck was glass. But some kind people gave us their spare winter panes. They didn't fit, of course, but we were able to brick up the space around them. There were enough bricks from the blown-up station and water tower, but breaking them off and cleaning them was quite a task.

Each department handled its own rooms—bricking up the windows, fitting the panes, rebuilding stoves, putting on doors. Everyone turned into a construction worker.

As we went through the houses left in the town, we could fully appreciate the misery of the civilians in this war. Many had been killed, many wounded, and no one seemed to worry about them. Soldiers had been attended to, but not the civilians. They were left to their own devices. Their wounds were wrapped in rags or just left unattended. We did what we could to help them, redressing some wounds, but many of them were doomed anyway without proper treatment. A little boy with both legs blown away died in front of our eyes before we could do anything.

In one hut we found a young girl with eight bullet wounds. She was executed by the Germans, who caught her and a group of other youngsters helping local partisans. They lined them up in front of a ditch which they had been forced to dig themselves, and shot them. By some miracle the girl stayed alive and succeeded in crawling out of the ditch at night before it was filled with earth. She said that there were others in the ditch who still moaned and moved, but they were all buried alive when a German bulldozer filled in the ditch with loose dirt. There was nothing we could do for her. She was dying of an anaerobic infection much too far gone to stop. She died a few hours after telling us her story. She had no one to mourn her. Her whole family had been exterminated by the Germans. An old woman was taking care of her, a complete stranger.

This whole area of Byelorussia was crawling with partisans, some operating in small groups and others forming large military units. The most famous of them was the unit commanded by one Sidor Kovpak, an old Bolshevik from the Ukraine. His commissar, Rudnev, was spoken of with special admiration. The unit consisted of three thousand men and women, organized into thirteen companies, well supplied and rigidly disciplined. It was known as the raiding detachment because they were constantly moving deep behind the German lines, blowing up bridges and railway lines, wrecking German trains, blowing up munition dumps, and generally terrorizing German rear organizations, and particularly local collaborators. The unit was constantly reinforced by local volunteers and small groups of Red Army soldiers left behind during our retreat. This unit had become legendary, and the single word *Kovpak* was enough to throw large areas into panic and demoralization. The Germans threw in large forces—whole regiments and even divisions—attempting to trap the Kovpak men, but the partisans had succeeded in breaking out of every trap. Their main tactic was not joining the advancing Red Army, but moving deeper and deeper into the German rear where they least expected them. According to local rumors Kovpak was now operating in Western Ukraine, in the Carpathian mountains, close to the Hungarian and German borders.

Of course we were interested to know what happened to the wounded among the partisans. The Kovpak unit had its own medical service, run by a woman doctor by the name of Mayevskaya.* But, of course, since the unit was in constant motion, untransportable cases had to be left behind, usually in peasant huts, together with some medical supplies. But all those who could be moved were taken in peasant carts and never left behind. Obviously, the wounded were the most difficult problem during this kind of mobile warfare. Later on in the war, Soviet planes came in to evacuate these hapless men and women, but generally, as always in any war, it is the wounded who pay the highest price. Whenever the Germans found a wounded partisan they would kill him, and also all those who gave him shelter. We saw proclamations, written in atrocious Russian, offering anyone "informing legal authorities about any wounded bandits" a reward of 20 kilograms of flour! Of course, whenever any partisans were captured by the Germans, they were always shot, often after hideous tortures.

Only now, going through Byelorussia, could we appreciate the work done by the "people's avengers." We saw burnt-out German trains and auto columns riddled by bullets, blown-up bridges, filled-in wells. They told us that at one point, during the Stalingrad

---

*This partisan unit, later reorganized into the First Ukrainian Partisan Division, performed some legendary feats. Kovpak survived the war, but Rudnev and his son were killed in the Carpathian mountains. (Dr. Mayevskaya also survived the war.)—Trans.

battle, the entire railway network of Byelorussia was brought to a standstill by the partisan rail war. Many small groups were trapped by the Germans and destroyed to the last man, but new groups always sprang up, in forests and marshes. Larger units, such as the one led by Kovpak and Rudnev, survived the entire period of German occupation and were now fighting hundreds and even thousands of miles behind the German lines. The help these courageous people rendered to our advancing troops was invaluable—they often so tied up all German communications that only planes could bring in supplies and evacuate the wounded. The psychological effect of this kind of warfare was devastating. German prisoners would grow pale and tremble at hearing the very word *partisans*.

I wondered if people abroad knew of the way our people fought this war. Yes, the people. Not merely the generals, whose exploits were reported and could be traced on maps, but countless thousands of our people—men, women, and even children—fought and died, often after atrocious tortures, without their names ever becoming known. Some of the larger units were known to our high command and were directed by it, but others fought on their own, and our soldiers would find their bodies hanging in liberated towns and villages. Some of these groups were led by boys and girls in their teens, some by old veterans of the Czar's armies in their sixties and seventies. And in all these groups women were always fighting side by side with men. Of course, there is no way by which human suffering can be measured, but it can be said that no people ever suffered so much in any modern war as our people did in this one.

Yes, we had our traitors. Usually one or two people could be found in any village who were willing to work with the Germans. But very often these helpers did more damage to the Germans than good because of their cruelties. Some of them were secretly helping local partisans and were expressly directed by the Party to stay behind, work with the Germans, and spy on their masters. Tragically, some of these brave men perished before their true identity could be established. This happened particularly whenever any village would be captured for an hour or so by some partisan unit that had no time and no desire to hold court hearings. The fate of those poor men who were forcibly mobilized by the Germans to act as local *polizei's* was particularly macabre. They could not refuse to serve the Germans without being shot, and they could not defend themselves when seized by the *partisans.* And the Germans would not take them along when they retreated. It was a vicious and tragic circle—the unwritten saga of this terrible war.

EARLY JANUARY, 1944

By the end of December our makeshift hospital was ready. We followed the plan we had worked out in Khorobichi and even improved upon it. We had 250 beds, the bathhouse, the laundry, and surgery, and the dressing station. Using our tents we could accommodate up to 600 wounded.

We were just in time. On December 26th, while our building was by no means ready, we started to work. This time the wounded were sorted at the Evacuation Center. The procedure was simple. A car column would arrive, and the man in charge woud command, "All those who can walk, get out. You'll be sent to the rear." Instantly all who could move would be out; the prospect of going to the rear was too alluring to miss. And others, those absolutely immobilized, would be turned over to us.

By this time, front-line hospitals had accumulated a good many wounded, and we were getting 50 to 60 complicated bed cases every day, all requiring surgery and special attention.

A new offensive started shortly thereafter, and the stream of wounded increased. There was no madness as there had been in Khorobichi—just 200 to 300 new cases a day. But there were also evacuation trains, and therefore we never had more than 700 cases on hand. Still we had to spread into the two neighboring streets.

The main problem during evacuation was to grab as many

cars as possible. The Evacuation Center was near the station, and the walking wounded assembled there were the first to grab every meter of space. We had to transport 200 to 400 bed cases to the station without any regular means of transport. But one becomes inventive in the crunch. During the evacuation days, we placed control points along all roads leading to Buda, to grab peasant horse carts and bring them to the hospital. They would take the wounded to the station until the train was completely filled. During evacuation the whole square in front of the station was filled with peasant sleighs pulled by skeleton-like horses. On each sleigh sat its owner, and also one soldier from our recovery battalion company, making sure that the requisitioned cart did not disappear.

Our army moved forward until February 20th. We didn't know in which direction it was attacking because this operation was never mentioned in any communiqués. Many battles are never mentioned anywhere, and there is as much blood shed in those nameless battles as during the most spectacular advances. We have learned that from experience.

We succeeded in organizing our work in Buda better than in Khorobichi: all the wounded went through preliminary examination and wound cleansing during the first 24 hours. Our dressing station could process 250 or even 300 cases with clockwork precision. But again all we could do was treat only those who were critical. And because there were too many needing constant attention, we could not treat any of them well. We could not use traction or put on plaster casts—we had neither the time nor the facilities. And suddenly there was an acute shortage of wound-dressing material. We had to recycle it, washing and disinfecting everything many times so that bandages became gray. So how could we put on any plaster casts under such conditions?

The chests were again our main problem. They ought not to be treated in front-line units, but must be immediately sent to special chest hospitals equipped with X-ray, where lung injuries can be operated on with constant draining and suction. Then they would recover. The way we handled them was senseless.

Our cold urologist came back. Of the 85 cases we left with

him, 21 died and many others were critical when he turned them over to a base hospital. How many of them would survive? Not many. And yet, with proper care, most of them could have been saved. I do not blame our urologist; I am sure he did everything he could, but there was something wrong with a system that forced us to leave the wounded without care, eventually to die.

Apparently it was the same with the Germans. We met a woman in Buda who had been drafted to work in a German hospital. Their equipment was excellent, "all sorts of machines," she said, but the wounded were dying every day. She thought that German doctors simply didn't bother at all with serious cases, those who could not be expected to get well enough to fight. German efficiency is gained by their lack of sentiment.

MARCH, 1944

Toward the end of February we had on hand over 200 untransportable cases, including some 60 with fistulas. We gave them better care than in Khorobichi. Fewer of them died, but none seemed to be recovering. We could not close the fistulas, and hospital trains refused to take them for evacuation. Finally the situation became impossible.

Our chief begged a hospital train commander to take some of them, and finally we evacuated most of our fistula and chest cases. They gave them the best cars, and we assigned a special nurse for them with all the necessary equipment. They safely reached the base hospital. In this way we evacuated almost 80 cases and breathed more easily.

We had fewer hemorrhages than in Khorobichi because the number of wounded rarely exceeded 500 and we could give them better supervision. Then the stream of the wounded started to slacken.

A very important change occurred in my private life. I got

married. The relationship between Lyda and me that started in Lavrischevo, had continued in Khorobichi despite the inhuman pressure. Finally, something had to be done to formalize the situation. I spoke to the commissar, but he had no authority to do anything. So we just announced to everyone that we were man and wife, and Lyda moved over to my billets.

It was the only honest solution: the situation was becoming embarrassing, particularly for Lyda. I had no right to compromise her. And it was Lina, of all people, who suggested it. "If you love each other, it's nobody's business. You can sign all the papers later on. And don't let the major stand in your way. If Tacia had wanted it, she could have had him living with her long ago. Remind him of that song of Darghomyjsky, which was Lenin's favorite: 'They did not marry us in a church.' " (Lina still cannot talk without song quotes!)

Lyda did not protest. It's a relief—like being forgiven some imaginary sin. Actually sin is not a part of the Soviet vocabulary, but conscience is a strange thing. Perhaps we Russians are more sensitive about these things than other people. With us *love* is a serious word.

Now everything has become simple and open. There is no longer any need to snatch minutes together here and there and talk formally to each other in other people's presence. Hiding and lying. I know Lyda did not like it, and neither did I. To both of us this is very serious.

So, my freedom has come to an end. Not that I had used it very much, but the feeling had been pleasant. For almost four years I had been a bachelor—my only true freedom, because the first time I married I was eighteen.

They found us a fine room near the hospital. It even had a radio in it. The owners of the house lived in another half of the house, and no one bothered us. We were newlyweds on our honeymoon. It would have been more romantic without gangrene and fecal fistulas, but we were happy together anyway.

In Buda we had several German bombing raids. Once it happened in daytime, when all our tables in the dressing station were occupied. We had not heard them approach, and suddenly there were explosions quite close to us. The windows were shattered. All our serious cases on the tables miraculously wound up on the floor. It's surprising what fear can do. Even our untransportable wounded found enough strength to crawl under their plank beds. It was quite a panic. We had forgotten what it was to be bombed, had taken it for granted that the Germans hadn't enough planes to bother us. But all our nurses and medics behaved very well. They all remained at their places and tried to calm their patients.

The second time we were bombed at night, and the Germans made several passes, dropping their bombs haphazardly. After the first pass they brought in a young lieutenant with an abdominal wound. He turned out to be a friend of our nurse Vera. Just as we opened up his wound, there were more explosions, and much closer than the first time. The whole building shook, and there was a sound of shattering glass. Again all our personnel behaved admirably, without in any way succumbing to panic. Lyda is frightened of planes—a reaction from the early stages of the war when she wandered in the forests with partisans while German planes were searching for them. But even she just went into a crouch, holding up her hands to keep her aseptic gloves clean. A brave girl.

We couldn't save the lieutenant; he died five days after the operation of acute peritonitis, which could not be arrested. Vera had been crying throughout those five days. During autopsy we couldn't find any surgical errors, but my conscience is not clear. Somewhere I must have erred. The man had no good reason to die.

While we were in Buda some collaborators and polizei's were tried. Most of them got long work-camp sentences, but two were sentenced to die. The execution was public and was held in a wooded knoll just outside the town, very close to our hospital. There was a tremendous crowd. Some of our men went to see it. We all felt the strain, knowing that the men were being executed. They told us about the "technology." The doomed men were placed on an open truck, the nooses were put over their heads, they read the sentences to them, and the truck started off. They were left dangling from a pine branch for three days, and I tried not to look through the windows in that direction. Somehow I felt an aversion to it all. Of course I am for the punishment of traitors, even for death sentences for the most vicious ones, but did they have to do it publicly? If we believed that the Germans might come back, there would have been some logic in it. A warning. But the Germans are hopelessly beaten and will never come back, so why kindle cruelty in people; why permit children to see it all? I can't understand.

The commissar told us that only those who were killing civilians and Soviet prisoners were being executed. All others would be put to work repairing war damage. That sounded logical. Actually German prisoners should have been used this way, particularly those caught setting villages on fire or wrecking and looting peasant houses. Does a uniform permit anyone to act as murderer and robber? There should be an international law that any soldier caught killing civilians or looting be treated as a common murderer and thief and punished accordingly.

EARLY APRIL, 1944

The third spring of the war has arrived. In the first week of April we were ordered to wrap up our hospital and turn all untransportable cases over to an evacuation hospital, which was to relieve us. Another stage of our work came to an end. We seem to have worked well, doing everything correctly, but somehow there is no feeling of satisfaction. Some six thousand wounded have gone through our hospital, and about two hundred died. That isn't a bad percentage, but we had no way of knowing how many of those who had been evacuated would recover and how many of those we had left behind would finally die.

We conducted as many autopsies as we could. We did not discover any bad surgical errors. Autopsies are important, one can learn surgery doing them. But nature is implacable, and it exacts its toll. A simple operation that one man can survive with ease and quickly recover from may prove fatal to another man. And there is no way of knowing in advance; each man is a special case.

Watching people die is quite an experience. It makes one

think. Soldiers—generally the older ones—who have religious faith, usually die easily. The Moslem soldiers almost always do. But it is difficult for those who have no faith. Dialectical materialism has theoretical answers to most human problems except the most difficult one—death. I have never had any religious training, but I feel that taking faith away from people is often cruel, particularly for those without an adequate education. And one thing is certain: atheism cannot replace religion at the point of death. It leaves a void in the human mind. It takes something away without replacing it with anything else.

Philosophy. A small army hospital is a good place to observe life, and to think.

We have time to think now. There is a lull at the front. Most hospitals are wrapped up, ready to move again. This is a time for inspections and conferences, and for study. Theoretically this is our rest period, and we all need it very badly, but everything depends on our immediate superiors and on how lax they are in fulfilling orders. If we followed all the instructions we would never have a free hour.

Our chief is lazy and not particularly good at following orders, but he's a bit of a coward. Our commissar is courageous and industrious, but everything depends on his mood . . . and on Tacia. Her boyfriend has been transferred somewhere, and our major once again is falling in love with her. He knows that it's hopeless, but he cannot help it.

EARLY MAY, 1944

In April our chief, Kansky, and I went to Rechitsa to attend our army's surgical conference. It was pompous and uninteresting. Some front-line generals sat at the Presidium table. Our chief army surgeon delivered a general report—repeated our *Doctrine* almost word by word. Not a word about the disasters we had in Ugolnaya and Khorobichi. According to him everything had gone smoothly and strictly in accordance with plans.

I don't know if the generals believed him. They probably knew that he could not say anything else, that it was the usual routine. They wrote their own reports the same way, the way their superiors wanted to hear them. That sort of conference is a terrible waste of time.

During the conference we spoke of our plaster cast technique. We demonstrated it on our medic, Stepa Kravchenko. Kansky worked like a true artist. When he finished we had an ancient classical statue standing there covered with plaster. Everyone liked the performance, and no one raised any question about whether it was practicable under war conditions when the wounded were lying on dressing station floors from wall to wall.

All the scientific lectures were rather insipid. I made a report; in fact, I made two of them. I told about our experiences with knees and pneumothoraxes, but apparently my remarks aroused no particular interest, because there were no critical questions. The most successful part of the conference was a banquet at its conclusion. Some of my colleagues got quite drunk, and we all behaved like a bunch of schoolchildren.

I made a few interesting acquaintances. The most interesting one was a middleaged woman doctor who stayed in Kiev during the German occupation. A sensitive, good looking woman, completely gray even though she was not yet fifty. She did not work for the Germans, except to load some railway cars for them. Her pay was two hundred grams of bread a day. Listening to her I felt as if I were listening to some crazy horror story, even though she spoke absolutely unemotionally. According to her, shortly after the Germans occupied Kiev, there was a series of explosions of undetermined origin* that wrecked the center of the town, killing many German officers and men. As a reprisal, the German military commandant of the city ordered all the Jews to assemble near the Jewish cemetery for evacuation. They were given precise instructions as to what to take with them, and some empty boxcar trains were prepared. When the Jews assembled—mostly old men, women, and children—they were surrounded by German soldiers, told to undress, and then all were killed in small bunches

---

*Recently it was disclosed that those explosions were touched off by remote control radio impulses—the technique developed by Soviet engineers before the war.—Trans.

by machine-gun fire in the place called Babi Yar. The killings went on for two days, and over one hundred thousand people* were killed. Many of them were merely wounded as they fell into the ravine and then were covered by earth. But that was only the beginning. Throughout the occupation the killings went on, and eventually fully one third of all civilians who remained in Kiev were murdered. She made it very clear that this was a routine German Army operation and not some excess of the Gestapo or the SS. "No, ordinary soldiers did the killing and the looting. They stole everything. Officers, too. I saw a German major throw a child out of a baby carriage and take it." She also spoke about the Ukrainian nationalists who came with the Germans, mostly from the Western Ukraine. They killed Jews and also every Pole they could find. Whole Polish villages were destroyed, with every old woman and child murdered. But, according to her, the Germans dealt with these collaborators quite simply. They threw them out of their evacuation trains and trucks, and the local partisans usually made short work of them just as soon as the Germans left. Quite a few of these nationalists wound up in Babi Yar, shot there by the Germans. Hitler planned to incorporate the Ukraine into Germany, and he had no intention of permitting any Ukrainians to set up an independent Ukrainian state. These collaborators were all slated for eventual liquidation from the very beginning. A few Russian anti-Soviet emigrés who joined the Germans in their crusade against the Bolsheviks all suffered the same fate, according to the woman. They were all killed by the Germans before their retreat.

During the conference we heard the news that Odessa was liberated—the last large Ukrainian city still held by the Germans. Everyone felt that Rumania would now certainly collapse. We all were overcome with joy.

I left for Buda with mixed feelings. It was good that my reports had been well received. It was pleasant to compare myself with others and find out that I was no worse than most of my

---

*This might be an exaggeration. Actually the German official records show that "only" 33,771 Jews were executed in Babi Yar on September 30, 1941. These executions continued throughout the German occupation, though on a smaller scale.—Trans.

colleagues, surgically speaking. It was good to meet so many interesting people. But it was nauseating to listen to all those banal, meaningless speeches full of bragging and trumped-up facts and figures, without a single word of criticism or even self-criticism. And the name of Stalin used ten times in every speech! Yes, we have learned to admire his conduct of the war, we have learned to respect him, but that endless repetition of his name with glorious epithets had become a distasteful performance to me. And it was sad to think that we could not hope for any improvement in our work—what with that orgy of self-admiration. The wounded would have to keep dying. And it was still so far to Berlin.

There was a continuous drizzle during the trip back, and our car got stuck in the mud the moment we left the main highway. I couldn't wait until it was pulled out, and I started walking—18 miles over a thick, sticky mud. I got home late at night, dead tired. Lyda had got some supper for me earlier in the day, and she prepared some tea. We sat around talking and exchanging news. In an hour or so I felt a little better.

The next day I received a letter from the First Moscow Medical Institute informing me that Professor Silischev had given a negative report on my dissertation, and that I needn't prepare to defend it. That was a bit of a blow. Even though I knew that it had been composed sloppily and I had had no particular hopes for it, secretly I hoped that it might pass.

When this war ends, who will care about my experiences with hips, knees and pneumothoraxes? I will again become an intern with two years' record.

LATE MAY, 1944

On May 20th we moved to Rechitsa, on a train this time. There is a lull at the front and there are enough empty boxcars. We were not permitted to stay in the town; once again we had to go to a village, ten miles outside of Rechitsa. The place was called Ozerschina, a very large village on the Dnieper. A prosperous place, almost undamaged. Large, well-built houses with multicolored window frames. The Germans had left so quickly that they hadn't had time to damage it. We established ourselves quite comfortably and would have been content were it not for the dull routine—including marching drills for our nurses and medics. It should be about time for our troops to move; the roads have become passable.

Now Lyda and I are legally married. We went to Rechitsa. A ZAGS* office was already working there, and we were duly registered and given our certificate. Now it is final. The commissar formally congratulated us. Strange man—secretly he has been upset about our "living in sin."

EARLY JUNE, 1944

All military units have been ordered to relocate into forest camps, probably so that the soldiers will not become demoralized by too much comfort. Our commissar is all for it; he's still worrying about our girls' morals.

Our chief and the commissar went out to look for a suitable place: some forest where we could set up our hospital. Of course they found nothing suitable, so our relocation has been indefinitely postponed.

JUNE 7, 1944

Yesterday we got some electrifying news. Our allies have finally landed on the European continent! So the long-delayed second front is now a reality. This must be quite a shock to the Ger-

---

*The Russian initials for special offices registering births, deaths, marriages, and divorces.—Trans.

mans. They probably thought that they would have to deal only with us and that all the talk about the second front was a bluff. Frankly, we thought so, too. Of course we have done all the hard work, breaking Germany's back, but if this shortens the war even by a few months, it would be wonderful. With luck we might finish the whole thing by autumn. Oh God, if that could only be true!

Finally we got our orders. We are again a part of the Army Hospital Base, but who cares? The main thing is to get back to work. Our new destination is the town of Pirevichi, near Buda. So our going back and forth was senseless, but our superiors have a positive talent for unnecessary moves. One should not be too critical, I suppose. It must be devilishly difficult to direct an army group. Even in our hospital department things are often a mess.

We load quickly and travel back along the familiar route, through Gomel. Now the town looks so much prettier. The apple trees are shedding their last blossoms. There is a great deal of greenery, hiding the burned ruins of wooden houses. It's strange to look at those sooty chimneys rising among the apple blossoms. The grass is not yet growing in the ashes, but it frames those ugly spots on all sides.

People are all over the place, cleaning up, rebuilding. This is already a living Soviet city, not a ghost of one. There are placards and streamers: "Let us rebuild our beloved Gomel!"

EARLY JUNE, 1944

We arived in Pirevichi in four trucks. Approaching the town we saw some large barracks and immediately felt better. All we needed were walls and roofs. Anything would do—storehouses, barns, even cow pens. We can clean up anything, given time. Our recovery battalion has practically melted away. No wonder, we've been inactive for almost four months. Most of the walking wounded got well and rejoined their units. All we have left is about fifteen men.

Of course all the barracks turned out to be occupied. How could it be otherwise? We found an engineering battalion there with all their equipment. The chief and the commissar went to the staff building, but without much hope. They returned smiling along with a lieutenant colonel, a fine looking man with engineer insignia on his shoulder straps.

"We'll give you all the space you need," he said. "Our men are well, and we'll help you get set up."

I couldn't believe my ears! A fairy tale?

But it was true. We immediately established contact on the lower levels with their captains, lieutenants, and sergeants, and went to work.

There was once a large woodworking plant in Perovichi. The Germans wrecked it, of course, but one long storehouse remained intact. That became our reception-sorting department. A large, partly damaged factory building became our evacuation ward. We cleared one small house for our dressing station and surgery. Soldiers put in window frames, and our girls whitewashed walls. Lyda worked on a high sawhorse, swinging her brush like a true house painter. We decided to prove that we could use plaster not only for casts.

Earlier in the spring we received a Yudin traction table, a portable orthopedic contraption, very well constructed. I couldn't wait to try it out, but there will probably be no time for it when the wounded really begin to pour in. Or perhaps the Germans will give up quickly now that they have to fight on two fronts. Doubtful. They know that they will have to pay for their crimes, and they will fight to the end against our troops.

MID-JUNE, 1944

Never before have we had such pleasant neighbors. No wonder—all the officers are graduate engineers and technicians, many of them Leningraders. It is surprising how this has held true since before the Revolution—that peculiar Leningrad finesse in speech and manner. Even common soldiers from Leningrad are always neater, more polite, and better mannered. And they have certainly behaved during this war with incredible courage and tenacity, holding out against all German assaults. They say that at least a third of all civilians have perished from bombs, hunger, and cold, but there is no longer any question of the Germans ever taking that city. And it was the second on Hitler's list, after Moscow.

In the evening the engineers come to our yard, bringing a record player with them, and there is dancing. One boy plays the guitar beautifully, singing, "You are far, far away, my beloved, and to death there are merely four steps . . . "

Those songs touch all of us almost to tears, particularly our girls. Even the most modest of them have acquired admirers, and this has plunged our poor commissar into the depths of despair. He is trying to build up discipline with reveille, lights-out, night checks. He even set up a guardhouse for those caught coming home late. All this irritates the engineers, and they've had a few fights with the commissar.

We are all waiting. We know that at any time now our armies must attack. We know about streams of supplies that have been going toward the front day and night. We are ready here. There is even an empty hospital train waiting at the station. This is a far cry from the first days of the war!

Many planes in the air, all ours. We haven't seen or heard a German plane since Buda.

LATE JUNE, 1944

On June 22nd, the third anniversary of the war, our engineering battalion left us. They got their orders. They say they will be building bridges across the Dnieper. A superb organization—they were loaded and gone within one hour.

Tension is growing. We all know that our holiday is about to end.

JUNE 25, 1944

Early yesterday morning we were awakened by the roar of gunfire. It didn't stop the whole day. We kept walking out and listening to see if it was getting more distant, less deafening, but it seemed to stay the same.

Toward evening they brought us some wounded in several ambulances, directly from front-line medical units. We asked what was happening at the front. "No, we didn't break through," they told us. "They're dug in . . . wouldn't give ground."

We worked all night, putting on three high plaster casts and several smaller ones. The wound debridement in front-line units was not suitable for plaster; we had to cut the wounds open. Each table was occupied for about an hour and a half. We hope to get more proficient later. The Yudin traction table is marvellous, but we need at least one more if we want to specialize in this kind of surgery.

Tomorrow we must expect a torrent of wounded men. The breakthrough seems to be going slowly.

JUNE 28, 1944

We have been working now for two days. The wounded are coming in steadily but in small groups. It is evident that the front is near and that transport facilities have improved. Our sorting place is large, it can accommodate all comers. Some of the wounded are taken directly to the evacuation wards because their wounds are clean and have been well attended to in the front-line units.

Yesterday we heard the steady hum of hundreds of planes throughout the day. We didn't see them but we heard them, and we also heard their bombs. It sounded as if the whole earth were exploding. We have never heard anything like it before.

In the evening the drivers brought in the news that we had broken through.

Now they will be rolling on. Thank God!

We can't do much plastering. No time. Gaseous gangrene has made its appearance. We had to do two deep resections and one amputation. By now we have about five hundred cases.

The wounded arrive in good shape. The summer's rest, good food, the sunshine—all have worked wonders. The general spirit is—onward to victory! Many are sorry to have been wounded just when we are beginning to move forward. Some are sorry about the missed booty, particularly the scouts—brave and adventurous lads. This is what we have come to—booty! Well, maybe it's a healthy stimulus. The Germans certainly looted everything they could lay their hands on.

JULY 9, 1944

On June 30th our troops made a great leap forward. Until now all the wounded have come from the Babruisk sector, but now they come from Osipovichi, and even farther. We looked at the map—60 miles! They say that near Babruisk they encircled the Germans, and there was a terrible slaughter. Our aviators had a field day. There are thousands of abandoned guns and vehicles. German soldiers are wandering in the forests, surrendering in droves.

On July 1st the stream of wounded all but stopped. On the 2nd we sent back our first evacuation train. All we had left were plaster-cast cases. They needed supervision; the gangrene danger point was not yet over.

On the 5th we sent off another train, leaving us with about 60 cases.

On the 6th we got orders to be ready for relocation the next day. The representatives of the front hospital base came in to take over our cases. They went through all the case histories, trying to pick up our mistakes. They looked sceptically at our high casts. "Isn't it too early for that?" I didn't try to convince them; with their self-assurance it would have been senseless. But I made a mental note: the farther to the rear hospital people are, the more important they try to appear, criticizing those who have done all the hard field work.

While we were getting ready to move, our troops advanced still farther. We don't even know where the front line is at the moment. Every day there are several orders of the day from Stalin. The whole country is watching this great offensive. Finally, today we got orders to move to the Babruisk region.

JULY 10, 1944

We're on our way to Babruisk. Both of our old trucks are loaded to capacity. The drivers, as always, walked around, sighing, "Poor rubber, hot weather, we'll get stuck for sure."

At Rogachev we cross the Dnieper. There is nothing left of the town—it was completely destroyed during the winter offensive. The grass has grown over the sooty ruins, and even the chimneys have collapsed.

At noon we approach the Berezina river, not far from Babruisk. This is the place where our troops surrounded the Germans and slaughtered them—an incredible sight. The field and the thin forest is completely covered with abandoned equipment—an incredible mass of twisted iron and steel. Vehicles are piled one on top of the other at all angles—broken, overturned artillery pieces, tow trucks, troop carriers, passenger cars. Among them, bomb craters, broken trees, rags and scattered papers. Large black spots—oil and blood—but no bodies, just pieces of flesh and brains still stuck to the sides of the vehicles. I can imagine what a hell this was when our planes were bombing these massed machines.

Of course we stop. It's impossible, absolutely impossible, to drive past such a wealth of equipment . . . what if some of the trucks are still operational? Our driver Fedya dived into this mass of junk like a falcon diving at partridges.

But we've arrived too late. Anything at all that could be removed has already been stripped. Our brother Slavs* have done themselves proud!

Fedya casts one last sorrowful look at this mess, and gets behind the wheel. The chief wants to get going.

What vehicles there were—Mercedes Benz, Fiat, Citroen, Opel, Horch, and some we had never heard of before—enormous diesel-powered monsters from Germany, Italy, Belgium, France, Czechoslovakia, Hungary. It's hard to understand how we could withstand the assault of so much first-class equipment collected from all over Europe and crush it with the products of bombed-out plants that had been dismantled, evacuated, and reassembled in the Urals and in Siberia by women and children working hurriedly in rain and snow, often with no roofs over their heads. Our success has been achieved by more than momentary heroism in battle. We are advancing because of our people's stubborn will to survive.

Our allies have sent us some cars, tanks, and planes, but none of them made their appearance before 1943, and even today, our officers say, ninety-five percent of all our weapons and supplies are Soviet-made!

JULY 12, 1944

Babruisk was more or less intact. It was pleasant to see a neat town after so many ruined villages. There we received orders to move toward Minsk. Now we are traveling on a highway. We

---

*An affectionate term for Russian soldiers. In use since the Balkan liberation wars of the eighteenth and nineteenth centuries.—Trans.

haven't seen one like this since Roslavl.

It wasn't easy for the Germans to keep this road open. All the trees were cut down on both sides for hundreds of yards to afford observation, and every few miles there are blockhouses and forts. And this after three years of occupation! No, the spirit of our people cannot be broken.

All wooden bridges have been blown up. Along the culverts lie dead, bloated horses with their legs up in the air, stinking to high heaven.

Now we have a chance to see thousands of the "invincible" Germans! They have been wandering in the forests, trying to surrender, afraid to fall into the hands of the partisans.

What miserable, bedraggled men! We pass a group of about fifty of them. They aren't even guarded: they are merely shown the way to prison camps and protected from the local people. In front walks a middle-aged soldier with a rifle slung behind his back. He is hot and tired and doesn't even look back at his prisoners. They follow him like sheep; he is their only hope of remaining alive, since the local peasants would not treat them kindly.

Is it possible that our soldiers went into captivity like that in 1941 and 1942? No, not like that. They say that they tried to escape at the slightest opportunity, even at the risk of being mowed down by German automatic weapons.

If we did not have to take detours around wrecked bridges we could move much faster. And we are often delayed by flat tires. It takes an hour or so to repair every flat.

Along the highway we pass an endless stream of our supply columns. We see many captured German vehicles, some painted yellow. They say that the Germans brought them from Africa. Until 1943 the Germans didn't bother to camouflage their equipment. But after Stalingrad they became cautious because of our aircraft. They seem to dominate the air these days.

Our troops have moved forward so fast that we cannot possibly catch up with them in our horse-drawn train.

LATE JULY, 1944

While we were still on the road, we received new orders to move to Bobovnya, somewhere near our prewar border. We drove the whole day. Fedya's Zis had three flat tires, and our 1½-ton truck had a broken magneto. We had to wait until we got a new one. There was no difficulty about getting any spare parts. We could get them all for alcohol, our hard currency.

We had a long and tedious wait at Bobovnya. Our horse train got lost somewhere behind us, and we had no news of it. I spent my time lying in a barn, reading some books I had found in Pirevichi and thinking about medicine and life. Our girls went to collect nuts in a nearby forest. Kansky and our finance officer, Mikhail Vasilievich, accompanied them to protect them from wandering Germans. Both men carried revolvers, but no one bothered them.

I also worked on my notes, trying to put them in order. Since my marriage I have become careless about my diary, making only occasional terse entries, sometimes missing whole weeks. I am no longer lonely as I was at the beginning of this war.

We are getting war news from passing cars. The communiqués have become shorter and more general. The German retreat has become more orderly, it seems, and there are no major new encirclements. A pity—with encirclements things go faster. Now and then we get some old newspapers. They are full of stories about our people's heroism at the front and in the rear. They also tell of our allies' successes in France, but they don't seem to be advancing very fast.

On July 18 our horse train caught up with us. We were a complete Mobile Field Hospital again, but we had nothing to do in Bobovnya. Then we got new orders to move in the direction of Bialystok. That was in Poland!

Our commissar delivered a lecture to us about how we should behave in Poland. He explained that the Poles are our brother Slavs who have been enslaved by the Fascists, and that we are liberating them. We must treat them as our friends and allies, he said, and particularly respect their religious beliefs. Catholicism is a strong force there. What he said was true enough, but we hardly needed such a lecture. Surely we are intelligent enough to know all that. But all political officers had been ordered to deliver a lecture to all military units crossing the border, and our major takes his work seriously.

AUGUST, 1944

We finally caught up with the front in the beginning of August, beyond Bialystok. The Germans were putting up a strong resistance, and our own advance had slackened. The troops were tired. The losses during the summer have been moderate, but the men have covered almost 500 miles, and have outrun all their supplies.

We set up our hospital in a small town called Bránsk. The town was completely undamaged, and we occupied one of the buildings of a local hospital. Soon the first wounded started to arrive, directly from their regiments. In effect we have become a front-line unit.

Finally, I performed an operation about which I had been dreaming for a long time: a radical chest surgery with debridement of a lung wound. The operation took two hours. I was scared stiff when I was ablating a section of the lung with a shell fragment; I doubted whether I would be able to stitch the wound up again. When the patient coughed, the lung ballooned out frighteningly.

We used local anesthesia. The patient—a captain—behaved magnificently. When we started to suck out the air, he started to smile and sat up firmly in a chair. His lips were no longer blue, only pale.

"I thought this was curtains for me. I've been fighting since

1942, was at Stalingrad . . . I've seen these things . . . I know that when the air begins to bubble inside, there's nothing anyone can do. This is like being born again. Thank you, doctors."

We placed him in a ward. The next day there was no more air in the drainage tube. We set up suction according to our own system, using three bottles. He seemed to be getting on well, our captain.

In general, I liked the operation, but it takes a lot of time and steady nerves.

All other surgery was routine. Well, not quite routine, because we put on many plaster casts.

They kept bringing in the wounded to us for eight days. Then the troops surged forward, and we were once again left behind.

One of our medics was blown up by a mine. He went to the outhouse in the garden, wandered off the trail, and stepped on a mine. We had to amputate his lower leg because the foot was completely smashed and there were many fragment wounds in both legs. We were sorry for the poor boy. He was a new one—had been with us for only a week.

One of our horses was killed, too—by a single German plane that dropped two bombs.

Those were the first battle casualties of our hospital since the air raid in Sukhinichi in 1941. Fate surely had been good to us up to now.

When the stream of new wounded slackened, life became interesting. New impressions: a neat Polish town with private stores, Catholic churches, former synagogues. It was terrible to hear the story about the extermination of the Jews. I cannot reconcile myself to the fact that such barbarism could exist in our century. But it is all true. And people speak about these atrocities matter-of-factly; they got used to them during the occupation.

Very soon we got orders to relocate to Ostrów Mazowiecka, about seventy miles away.

We evacuated our captain in good condition in one of the last cars. We had removed the tube and found no fluid. I was very pleased that the operation had been a success.

SEPTEMBER, 1944

We are driving through Poland. This is the Warsaw province, the most Polish Poland. Once this was a part of the Russian Empire, and therefore we have no linguistic difficulties. All the older people speak good Russian.

The population is friendly but reserved. The Germans had been spreading rumors that the Red Army was coming here in order to annex Poland to Russia. Our political officers have to do a good deal of educational work to convince the Poles that we have no such intentions.

The landscape does not differ much from that of Central Russia or Byelorussia. Flat fields, small forests, little brooks—there are many private little farms, and small towns with large, gloomy churches. We went inside some of them. They are impressive, but not as cheerful as our village churches. At all road crossings there are large crosses with the crucified Jesus on them, or statues of the Virgin Mary. There are always wilted or fresh flowers at these shrines. We saw a company of our soldiers passing a funeral procession. There was a command, and our men removed their helmets. The Poles looked surprised, and some of them smiled. A thing like that works better than hundreds of propaganda leaflets. We are supposed to be a godless people. It is strange for us to see so many churches, priests in black soutanes, nuns, and crucifixes. But Polish peasants look very much like our own, and their villages look very much like our own, small, modest huts.

DATE UNKNOWN

We set up our hospital not in Ostrów Mazowiecka but in a suburb called Komorowo. There are some cavalry barracks there, left from the Czar's time, completely undamaged, and it was an easy task for us to get organized.

Here we were close to the front. We could hear the artillery fire and machine guns even at night. They say that we are within range of German heavy artillery.

We are working like a front-line hospital. The wounded come to us directly from regimental units. We have set up a shock ward and keep the temperature there an even 28°C. But the laws of nature are cruel. If the low blood pressure lasts for two hours, there is no way of bringing a man out of shock.

During the first day I operated on abdomens and pneumothoraxes. It was a hectic day. Unfortunately, when the sorting room is crowded with waiting cases, one has to hurry. We sewed up seven pneumothoraxes and only one lung, without ablation. All the men are in satisfactory condition; most of them will probably survive.

Abdominal wounds are more bothersome. We performed eleven laparotomies, but five men died of peritonitis. Maybe I don't know how to do this kind of surgery well enough.

We have created fairly good conditions for our wounded, and they do not suffer as they did during the first years of the war. When their number reached 600, we could not provide fresh linen for all, but nobody lies on bare straw. However, we must not feel satisfied. The main problems have remained—suffering, dangers of gangrene, peritonitis, sepsis—they all are still with us. And the fatality rate hasn't improved much. What we need are new scientific approaches and an absolutely new organizational scheme, but it seems that we will have to finish the war pretty much the way we started it.

Our living quarters are good. Lyda and I have a separate room in the barracks, close to the operating theater. Others live in the hospital buildings; one building is used as a dormitory for medics.

The pressure lasted for about a week; then the wounded stopped coming. Altogether we processed 1,100 cases; 220 were operated on, 24 died.

The Germans are committing incredible atrocities. A death camp, Treblinka, is not far from us. Now there is a special commission to investigate Fascist crimes. They have opened up ditches filled with corpses and are conducting autopsies. A pathologist of our own army is on the commission. He comes from there almost in a state of shock. Layer after layer of corpses, all with bullet holes at the base of the skull—that is how they killed them. Many women, many children. One would think that some monstrous machine was firing those bullets. But no—a man was holding that gun! How horrible human nature is, if things like that are still possible. It seems that civilization has given us nothing—absolutely nothing!

When someone tells about all this twenty years from now, no one will believe it. But it is all true—thousands, hundreds of thousands, maybe even millions of helpless men, women, and small children with bullet holes in their skulls.

DATE UNKNOWN

We have finished our work here and evacuated all our cases by air. Wonderful. Why are there so few of those hospital planes?

Again I am trying to find the truth. They say there is a larger truth in the war and a smaller truth. The larger truth is strategy, national politics, that sort of thing. The smaller truth is the way soldiers see the war, or even doctors. They do not fit together, those truths. The arguments for the larger truth are logical. They say that in accordance with the larger truth it was impossible to build a thousand hospital planes; that would mean a hundred fewer fighter planes, and without the hundred fighter planes the war could not be won. Maybe, but I doubt it—particularly after Stalingrad, when there was a definite turning point. Then, a thousand hospital planes would have done more good than a hundred fighters.

We are packed and ready to move to a place called

Dlugasiodlo. A colonel from the hospital base told us that we are going to work as a specialized hospital, hips and joints. But I have my doubts!

We must treat our cases even better than Yudin! We know the value of traction, and we are not going to be too inflexible about plaster casts. We know the methods of primary debridement and primary joint resections.

OCTOBER, 1944

Alas, Dlugosiodlo turned out to be a tiny town without a single suitable building except a church and a priest's house. In Russia we would have requisitioned them, but we were in Poland and we had our orders. I wonder what Jesus would have said about it? Isn't saving human lives more Christian than praying? But orders are orders, so we moved to a village about two miles farther on, a neat little place with masses of greenery. It is called Karnacycka. We set up our tents in the orchards, and the wounded started to come in almost at once.

We set up six tables, including three special ones—the Yudins, and two of our own. If, after a bandage is removed, we see that the wound is in bad shape and that gaseous gangrene is possible, we cut the wound open and insert a drainage tube. Then we leave the wounded in a splint for one or two weeks until the danger of acute infection is over. Then a plaster cast. Of course, we watch all casts for at least seven days in order to catch any sign of gangrene. If, after the cast is put on, the general condition of a patient worsens, we do not hesitate; we remove the cast and use traction. We must not overlook infection. We must not repeat the Kaluga mistakes.

A joint wound—knee or pelvis—is a special case. If the wound shows no signs of infection, we keep the patient in a Dietrich splint for five days, and if everything is normal we put on a high closed cast. The wounds with extended damage and infection go through a thorough primary debridement, and only then do we use plaster.

Our two terribly heavy trunks filled with plaster bandages have come in handy. It isn't for nothing that we have been carrying them for 500 miles, all the way from Pirevichi.

Our main plaster cast specialist is Kansky. To help him we have Marusia, a volunteer nurse, and if necessary, Lyda joins in.

The colonel was right. All the wounded coming our way are marked "serious extremity wounds." During the very first day we put on 27 high plaster casts, three with drainage tubes. We worked as usual—18 hours. Kansky was so tired that he practically crawled out of the wound-dressing station. We set up a special ward for plaster cases. These men are always cold, but we must dry the plaster as quickly as possible, so we had to organize special ventilation. Besides high casts, we put on about thirty light ones—foot, leg, shoulder. But that is easy stuff.

The next day our production reached 33 high casts. Then the new wounded started to arrive more slowly, and finally the new arrivals stopped altogether. We heard that our troops ran up against strong German counterattacks. Small wonder, after three and a half months of constant fighting.

We were allowed to treat our wounded for three weeks, but then we had to evacuate them. Senselessly, really, because we just packed up and then did nothing for almost two months, waiting for new orders.

Was our last operation successful? Undoubtedly. Here are the statistics:

Gun-wound hip fractures, operated on and put in plaster—55 cases. Five of them, after traction treatment for 7 to 16 days. Only one case of gaseous gangrene under cast, but a timely amputation saved his life. Knee injuries—37 cases. Three primary amputations, 10 primary resections, all the rest, simple debridement. All put in casts. Only one man died of hemorrhage, at night. We couldn't help him in time. There were no untransportable cases. The chief of the Evacuation Area told us that we will work the same way in the future. We were glad to hear that.

Our hospital unit has received many decorations. The chief,

the major, and myself have been awarded Second Degree Orders of the Patriotic War; Lina and Lyda have received Orders of the Red Star. And others in our unit have received various medals.

NOVEMBER, 1944

A lull in the fighting. A wet, cold November. A small, miserable Polish village. Training sessions for possible chemical warfare. "The wounded beast might do anything." Lectures, gas masks. Probably needless, but it is better to be ready than to be caught by surprise.

We have seen some films. A mobile theater came in and put up a screen in a big barn. They showed us two full-length films and a newsreel. The newsreel was interesting. We saw 60,000 German prisoners being walked along the Moscow Garden Ring.

The war seems to have come to a standstill temporarily. Our troops have moved forward farther than the Germans did in 1941. We have not only liberated our Soviet territory, but have gone deep across our borders. Rumania has gone over to our side; Czechoslovakia, Bulgaria, and Yugoslavia are all helping us. But the Germans are still fighting stubbornly on our front.

DATE UNKNOWN

In Karnacycka I met a very interesting man. He was a Russian, but he had lived in Poland for many years. He was probably about 75, and he didn't like to speak about his past. It's an old story. He was married to a Polish woman. She had been dead for many years, and their two sons were killed when the Germans invaded Poland.

He owned a small house with a plot behind it, and he had a little cobbler's shop. I had brought my boots to him to be mended. When I spoke to him I knew that he was a well-educated man, and he invited me in to have some tea. He lived in a tiny room at the back of his shop. The first thing I saw was an old Bible, in Russian, lying on the table.

Ivan Petrovich told me he was a religious man. His family were "old believers"—a religious sect persecuted during the Czar's time because they refused to serve in the army.

When I looked at his Bible, he said, "A beautiful book. I have probably read it three hundred times from cover to cover, and every time I find something new there."

I have never read the Bible. We never had one in our house. I think my mother was an agnostic. And I was told in school that it was a collection of old legends, myths, rituals, and superstitions. While Ivan Petrovich was making tea, I told him that with us it was considered counter-revolutionary. The old man just smiled. "That's stupid," he said. "You know, before the war, Polish policemen kept bothering me, thinking that because I was a Russian I was a Communist. Once they arrested me and took me to Dlugosiodlo to see a commissar. He asked me whether I was a Communist. And do you know what I said? 'Of course I am,' I said, 'because I'm a Christian.' I don't think he understood me, but he let me go. Probably thought I was a harmless fool."

Maybe Ivan Petrovich was harmless, but he was no fool. He had a quick and original mind. "You know," he said, "there's nothing in Christ's teaching that is reactionary. He was a revolutionary. But then churches perverted his teachings. Even Lenin once said that Christ was the first Bolshevik."

I had never heard such a quote, but I didn't argue with the old man. As we had tea, we spoke about the Germans. Ivan Petrovich was full of surprising ideas. "You know," he said, "Hitler stole everything from the Bible—all his mad ideas. He is trying to turn the clock back three thousand years—back to Moses."

"But wasn't Moses a Jew?" I asked. "Hitler has been destroying Jews."

"Because he stole everything from their old books, that's why. Like every thief he is trying to get rid of the people whom he robbed. And while the Jews have long since grown out of those old barbaric ideas, Hitler has revived them."

I thought that the old man was exaggerating, but he picked up his Bible. "I can prove it to you. Who originated the doctrine of the *Herrenvolk*—the chosen people? Moses. And who spoke about the promised land? Moses. And Moses decreed that in that promised land everything was to be destroyed—every man, woman, and child. 'Everything that breathes' it says here. That was the first blueprint for a genocide. Here it is—and here." He was quoting from the Bible, passages I had never heard of. He made me read them. I was really surprised at the descriptions of the barbarities.

"But that was thousands of years ago," I said. "Probably then everybody was doing those things—everyone was at war."

"Oh yes," Ivan Petrovich said. "But only Moses proclaimed it to be orders from God. You read the Bible, Doctor. Then you won't be surprised about the Germans killing off people in the places they occupy. That maniac in Berlin took the Bible seriously."

One day I will read the Bible, if I ever get hold of one. And if I have time.

Ivan Petrovich was a better theologist than he was a cobbler. He used some German artificial leather on my boots, and it fell apart in two weeks.

JANUARY, 1945

At the end of December we got orders to move closer to the front—to a forest near Orlowo on the Narew river. We were supposed to receive the wounded during our new offensive, probably the last of the war.

Why a forest? This mystery remained locked in the minds of our superiors. The order evoked no enthusiasm in us. Winter, forest, hospital—a strange combination. But we had to obey.

We drove to see our new place, a dense forest with three small houses in it. We became discouraged and our chief went to the Evacuation Center to complain. A miracle occurred. We were given an engineering battalion to help us! Their orders were to prepare dugouts for 200 beds. We knew that that would be insufficient, and we asked for 300.

The engineers and our own personnel worked like men possessed, and on the last day of 1944 we moved into our new home. One house was taken up by our pharmacy and supplies, another by our office, and the third by our superiors. The personnel moved into dugouts.

We have almost everything ready for the wounded. The dugouts have stoves, and they have been going for days. Unfortunately the wood is damp, and burns slowly. And it's important to have dry air for plaster casts. But our boys have promised to get in some dry wood. "Forty high plaster casts a day!"—that has become our motto. All our trunks are filled with plaster bandages. Now we can get as much surgical material as we need. It is difficult to understand how so much medical stuff could be made ready for the millions of wounded. Our medical supply people have proved to be miracle workers. The reserve capacity of our people under stress seems to be unlimited.

The front-line officers tell us that they do not expect many casualties. We have an overwhelming superiority in artillery and aviation.

We celebrated New Year's Eve in our pharmacy. We had warm, tasty food and a bit of drink. It was a happy evening. We had music, danced, and told funny stories. Traditional and non-traditional toasts were offered. But it was all very modest. We are a modest little hospital. Our girls would have liked to celebrate the New Year with their officer friends, but they got no leaves. The commissar was determined to see our girls' morals through to the end.

(If he only knew! During our interlude at Karnacycka, Lina took me aside one night and told me that one of our girls had got into trouble, and was in a state of despair. She begged me to help her, but I had had absolutely no experience, outside of medical textbooks. But something had to be done. Finally we found an old Polish midwife, who performed the operation at her home for two bottles of alcohol. It was surprisingly easy. No one except Lina and I knew about it, except our pharmacist, Zina, I think. Otherwise, why would she have given Lina two bottles of alcohol? That was the only case in our hospital, as far as I know, and the major knew nothing.)

JANUARY 18, 1945

On January 12th we heard a steady roar in the direction of the highway, two miles away. It was our tanks and self-propelled guns going toward the front. For two days and nights the roar continued. On the 13th a thaw began, and the whole country was enveloped in fog so thick that one could see nothing ten meters away.

The offensive started on the 14th. We knew it had begun because heavy guns kept firing without interruption for several hours. The planes did not take off because of the fog. We were all surprised that the attack had not been postponed, but our generals must have had their reasons.

The first wounded started coming around noon.

"No, we didn't break through," they said.

"They have dug in deep, the bastards. They know this is their last fight. But we'll rip their guts out anyway."

I did not envy the Germans. So much hatred, justifiable hatred, had accumulated that it would be difficult to keep it within bounds. When I think about it, I can't help worrying about the German women and children who will have to pay for their men's crimes. But then, who asked them to attack us? And the same old unanswerable question—can any people as a whole be held responsible for the crimes of their government, their generals, and their soldiers? There is no satisfying answer to that one.

We worked methodically from the very beginning. It was almost an exact repetition of Karnacycka. We could not manage 40 high plaster casts a day. There simply wasn't enough time, but we went over 30.

The wounded came in for seven days. They said that the breakthrough was difficult, but we did not feel it because on our front sectors at least five field hospitals were working.

END OF JANUARY, 1945

On January 19th they announced that our troops had reached the borders of East Prussia, and on the 23rd we were ordered to get ready to move. At that time we had over a hundred plaster cast cases and 16 in traction.

By the 26th we had evacuated everyone. Those in traction went in Dietrich splints. We could not use plaster for them.

Then we briefly reviewed our two last operations—Karnacycka and the forest. The figures were not bad, even though we had four percent fatalities in hip cases and one percent in knee injuries. We had coped quite well with suppuration infection, but gaseous gangrene and shock still remain unsolved problems.

All our plaster cast cases are fine boys. They will all survive—with their legs! This one thought makes all the difference in the world.

MAY 6, 1945

It seems that the war is coming to an end for us. We are in Germany, not working but moving from place to place like tourists. Either there are more hospitals now than we need, or there is some deficiency in organization. Most likely there are few casualties. Otherwise they would have found a place for us. After all, our PPG-2266 has earned for itself a certain reputation. It is good that our generals are sparing the men now that the war is practically over. Now every man that can be spared must be spared. Let the guns and planes fight from now on.

My diary for the last few months has been so fragmentary that I must reconstruct the events mostly from memory. Now that I have some time I must try to bring it up to date.

We left our forest on January 28th, toward evening. We already knew that our troops had reached the Baltic coast and that East Prussia had been cut off, but the Germans continued fighting in the encirclement. Late at night, in a raging snowstorm, we reached the Polish border town of Mlawa. We slept in an empty house under red German eiderdown quilts. Early next morning we crossed the border.

There it was—"the Lair of the Fascist Beast." Everything looked new and strange to us. Neat brick houses and brick barns. Well-planned fields. Small postcard towns. And not a single person! Not a soul! A fairy-tale scene: not a house is damaged, but not a single man, woman, or child lives in them. It looked like a page from some science fiction story. The damned Fritzes had fled in advance of our troops.

For about ten days we stayed in some small, empty village, not far from the border, in some Junker's large house. Everything inside was intact—even a decorated Christmas tree. But there wasn't a living soul in sight—not even dogs, cats, or farm animals.

Then we were ordered to relocate to Hochenstein, about 80 miles to the north. We found Hochenstein more interesting. We wandered all over the small abandoned town, entering empty houses, getting acquainted with Prussia. It was a weird feeling to walk through rich apartments and mentally reconstruct the life that once had been there.

The front was far away, and there was nothing to remind us of the war. There was a Soviet commandant here and a small detachment of soldiers, but there seemed to have been no looting. Special commandos drove around neighboring villages rounding up abandoned cattle and registering all supply stores. The Germans lived well; there was plenty of everything. It was so strange to see articles that had suddenly lost all value—grand pianos, fine furniture, paintings. . . .

Our hospital got rich. We now had plenty of blankets, linen, mattresses, dishes. We were a bit too greedy, as though we were expecting thousands of cases. We could have taken care of them on the highest level. Some people were even picking up abandoned clothes. One could not blame them too much. Their families back home were walking around in rags, and here there were heaps of abandoned things. Lyda and I looked for medical equipment and books. The Germans were famous for their *Handbücher*—medical manuals covering every scientific subject.

Our dream was to find some X-ray equipment. We looked through all the abandoned hospitals. We needed a portable machine. A large one would be difficult to carry, and our generators were too weak for them. Kansky and I had converted one to alternate current, but that would not be sufficient.

On February 28th we were suddenly relocated farther north, to the town of Liebstadt. We drove along a road that showed signs of a panicky German retreat. The culverts were strewn with abandoned things—baby carriages, pillows, empty suitcases. Apparently there was a thaw then, but now all this junk was frozen stiff to the ground. On tree trunks we saw the frozen down from gutted mattresses. I could not suppress a secret malicious thought: "Aha, so you, too, had to experience all this!"

We immediately got set up in the railway station building, and prepared to take in the wounded. A large German division was being destroyed by our troops in the center of Prussia. Everything was easy—plenty of space, mattresses, linen, food. We put up beds in our sorting ward and covered them with rugs. It looked like the palace of a Turkish sultan.

There were no particular surgical problems. We received about three hundred cases, some of them with light injuries, and all very well treated in medical battalions. Only two men died—peritonitis and gaseous gangrene. We couldn't save them. We needed advanced medicine, not Oriental rugs. But there was a consolation. The war was obviously ending.

On March 10th we evacuated all our cases and moved over to Morungen, a fairly large town. Once there were probably about twenty thousand people living there, but now, not a soul. We were again allowed to specialize in the lower extremities, but there were few wounded and no surgical problems at all.

We finally found an abandoned hospital and two X-ray machines—both portable, and one even on wheels! And enough film and chemicals to last us a long time. Kansky read the German instructions, and he wheeled the machine around from table to table, taking X-ray photographs. Even in our Arkhangelsk hospital we did not have such luxury.

We worked in Morungen almost a month and a half, quietly and pleasantly. We slept in soft beds, sat in upholstered armchairs, read books—some were in Russian and bore the stamps of the Kiev and Kharkov libraries. We found many luxurious French art albums. It was all very well, but the damned war still continued and men were still dying.

On April 9th our troops took Koenigsberg, the cradle of Prussian militarism. The chief and I visited the city two days after it had been taken. We saw many damaged buildings and white flags hanging from balconies. We learned that it was the 5th Army—the one in which Bocharoff was serving—that had taken the city. But they had already been withdrawn to another sector. I was sorry to have missed him.

At the end of April we were ordered to move to Elblag. Elblag was a beautiful city of about 200,000 population, but only a very few people remained there. Streetcars had once run there, and the shipbuilding wharves had built submarines. There were leaves on the trees, and the entire city looked wrapped in pale green lace.

We occupied a large new school—four stories, with a basement kitchen and dining room and a stadium. The Germans had also had a hospital there. Beds and heavy glassware and dishes were left behind, but all the medical equipment had been taken away.

We set up an excellent wound-dressing station and an operating room. Everything was ready by May 1st. The last battle for Berlin was raging, and in East Prussia the Germans were still holding the Pilau fortress and a long Frischof promontory and fighting stubbornly.

We celebrated May Day as we used to celebrate it during the prewar days. We had a ceremonial meeting, and the commissar spoke about the international situation. Then we had an excellent dinner in the basement dining room. We expected a radio announcement about the fall of Berlin, but it did not come. Just "hard fighting in the center of the city."

MAY 9, 1945

The announcement came the next day, on May 2nd. We all knew that this was the end, but still there was no news of an official German surrender. Technically, the war was still on.

They brought us about a hundred wounded from the divisions fighting on the Frischof. The Germans were still resisting there bitterly—for no reason at all.

One of our last patients was a girl sniper with one leg amputated to the hip and in an extremely grave septic condition. A pretty blonde girl with a handsome and typical Russian face, she had four battle decorations, including two Orders of the Red Banner. She was now recommended for the Hero of the Soviet Union star, but it was doubtful if she would live long enough to receive it.

"Am I going to die, Doctor? Tell me," she asked.

"No, Zoya, no, darling." I said. "I'm sorry about the leg, but life is more important. They will fit you with an artificial leg."

She shook her head. "No, I feel that the life is draining out of me . . . I'll go to sleep or just drift off, and I am afraid I won't wake up."

We did everything possible for her. We transfused whole blood every day, glucose solution, various vitamin preparations. The stub was covered with dead tissue and a sharp piece of bone was protruding from it. In all probability the infection had spread into the pelvis. I operated to remove the remainder of the bone. There was pus on it.

The operation didn't help her. The sepsis spread very fast. She had chills several times a day and was sweating in between. She lay there so pale, like a corpse. Despite the daily transfusions the hemoglobin fell to 30. Shura Matashkova watched her day and night. Zoya asked her several times each day, "Shurochka, did they announce the victory yet?"

"No, Zoya . . . not yet."

"Please wake me up when they announce it . . . I want to live long enough to hear it."

She did live long enough.

On the evening of May 8th the signal officers from the radio battalion told us that the official surrender in Berlin was being prepared. The next morning we worked in the hospital as usual, but we were all nervously awaiting the official announcement. All the tables were occupied. Some men were being examined; others were ready for wound dressing and plaster casts. Kansky was working with our X-ray machine, taking photos, wheeling it from one table to another. It was about eleven o'clock.

Suddenly we heard a flurry of rifle fire and machine-gun bursts. At first we did not understand.

"What's that?" I said. "Have they gone crazy?"

Suddenly Stepa Kravchenko appeared in the doorway.

"Victory! Victory! Come outside!"

We all ran out. Only Lyda, who was dressing a wound, stayed behind. The soldiers begged her to stay with them. She walked from table to table, congratulating the men, squeezing their hands, kissing them.

In the stadium outside the hospital there was a crowd—our people in white gowns, officers and soldiers from different units—and the rifle firing continued all over the town.

The major climbed on a large crate and made the announcement. "Comrades! Fascist Germany has surrendered! Hurrah!"

Everyone yelled, cried, embraced. The major took out his revolver and fired it into the air. The few others who were armed fired their guns. It was a meager little salute. After all, we were a hospital.

No one wanted to leave the stadium. The girls were kissing and embracing everyone, and some of them were crying. It took me some time to herd them all back to their posts.

Meanwhile Lyda had finished her wound dressing, and now I went from table to table congratulating the men.

Then Shura Matashkova looked in.

"Nikolai Mikhailovich, let's go see Zoya."

"Why? Something happened?"

"No, but she has asked to be told . . . and I think it is up to you to do it."

I didn't want to go. It was very difficult. But Shura was right. It was my duty.

Zoya was lying in a small private ward, pale blue face, eyes closed. It was hard to tell whether she was dead or alive. Shura whispered to me, "She had chills at eight o'clock. Then she drifted off. But she begged us to wake her up."

"Perhaps she'd better sleep, Shura? We can tell her when she wakes up."

"No, Nikolai Mikhailovich, wake her. Perhaps she won't wake up again."

I touched her shoulder.

"Zoya . . . Zoyachka . . . "

Her eyelids fluttered, and she ran her tongue over her blue lips.

"Drink . . . "

Shura gave her some fruit juice from a bottle. She opened her eyes.

"Zoya, Germany has surrendered. I congratulate you on the victory."

She stirred and smiled, a sad little smile. I saw a single tear rolling down her cheek.

"And I congratulate . . . congratulate you . . . Now I must get well . . . I must . . . "

I sat at the edge of her bed and took her hand. It was white and bloodless, with rough skin and uneven broken nails. I tried to comfort her.

"Yes, Zoyachka, yes . . . Now you must sleep . . . to regain your strength."

She went to sleep almost at once.

Toward evening she again had chills, and then a complete collapse, and cardiac arrest. There was absolutely nothing we could do.

That was the last death in our hospital.

But there was no grief. We were all so filled with happiness and had become so accustomed to death that nothing could kill our joy at the victory.

It was hard to believe that men were no longer dying.

EPILOGUE

That was the last entry in my diary. I will try to reconstruct the further history of PPG-2266 from memory. It did not come to an end at once. While the war was going on, we thought that as soon as Germany collapsed we could return to a happy, peaceful life. But it did not happen that way. There was still Japan and some international political considerations. Whatever it was, there were still a few more dull, uninteresting months. The main connection holding our little group together was now gone—our common work, the wounded, the overriding desire to win the war—and our unit had become fragmented.

Each of us had to face his future. To many, it did not look promising. What was in store for Liubov Vladimirovna, for instance, or Zinochka? Routine work, a small room, loneliness. And our major? He had separated from his family before the war. They all hoped to meet someone, to find companionship, but four years had passed, and at their age, these hopes had become unrealistic. Yes, many of us felt uneasy, even sad.

Perhaps the most difficult thing was to find out suddenly that we had to act on our own. For four years someone had been thinking for us. Now we all had to choose for ourselves, and the choice was often brutally limited.

It was better for us, the young ones. We were not overburdened by memories and disappointments. We were still hungry for life, ready to meet any challenge. I felt very happy during those first days of peace. I felt vast relief and eagerness to tackle a new life.

But back to history. We worked in Elblag for about six weeks treating our wounded and taking care of accidental injuries. But the main stimulus was gone, and we worked without our former spirit.

We had our army's surgical conference in our hospital—the summing up. The atmosphere was formal rather than creative. We still argued about surgical problems, but all that now sounded academic. I made two reports about joints and hips. I had amassed some solid material, almost 1,300 knees and 1,600 hips. Toward the end of the conference, Banaitis and Gurvich, two leading surgeons of the Soviet Army, joined us, and I had to repeat my reports for them. I even argued with Banaitis about certain of his remarks. I felt my new freedom. I no longer had to adhere to any unified doctrine. I don't think that we convinced each other.

During that time I wrote eight scientific papers as well—on Hips, Gaseous Gangrene, Blood Transfusion, Secondary Hemorrhages, two papers about chest injuries, and two about knees. (I still have them. I have reread them recently. Not bad at all. Some convincing statistics. But after the failure of my dissertation, I did not risk submitting them anywhere.)

We went to the general staff headquarters of our army to receive decorations. It was a pleasant trip. All of us got some new medals: "For the Victory against Germany," "For the Defense of Moscow," "For the Koenigsberg Operation." It was fashionable to wear all one's medals then, but I always wore only ribbons.

In the middle of July we got orders to turn in our horses, our trucks, and all excess equipment, and get ready to leave. We were excited. We thought that we were going home to be demobilized.

We again loaded everything into boxcars and went back to Russia. Passing Moscow, we headed eastward, and when we passed the Urals, we knew that the war was not yet over for us. Was it to be the Maritime Province, or Mongolia?

That was a rather sad trip. It lasted for a whole month. We passed through a hungry, disorganized country, filled with bedraggled men and women and many cripples both with and without medals. The thought of another war was sickening.

We unloaded at Lesozavodsk, not far from Vladivostok. We had all our equipment, including the X-ray apparatus. We were then attached to the 35th Army,which had spent the whole war sitting in the Far East.

The next day I went out to look for Bocharoff because I knew that the 5th Army was also here. Finally I found the staff of his army in the border hills. Bocharoff came toward evening, and we spent the whole night talking. I told him all about our work—I knew that no one understood military surgery better than Bocharoff. And he told me about his army. Things were better for them than for us—more hospitals, more transport facilities, lower fatality figures. But my experience with traction and knee resections impressed him, and that pleased me. In the morning he drove me in his staff car to the station, and we parted. (Our friendship continued for 25 years, until his death. He was a professor, lieutenant-general, and the first head surgeon deputy of the Soviet Army. Many people change with time and distinctions, but not Arkady Alexeievich Bocharoff. To me he always remained my friend and my brother.)

Then we went through another war. Luckily, a short and practically bloodless one.

First of all we were sent for some reason into the Ussuri border hills. We stayed there for three days, being almost eaten alive by mosquitoes. Then we were pulled back and relocated in some village the name of which I no longer remember, near Shmakovka.

On the morning of August 9th we heard the rumble of guns. That aroused nothing but irritation in us. In a few hours the first wounded started to arrive: all Far Eastern boys who had never experienced any war and were all scared stiff. We had about twenty cases, a mere nothing to us. We worked for two days and processed about forty cases. All were operated on, put in plaster casts, and swiftly evacuated.

On the 14th we got orders to relocate to Manchuria. Almost at the same time we heard that Japan had surrendered. Our trip looked doubly senseless to us.

The next twenty-four hours were the last heroic ones for PPG-2266. In cars, under a thin drizzle, we were driven towards the Ussuri river. Then we alighted and went toward the bridge. It was blocked by a boom, and a colonel and a few of his officers ordered everybody to get back. The roads on the other side of the river were absolutely impassable for motor traffic because of the rain. There were many cars from other units. There were shouts, arguments, obscenities. But we were not sorry to be so detained.

Our superiors felt differently. We got orders to proceed on foot to a certain place beyond the border and to "render surgical service." The order sounded strange to us, but when our chief spoke to a Far Eastern colonel who had never seen any war, the colonel just snapped at him, "Carry out your orders!"

So we quickly collected the most necessary equipment that we could carry and started off. We probably looked ridiculous. Our fat chief walked in front, then the major, then I, Lina, Anna, Lyda, Bykova, Shura, Tacia and the other nurses. We had only eight medics with us, including Kansky, Bessonoff, and Kravchenko.

The colonel on the bridge laughed at us, but let us pass. "I have orders only about motor traffic."

We made little progress until nightfall. The road was a sea of mud, often knee deep, marshes all around, overgrown with very tall grass. No sign of human habitation. Many vehicles stuck in the mud and abandoned. And clouds of mosquitoes. Since our hands were taken by the things we were carrying, we had no defense against these tormentors.

When it got dark, it became scary. Our armaments consisted of two revolvers and a submachine gun. One Japanese could easily have dispatched all of us, firing from the grass. But we were of no interest to the Japanese. By about midnight we saw some lights ahead. There were a few Chinese clay huts, the *fanzas*, and a few soldiers, warming themselves around a campfire. We all collapsed dead with fatigue. In the morning we found our destination, a kilometer away. It was something like an abandoned Japanese border post. During the day they indeed brought in a soldier with an abdominal wound. Using our limited means we performed a laparotomy. But it was too late, and the man died the next morning. "Heroic" operations are rarely successful.

Toward the next evening the roads had dried up, our cars brought in our equipment, and we started a trip across Manchuria for two days, loudly acclaimed by the Chinese population. Finally we stopped at a small town, and here we received about a hundred wounded: the result of the liquidation of a group of Japanese suicidal maniacs. In two days our wounded were all evacuated safely, and that was the end of our second war.

In the second half of September we were pulled back to Sedanka, near Vladivostok, and put in an empty pioneer* camp. Here the process of liquidation of our PPG started in earnest. First of all, we received a bunch of decorations for our second war—I do not remember who got what.

Our hospital agonized for about six more weeks before it expired. First our medics were demobilized and left to face the uncertainty of their future. Our ward nurses left next: Masha Poletova, Liucia Brashina, Anya Menzhes, Anya Suchkova, Shura Matashkova, Anya Manerkina, all dedicated girls who had been with us since Kaluga. Next to go were our doctors and chief nurses, Liubov Vladimirovna Bykova, Tacia, Shura Filina, and our pharmacist, Zinochka. Lyda and I were transferred to another PPG. The Chief, Kansky, and the supply people were left behind to formalize the final dissolution of our unit. Thus, PPG-2266 was no more.

We have met many of our co-workers since the war. Anna Vasilievna still works in our clinic. Lyda and I had a friendly relationship with Liubov V. Bykova until her death in Briansk. For many years when we visited Moscow, we would look up Zinochka and Anya Suchkova. We also met Liuda Yankevich, Vera Tarasenko, Anya Manerkina, Lucia, Shura Filina, and Nina. I went once to Cherepovets and saw Tamara. Fate has treated the girls differently, and not always kindly. Once the chief came to

---

*A Soviet scout-like organization.—Trans.

see me, but we had no real contact. Not a word about Kolia Kansky—he seemed to have disappeared altogether.

I suppose I must say something in conclusion. While rereading my notes I have been trying to evaluate myself, my colleagues, the war, surgery, society, our people. I thought that I should draw some conclusions. But now that the work is completed, I know that one just cannot evaluate such things in any logical terms.

The sea of human suffering . . . almost 50,000 wounded, most of them badly injured. Over a thousand fatalities. Several thousand cripples. And this only in our small Mobile Field Hospital, horse-drawn, and slated to care for 200 cases at any one time, with five doctors! And our hospital was lucky enough not to be involved in any really bloody battles of the war—the Ukraine, the Crimea, Stalingrad, Kursk, Berlin. What can one say after these figures?

I would like to say a few words about heroism. What kind of heroism can one see in a small field hospital? The Germans did not attack us; our men did not fight hand to hand with them. During the entire war I did not treat a single bayonet wound. I did not see with my own eyes any heroic exploits, besides that one occurrence in October, 1941, at Sukhinichi, when our single fighter plane attacked eight German bombers. Of course, that does not mean that there were no heroic exploits in the war. I am sure there were. I am reminded of that girl sniper who died on Victory Day. It is simply that in mass the wounded do not look like heroes, and they usually speak of their war work stingily and matter-of-factly. No, we did not win the war by individual heroics.

What I did see was courage. Boundless, quiet courage. One needs courage to bear suffering. Suffering is a sharp pain when a dry bandage is torn off an open wound or when one works on a broken leg. It is the dull, constant pain of gaseous gangrene. The agonizing headaches of pierced skulls. Suffering is hunger and thirst—the hunger and thirst of a man with a smashed mouth who cannot swallow, the chronic hunger and thirst of a man with an abdominal wound or high fecal fistula. Suffering is cold, lice, and maggots, and absence of bed, food, and shelter.

How many had cried and complained? Just a few. How many had begged for special treatment because of their ranks? Very few.

There is also the courage of decision—"We must amputate your legs." "We must operate on your knee." "No, it will never bend." "Yes, there is a great risk of death."—men who can take decisions like this can also be firm in battle.

Yes, there is heroism in our people, but I prefer to call it courage and patience. And it is not a matter of discipline—discipline ends when a bullet pierces one's stomach. No, it is the majesty of the human spirit.

I humbly bow to you, the wounded who went through our little hospital—to all the wounded who went through all the hospitals, large and small, and to those who never got out of them alive. With their suffering they bought peace for all humanity.